IMAGES
of America

MURRYSVILLE AND EXPORT

I0807081

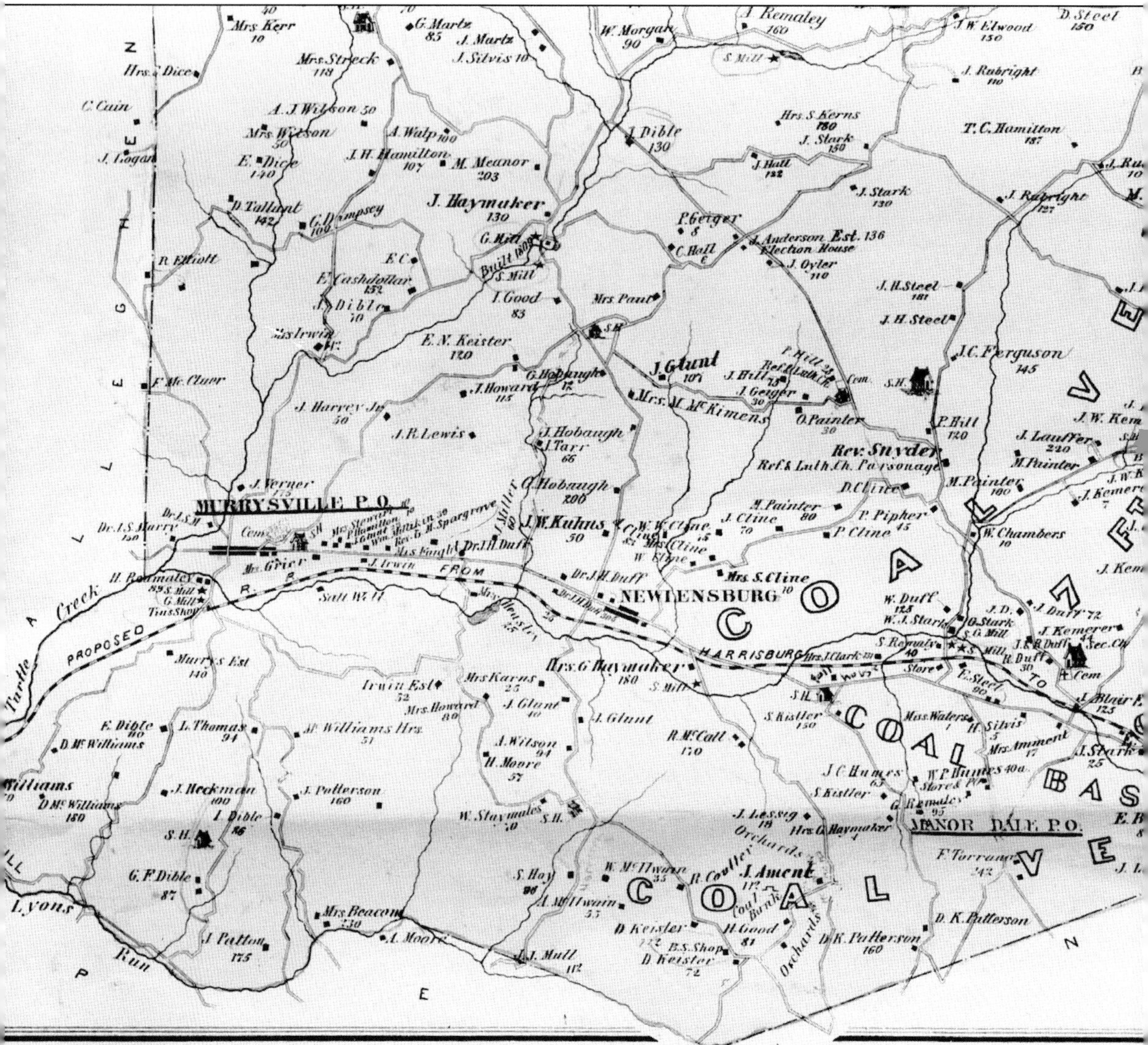

In the *New Illustrated Atlas of Westmoreland County, Pennsylvania, 1876*, the seven-foot coal basin in Turtle Creek Valley is very prominent in the southeastern section of Murrysville-Export. The intersection of Harrison City and Berlin Farm Roads, New US 22, is in Export, which saw the advent of the area's bituminous coal industry. Murrysville was incorporated in 1976 (officially 1978), and Export's incorporation as a borough was November 11, 1911, with the first council meeting held in the First National Bank. The town's 100th anniversary is November 11, 2011. The original bank in Manordale (also Manor Dale) was William P. Humes's iron safe, with business conducted in S.W. Blair's house and file drawer. Export's Town Square is along Old William Penn Highway, Old US 22, Northern Pike. Murrysville's Town Square is at the intersection of Mill Street (Vincent B. Hall Road) and Old US 22, Northern Pike. Newlonsburg, sometimes spelled differently, is now part of the municipality. (Author's collection.)

On the Cover: Nurses stand in a row as part of a 1918 Columbus Day ceremony at the Export Town Square. For additional information, please see page 80. (Courtesy of Raymond and Helen Meehan.)

IMAGES
of America

MURRYSVILLE AND EXPORT

Helene Smith

ARCADIA
PUBLISHING

Copyright © 2011 by Helene Smith
ISBN 978-0-7385-7463-9

Published by Arcadia Publishing
Charleston, South Carolina

Printed in the United States of America

Library of Congress Control Number: 2010937244

For all general information, please contact Arcadia Publishing:
Telephone 843-853-2070
Fax 843-853-0044
E-mail sales@arcadiapublishing.com
For customer service and orders:
Toll-Free 1-888-313-2665

Visit us on the Internet at www.arcadiapublishing.com

To my husband, Wayne, and children and sons-in-law who help me with my books—Cheryl, Gregory, Jennifer, Laurel and Michael Smith, Michael Benzer, and Howard Bowen

Contents

Acknowledgments		6
Introduction		7
1.	Roads and Ways	9
2.	Murrysville's Wildcat Gas Industry	21
3.	Export's First Coal to Go Global	37
4.	Between a Rock and a Hard Place	51
5.	Children of the Gas-Coal Region	57
6.	For Dedication in Helping Others	71
7.	Good Sports, Community Spirit	81
8.	People, Their Homes, and Places	99
9.	Businesses and Historic Buildings	111
Bibliography		126
Index		127

Acknowledgments

My sincere thanks are extended to Erin L. Vosgien, acquisitions editor and assistant publisher, for her enthusiasm, professional assistance, and devoted guidance on behalf of this Arcadia publication, and to all the kindhearted people who contributed to this undertaking—especially the productive administration at Arcadia Publishing, the leading publisher of United States regional history. My thanks also go to Allyson Reese and the Greensburg librarians.

My heartfelt gratitude goes to my daughters for their skills and expertise: my proficient and competent agent and liaison, Cheryl Smith, a tenacious business-growth strategist who read my manuscript and helped me considerably; and my daughter Laurel Smith, a computer guru and my creative website designer whom I depend upon for specialized technical advice and the well-organized efficiency she possesses. I could not have achieved what needed to be done without their help. I am grateful for Howard Bowen and Vincent A. Geiger, who also read my manuscript and offered good points.

For sharing information and fascinating photographs that portray the communities of Murrysville-Export and their environs, my wholehearted appreciation goes to contributors Edward Banks, Joan Kearns, and those named in courtesy lines throughout; in particular, the president of the Murrysville Historical and Preservation Society (MHPS), Ralph Carl Patty, who also generously made possible the use of vintage images. Unless otherwise noted, images and photographs are from the collection of Karl Koch and his wife, Katherine, to whom I am most thankful. Other images not acknowledged as from someone are from my own archives. All these photographs have been returned to their owners with complimentary copies of my previous books and sincere appreciation. Special thanks go to Stephen Simpson (www.takeavirtualhike.com) for sharing pictures he developed from glass negatives. He also provided rare woodcut images ordered from the historical archives of the world-famous Murrysville-Haymaker Gas Well and now published for the first time since the late 1800s. At last, these treasures can be enjoyed by all who would otherwise have never seen them.

Appreciation is extended to Murrysville's *Penn Franklin News* for publishing my article requesting photographs from both communities. The press's founder, Charles K. Cooper, started the newspaper in 1947, and it is still family-operated. His philosophy in life was, "A good newspaper is the best backbone of a community."

INTRODUCTION

One picture is worth a thousand words. Vintage photographs reflect common characteristics of and differences between Murrysville and Export, located atop Pittsburgh's vast gas-coal vein that fueled the nation's industries for many years. These images conjure up nostalgia, which is by definition a sense of mixed emotions of happiness and sadness over times now gone. In compiling a book such as this, a story emerges chapter by chapter. Through clashing of indigenous nations with foreign nations sailing over the horizon from distant shores, there was a period of violent struggle. Eventually, harmony and tolerance emerged among varied cultures. In his book *A Gold Dollar*, the Reverend Joseph M. Duff, DD (a descendant of Turtle Creek Valley pioneer John McIlduff), reflects on a natural harmony: "These hills and valleys have been here from the first, and yonder stream winds its course today as when the settlers saw it shimmer among the forest trees."

Franklin Township was settled mostly by Scottish, German, and Irish immigrants, with competitors Britain and France fighting over indigenous lands during the French and Indian Wars (including the American phase of the Seven Years' War in Europe), staged for control of North America. Colonels Bouquet, Montgomery, and Washington led Brig. Gen. John Forbes's brigades. They met November 19, 1758, in old Franklin Township before seizing Pittsburgh's Fort Duquesne. On this dangerous trail originally formed by American bison and later known as the Raystown Indian Path, Forbes's army quickly cleared its way to take over Fort Duquesne as fast as possible. Col. Bouquet reported that the path from three redoubts at Hannas Town, where residents of Murrysville and Manordale (later Export) traveled to their courthouse, was especially treacherous. Prior to Forbes's strategic capture of the fort, the French had torched their own garrison. Upon arrival, Forbes's men buried the corpses of Gen. James Grant's soldiers killed in an unauthorized attack that fueled a French–Native American skirmish at Fort Ligonier in 1759. Sun-bleached bones of Major General Braddock's men the French had not buried since the ill-fated 1755 battle of Monongahela River were also interred. Bears, having fed on the slain, became fierce and totally unafraid of man. The garrison was renamed Fort Pitt for William Pitt the Elder, British secretary of state.

In 1764, Swiss soldier of fortune Col. Henry Bouquet built a brick blockhouse at the site of the garrison. A year before, a flour-bag fort was quickly assembled to defend against Ottawa Chief Pontiac's allied nations, who attacked a 400-packhorse supply train in the Battle of Bushy Run. The sachem was conducting a siege on Pittsburgh for reneging on a treaty. One of the frequent conflict that occurred between Fort Ligonier and Pittsburgh was the so-called Battle of Murrysville, causing eight Americans and four Indians to die in a rugged defile overshadowed by gigantic virgin trees—what First Americans called "endless mountains." This sets the scene for the perilous stage Jeremiah Murry faced when he first came over the Allegheny Mountains to settle in the Turtle Creek Valley.

The importance of the pioneer Forbes Road cannot be emphasized enough. Westmoreland County's purchasing office opened April 6, 1769, after a peace treaty with Iroquois nations in

1768 at Fort Stanwix, New York. Maj. Gen. Anthony Wayne defeated Indian forces at Fallen Timbers battle in Greenville, Ohio, in 1794, and a treaty a year after the battle forced indigenous people west.

Following the American Revolution, Forbes's soldiers from the east, who fought along with the Westmoreland County Rangers and were impressed with the area, returned with their families in wagons loaded with belongings. They had been given government land grants in lieu of payment. Fur traders passed through prior to 1769. Area residents such as the Larimers and members of Col. Archibald Loughry's family asked permission from First Americans to build on their lands. Maj. Hugh Torrance lived "a rifle shot away" from Washington's camp and Caggey's (meaning "cockeye") log cabin, in the late 1700s and early 1800s. Nearby lived David Logan, George Keister, and John Rose. One neighbor avoided Indian capture three times, and a baby was taken from Maj. Hugh and Mary Fenton Torrance's home and returned wearing newly made beaded moccasins. Later, a freshly baked berry pie cooling on a local windowsill disappeared. Soon, a newly slain deer was dropped off at the front door. This was a native way of fulfilling a need and paying for it later. This happened in Manor Dale (later Manordale), which eventually became Export.

When natural resources became competitive, original farmers gained wealth from their first deeds and mineral rights. Judge Thomas Mellon, a banker and industrialist and the father of Andrew Mellon, who was the United States secretary of the treasury, wrote, "Their labor was incessant; farm work during the day, and spinning and weaving at night." It was the pioneers who fought nature's elements and the later settlers who labored in the coal dust underground. The so-called Wild East was just as unruly as the Wild West, with overcrowded boardinghouses and prominent drinking and gambling; even children drank whisky in those days. In Export's First National Bank (later Borough) Building was Scott's Barber Shop. Its red-and-white-striped pole indicated medical help, with jars of leeches for customers having black eyes from frequent fistfights. The town had a jail where "the best way to stay clear of the law and lockup" was a bottle of moonshine for the squire.

Through immigration came the fabled *melting pot*. Although languages were lost as First Americans and African Americans were chastised for speaking native tongues, each group still kept its distinction. Immigrants retained their cultural identities through festivals, clubs, and recipes. The population of Murrysville in 2010 was 18,872. According to the US Census, Export had 895 people that same year. Demographics that indicate no Native Americans and only a few African Americans are misleading, as many residents have indigenous inheritance as well as African descent. Various cultures, once fearfully shunned, are now appreciated for their values, arts, and herbal health remedies.

Original industrial frenzy was transformed to pride. Lee A. Iacocca, former chairman and chief executive of Chrysler Corporation, writes in his autobiography when commenting on his father (who once worked in a coal mine), "Roots are what this country is yearning for. People ache to return to basic values. Hard work, the dignity of labor, the fight for what's right, these are the things the Statue of Liberty and Ellis Island stand for . . . Somehow they have managed to keep their cultures intact as each rubbed off on the other." There were good and bad times in the gas-coalfields as international peoples battled differences. However, they finally realized "everyone was for everyone" to survive. As residents shared vintage photographs for this book, they told stories, some with humor as well as a sense of longing. One person said, "At times, things were bitter, but now with the complexity of modern life, these pictures look good."

In general, Old William Penn Highway (also called Old US 22) is often confused with two roads in Export: the Northern Pike, whose route it follows through the towns, and the newer Old William Penn Highway. Industry rerouted roads and a creek to make room for its coal yards that required much land. The New US 22 (the new Old William Penn Highway) loosely follows the old Forbes Road. This great thoroughfare runs back and forth across Turtle Creek. Along with the Turtle Creek Valley Railroad, it brings wistfulness of the past, reminding us of what we often forget and giving us pause to think about the future of the next transformation.

One

Roads and Ways

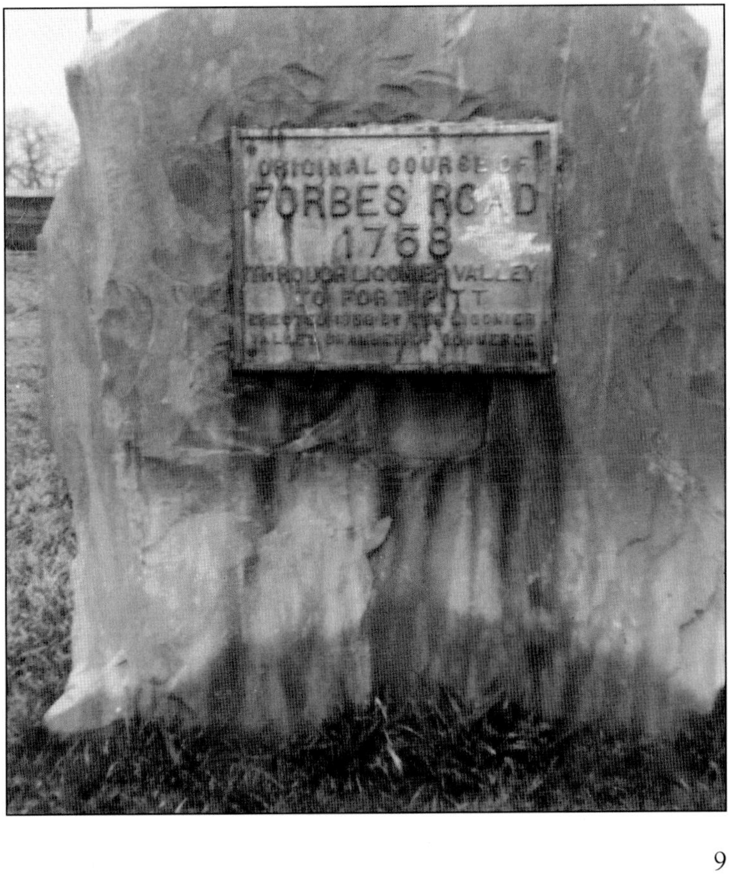

In 1758, General Forbes's "Great Road," with few wagon wheel ruts remaining, was America's first strategic highway, essential for industrial success. Ill during his expedition, Forbes was carried on a horse-borne litter as he cursed the bumpy road under construction. He died after his return to Philadelphia.

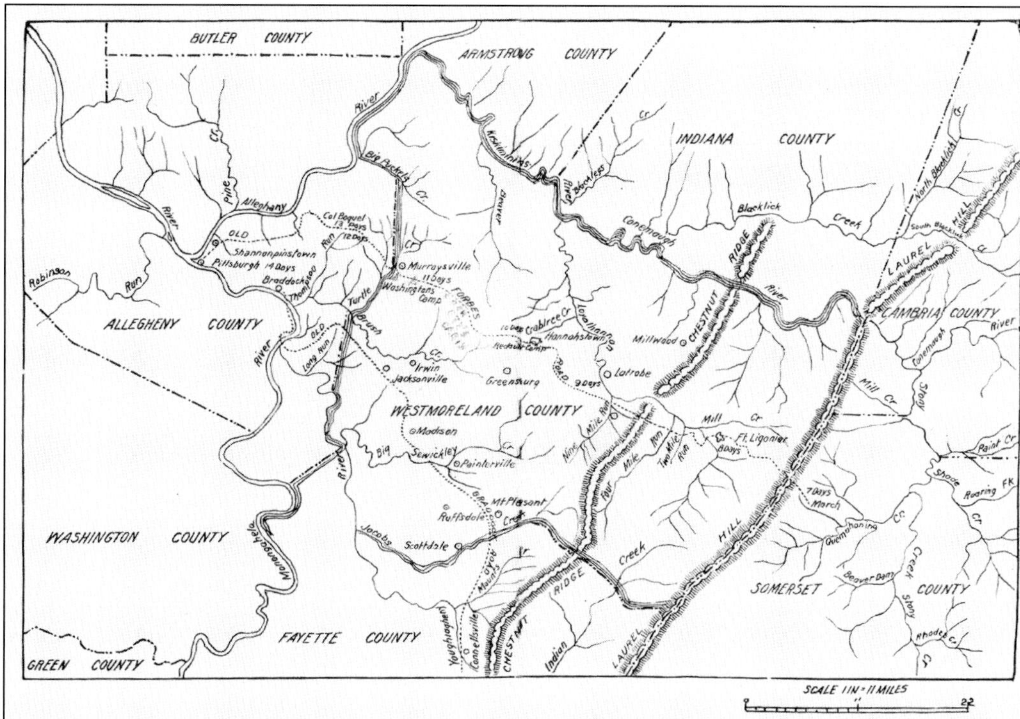

MAP OF WESTMORELAND COUNTY, SHOWING ROUTE TAKEN BY GEN. FORBES

On February 26, 1773, Westmoreland County was formed. A map of Forbes Road shows Hannas Town (misspelled as Hannahstown), the first British county seat west of the Allegheny Mountains, and Manordale's log cabin spring, site of Delaware Chief Cockeye's fur-trading inn. Washington's agent in 1753, Christopher Gist, visited east of Newlonsburg Country Place off New US 22.

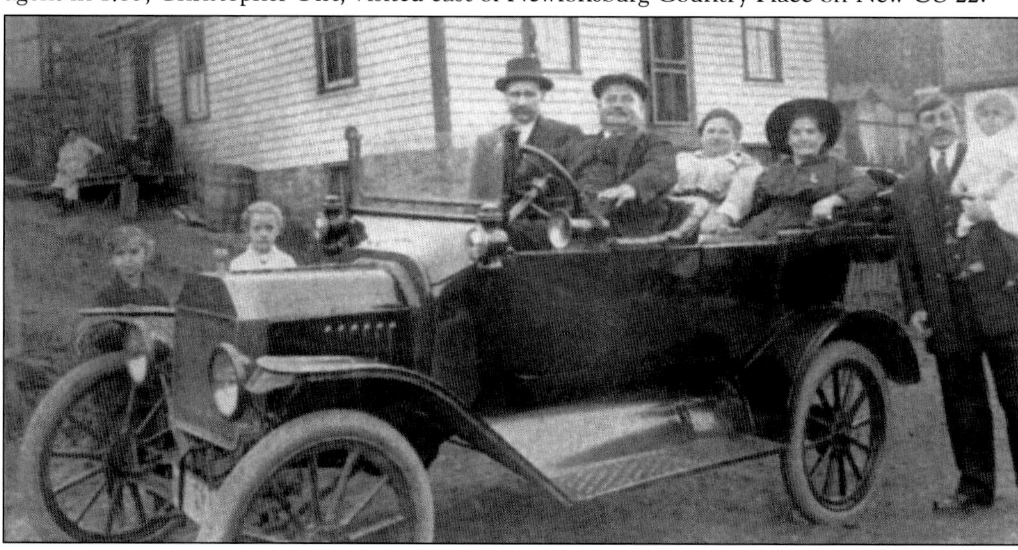

Christopher Gist wrote: "I was very sick and sweated myself according to the Indian custom in a Sweat House, which gave me Ease, and my fever abated." At a spring a mile west of Cockeye's was Washington's camp breastworks, later owned by McMullen, Coulter, Wilson, and Putkovic, near Frank Kusnick's spring. Over this same road where Hugh Torrance once lived, Joseph Wonce drove a 1920s quad car with four steerable wheels.

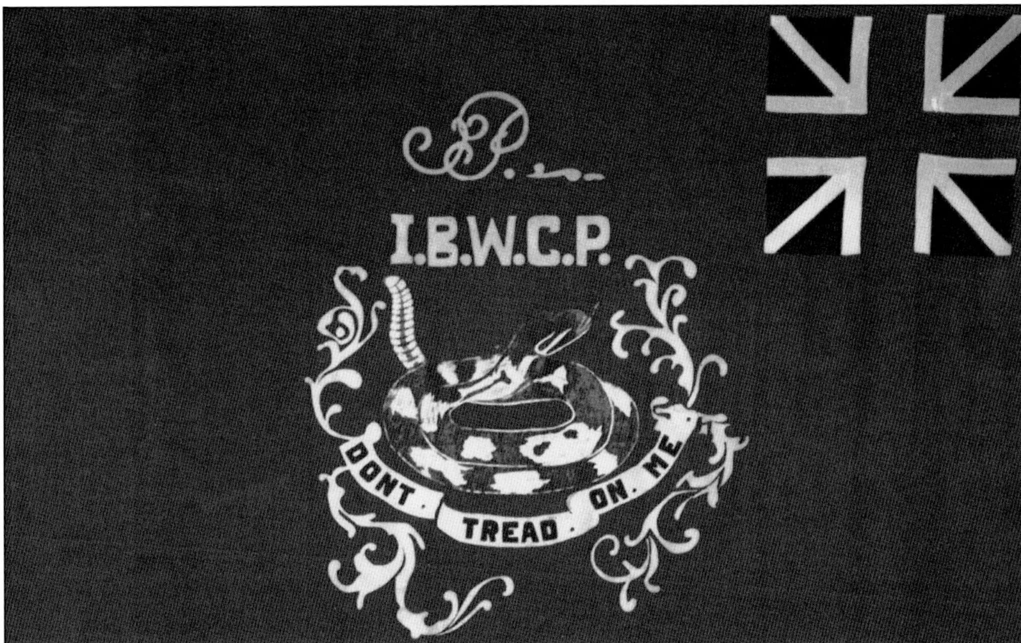

Old Westmoreland County Revolutionary Flag

Col. John Proctor, carrying this flag (Independent Battalion, Westmoreland County, Pennsylvania), led his men—George Ament, Capt. Dan Carpenter, Jacob Fink, and Maj. Hugh Torrance—over Forbes Road. In 1775, Revolutionary patriots composed the Hannas Town Resolves, a precedent to the Declaration of Independence in which the men of Westmoreland promise to fight tyranny with "our lives and our fortunes."

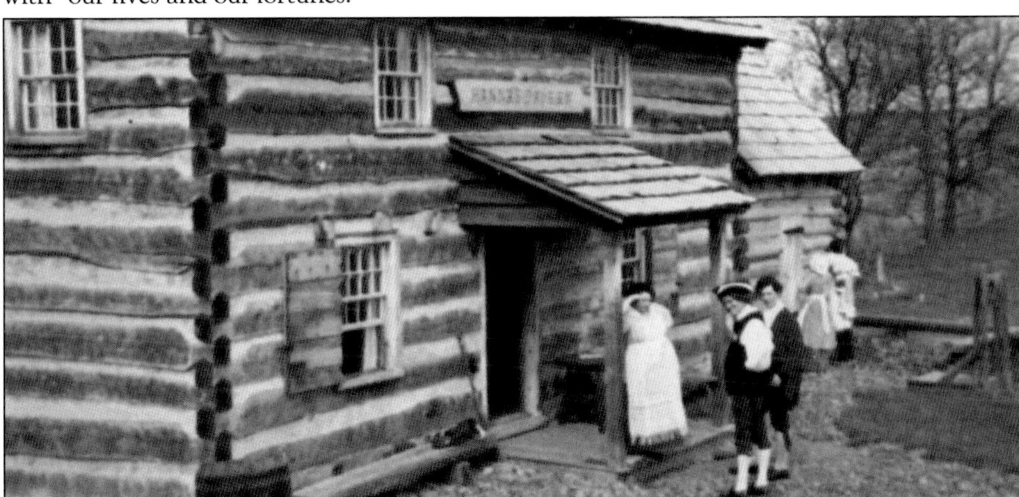

Farmers Brother (born between 1716 and 1732), a member of the Seneca of the Iroquois Confederacy, led the British/Native American attack at Hannas Town (perhaps with help of Chief Guyasuta) on July 13, 1782, avenging the Ohio Gnadenhütten massacre of Christian Native Americans. Farmers feared harvesting during the revenge. Members of the Peter Uber (a Kepple ancestor), Tarr, and Sloan families were captives. John Duff rescued his baby from his house, set afire because Hannas Town justice Col. William Crawford falsely was blamed for the county seat attack by David Williamson and his militia. This image was made at the Hannas Town historical park.

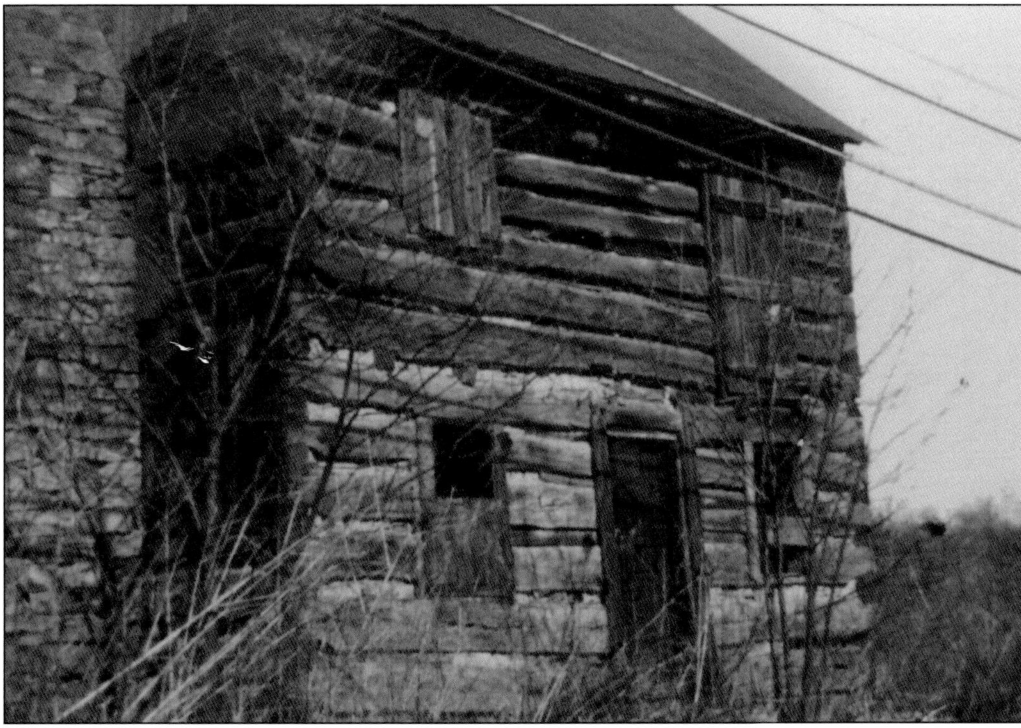

The last log tollhouse (believed to have been built by a Sampson ancestor in 1784 and privately owned in Murrysville) was reconstructed on its original site on Kistler and West Pike Roads. Tolls started in 1818–1819. Simeon Clark and his daughter, Nancy, lived here as toll keepers. She made apple butter in the stone fireplace and swept her garden rows with a broom. Harolds and Clarks were among the structure's early owners. The last person to live here, besides Louis Geiger, was Nevin Kemerer. In 1928, the original tollhouse site and an adjacent Victorian house built in 1890 by the Kemerers was sold to Manuel Viola.

Turnpike Rates of Toll 1819

	For every 10 miles
For every score of swine	6¢
For every half score of swine	3¢
For every score of sheep	6¢
For every half score of sheep	3¢
For every score of cattle	10¢
For every half score of cattle	5¢
For every horse or mule laden or unladen led or drove	6¢
For every sulky, chair, or chaise with one horse	12¢
For every chair coach, phaeton chaise, sulky, and light wagon with 2 horses	25¢
For either or more with 4 horses	50¢
For every carriage of pleasure—may go higher according to number of horses	
Sled or sleigh, for each horse	6¢
For every cart, wagon, or other cariage of burthen, the wheels of which do not exceed in breadth 4 inches, per horse	12¢
For every cart, wagon, or other carriage of burthen, the wheels of which do exceed 4 inches, per horse	8¢

When any carriage aforesaid, whole or part, is drawn by oxen, 2 oxen shall be estimated as equal to one horse and charged the aforesaid toll.

No toll shall be demanded from any person or persons passing or repassing from one part of their farm to another, nor from any persons attending funerals or going to and from places of worship.

Tollhouse rates were fixed for sheep, with less than 20 passing free. This road running through Export and Murrysville to Pittsburgh follows the 1787 Frankstown Road. The toll keeper turned a pike when a fee was paid. These tollhouses were a forerunner of tollbooths on modern turnpikes.

The advent of railways ended the drover era. On modern turnpikes, 18-wheeled trucks replaced teamster horse wagons. On the tollhouse (later a stable) is an overhanging balcony that was later removed. Benjamin Sampson, a building contractor and the great-great-great-grandson of original owner Charles Sampson, rebuilt the tollhouse around 2010, preserving its indoor-outdoor fireplace. It is now a park.

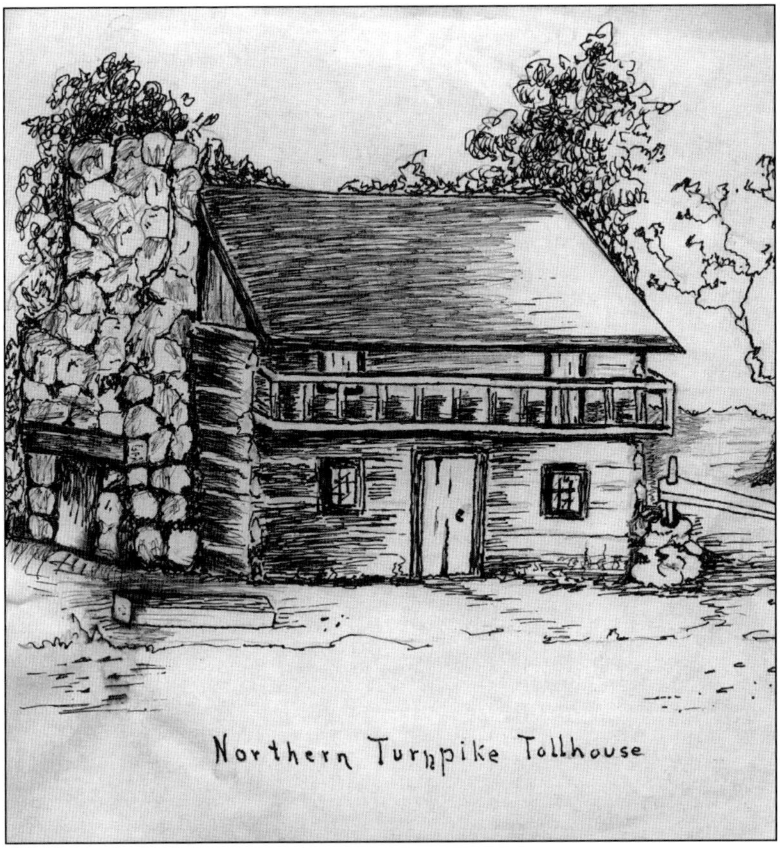

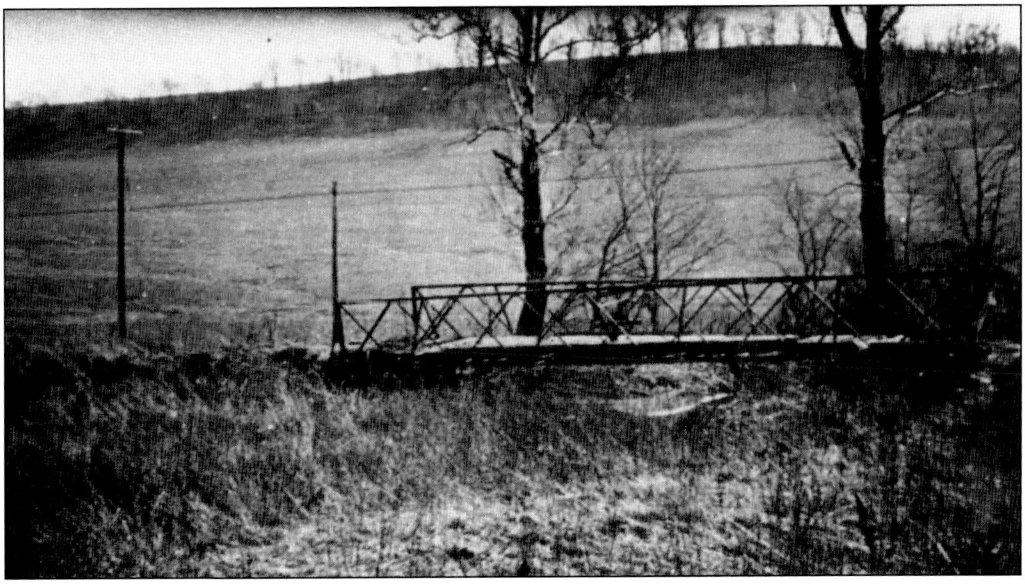

This tollhouse bridge was on the old Northern Pike running through Export and Murrysville. It accommodated horse-drawn vehicles and hand-cranked cars with Prest-O-Lite tanks used to fuel the acetylene gas headlights. When the driver turned a key in back, he had to run to the front to light the gas.

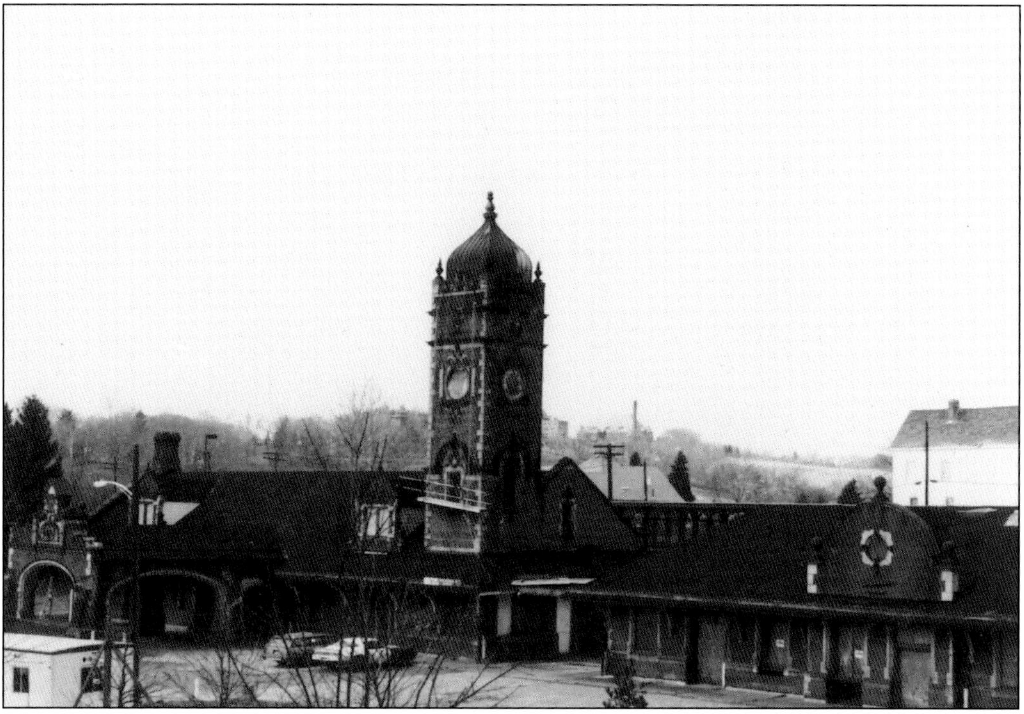

The nearby train station in Greensburg (the county seat after Hannas Town) was the site where immigrants arrived from Eastern and Southern Europe. Andrew Carnegie hired composer Stephen Foster's wife, Jane McDowell, to work here as a telegraph operator. Before finding employment in gas-coal fields, men stayed at a boardinghouse called Castle Garden, after America's major immigrant reception facility at Ellis Island. One Serbian saying was, "*Nema robic* ("neema robich")," meaning "no work today"; it was familiar to many miners and was handed down over the generations.

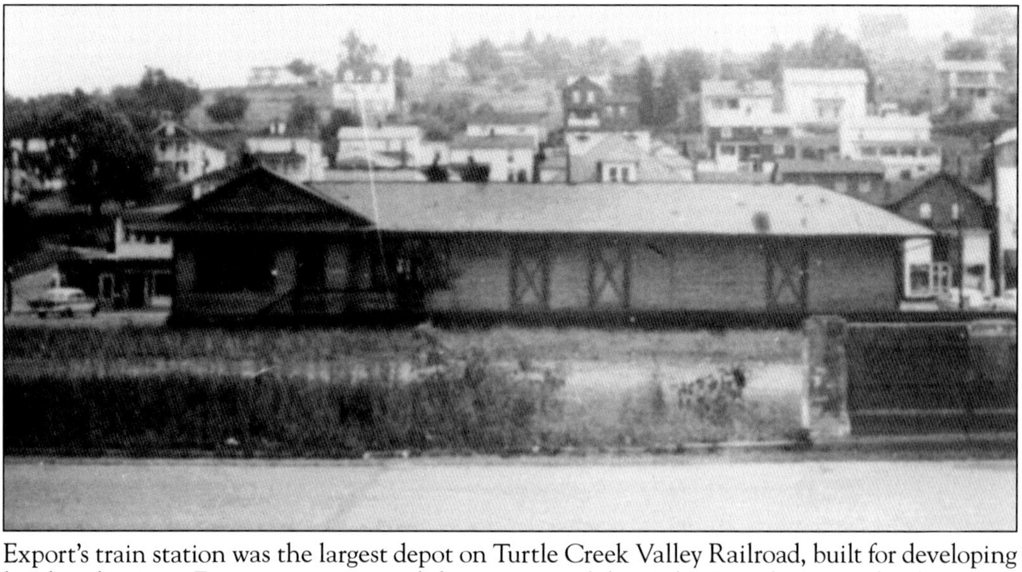

Export's train station was the largest depot on Turtle Creek Valley Railroad, built for developing local coal regions. Five-passenger trains left town on weekdays. The Saturday train, the "bummer," left for Braddock and Pittsburgh with shoppers in the early morning and returned at 1:00 a.m. The station closed December 7, 1970, and later burned. (Courtesy of Raymond Meehan.)

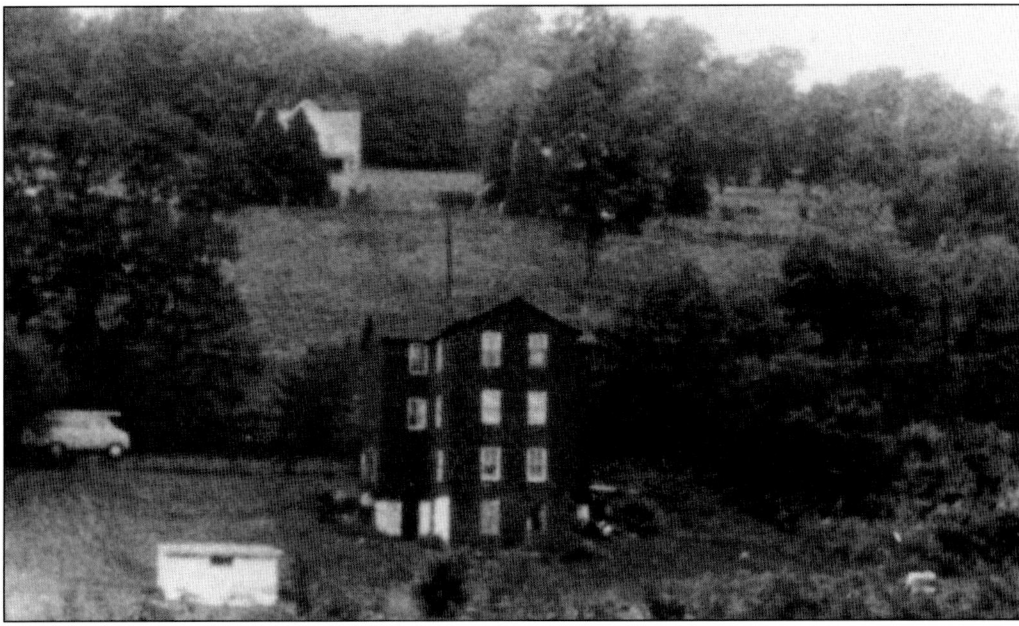

Immigrants waited until 5:00 p.m. for a bell indicating available employment from the headquarters of Westmoreland Coal Company in Irwin, Pennsylvania. This red frame boardinghouse was also called Castle Garden. Located on West Pike Street and erected by coal dealer W.B. Skelly, it was the tallest building in Export and boasted 12 rooms with fireplaces. It first housed Irish railroad workers (known as gandy dancers) who laid track for the Pennsylvania Railroad.

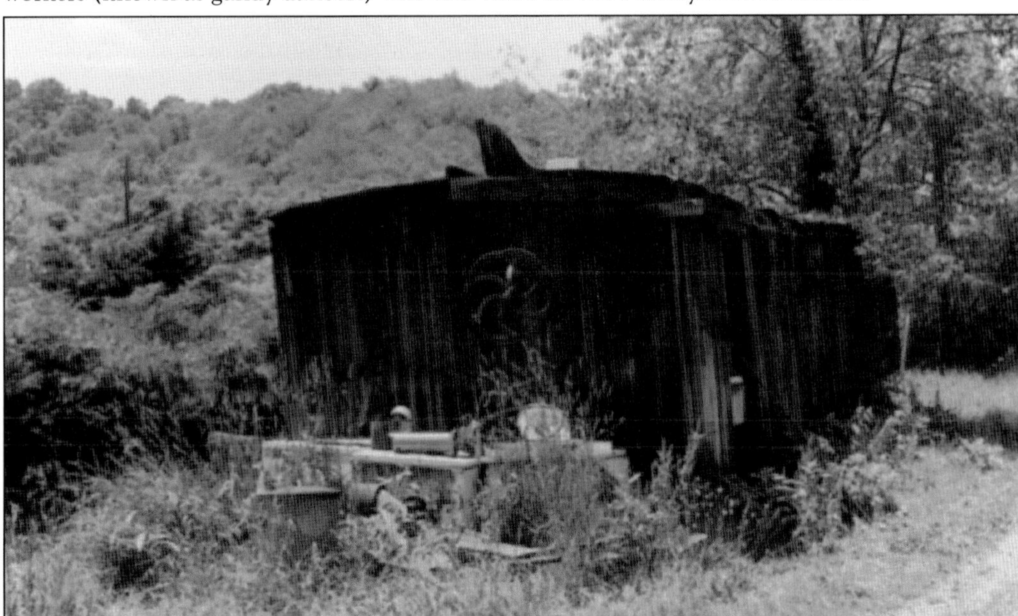

Refrigerator cars provided temporary housing at what was called Boxcar Town in Esler (the location of the Irwin Gas coal tipple), which was a 30-minute ride by canoe for inspectors from Export. The boxcars were set up with four double bunks and a stove. Women were paid to assist the workers; for every 10 immigrants, there was one female helper. Miners also slept on straw-filled burlap bags referred to as "zulus."

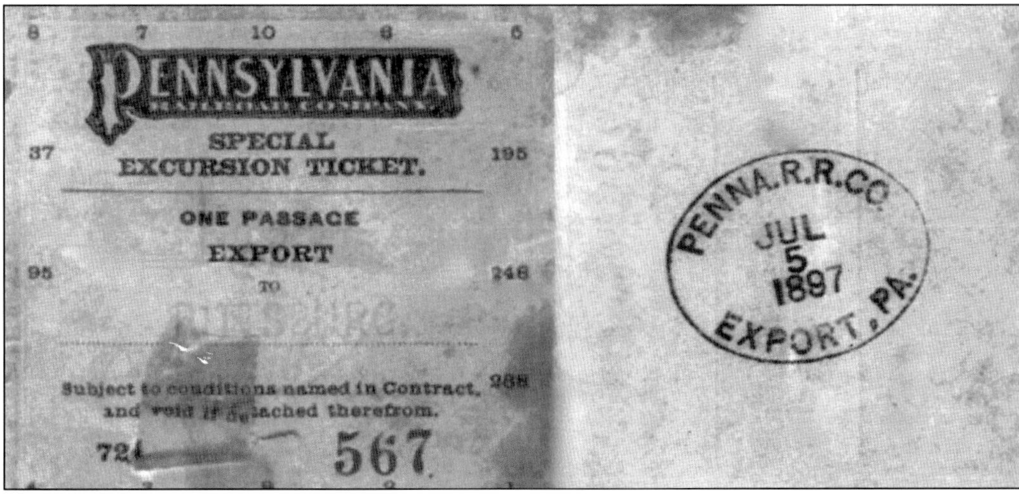

This 1897 ticket is reminiscent of early railroad travel. From neighboring Delmont (Old Salem Crossroads, a stagecoach stop), people arrived at Export's station in surreys. Roy Paul operated a horse-drawn hackney (with rolled-up rainproof cloth) because the train did not go to Delmont. Before trains, a stagecoach trip to Philadelphia from Export, with nine passengers inside and six outside, cost $17. (Courtesy of Carl Patty.)

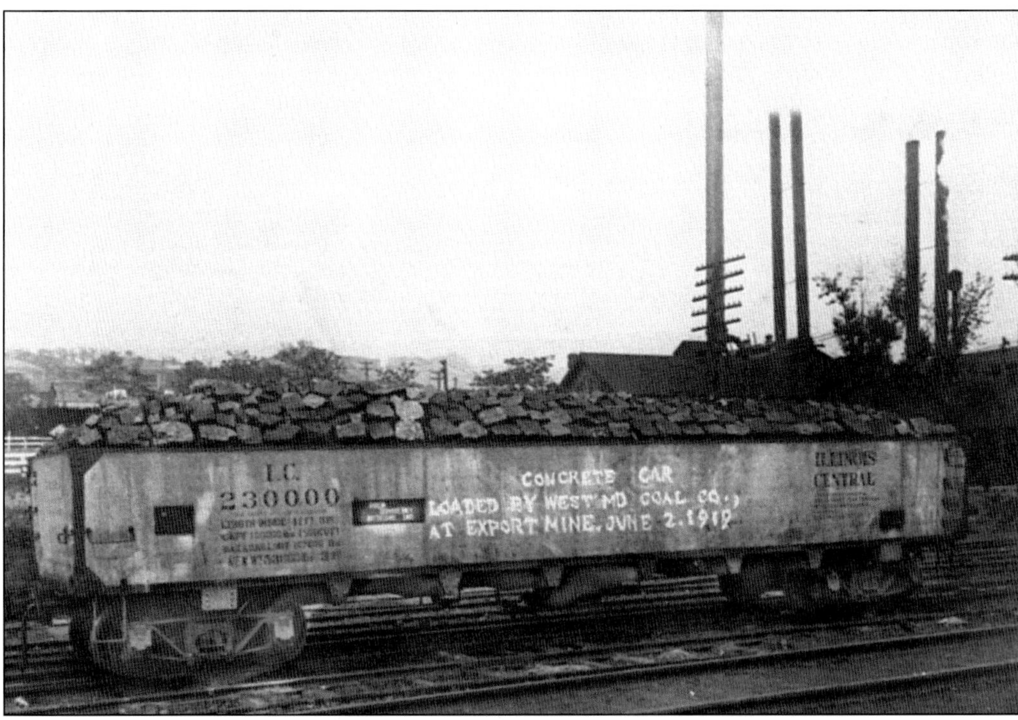

A unique concrete gondola railroad car was loaded with coal from Export on July 2, 1919. Illinois Central Railroad, due to a shortage of steel in World War II, constructed this experimental railcar. The Pennsylvania Railroad (1846 charter, 1885 passenger service) hauled coal overseas during World War II, in addition to supplying the United States. Black walnut trees used for rifle stocks as well as coal were exported from Export to Europe.

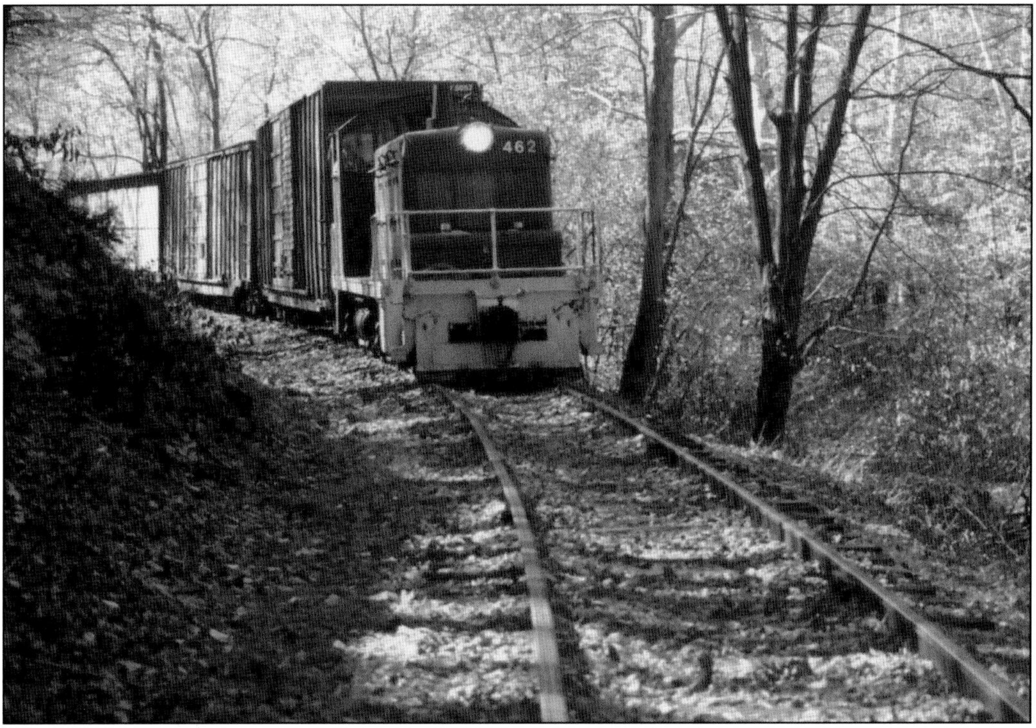

Farmers rose at 3:00 a.m. to deliver 10-gallon cans of milk by wagon in time for the 6:00 a.m. iron horse. The Norrises (owners of Dura-Bond) purchased this branch from Conrail when coal dwindled. The Dura-Bond Steel fabricating firm (that supplied the World Trade Center site in New York City with steel salvage support services after 9/11) and other businesses depended on the line for moving piping from US Steel and Bethlehem Steel Companies. (Courtesy of Cindy Norris.)

This Murrysville's railroad station was built in 1891. J. Edgar Thomson was the master of the Pennsylvania Railroad. Its subsidiary, Turtle Creek Valley Railroad, was incorporated in 1886, as George Westinghouse's air brake was transforming rail safety. On September 28, 1891, Turtle Creek Valley opened its first stretch of 6.5 miles from Stewart's Station (Trafford) to Murrysville. In 1892, the line was extended to Export. (Courtesy of Carl Patty.)

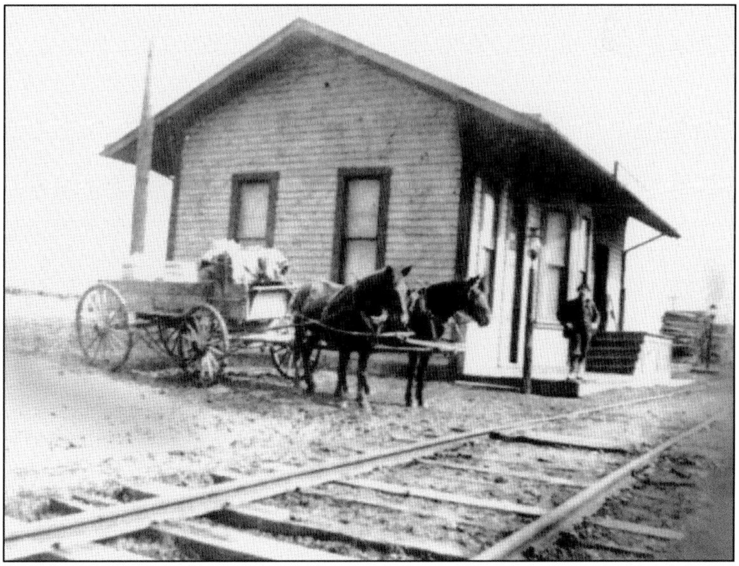

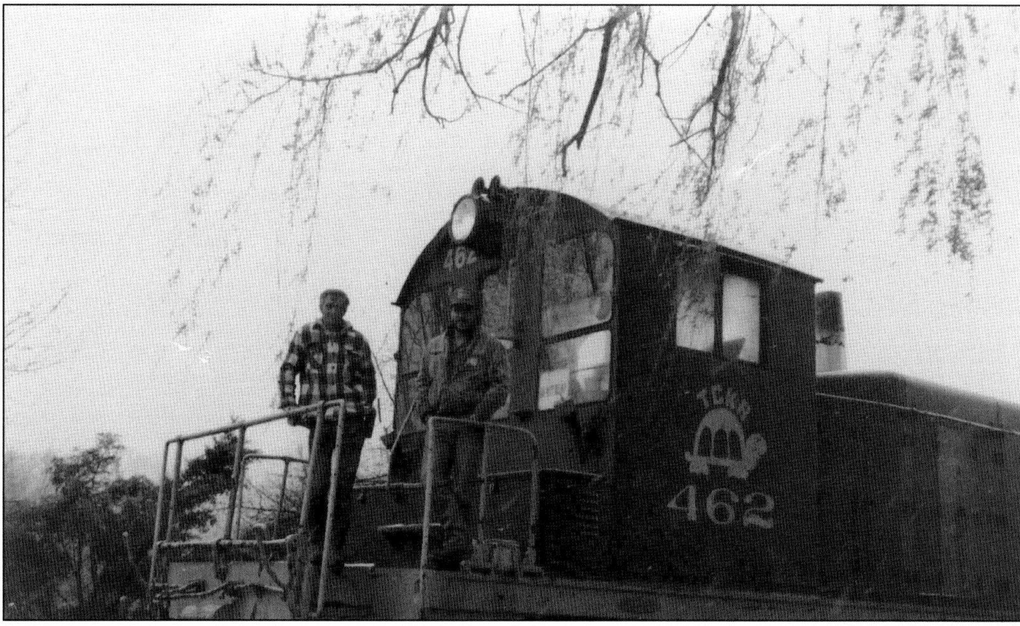

In Export, Charles Rubright (left) and James Norris stand on the Turtle Creek Valley Railroad caboose. Civic-minded J.M. "Buster" Norris founded Dura-Bond, a fabricator of protective steel coatings in 1960. He started his company at his home, at the end of Export's Turtle Creek Valley Branch of the Pennsylvania Railroad. Norris came from Alabama with the Civilian Conservation Corps (CCC) in the 1930s, during the Great Depression.

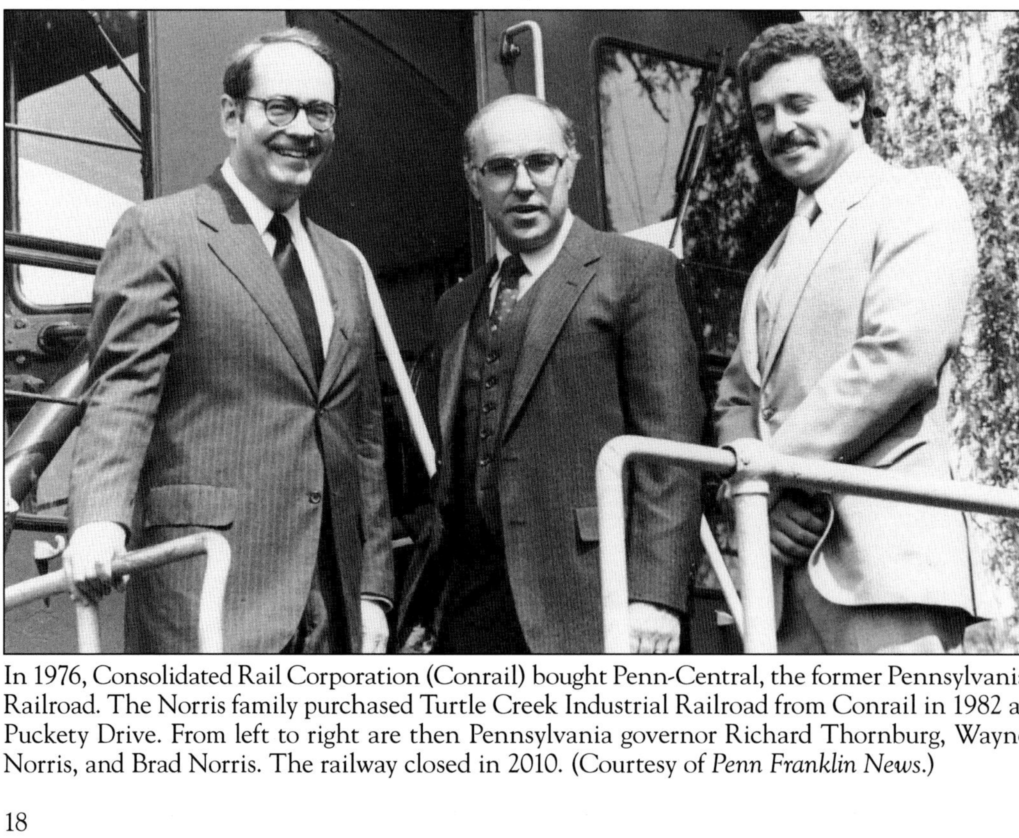

In 1976, Consolidated Rail Corporation (Conrail) bought Penn-Central, the former Pennsylvania Railroad. The Norris family purchased Turtle Creek Industrial Railroad from Conrail in 1982 at Puckety Drive. From left to right are then Pennsylvania governor Richard Thornburg, Wayne Norris, and Brad Norris. The railway closed in 2010. (Courtesy of *Penn Franklin News*.)

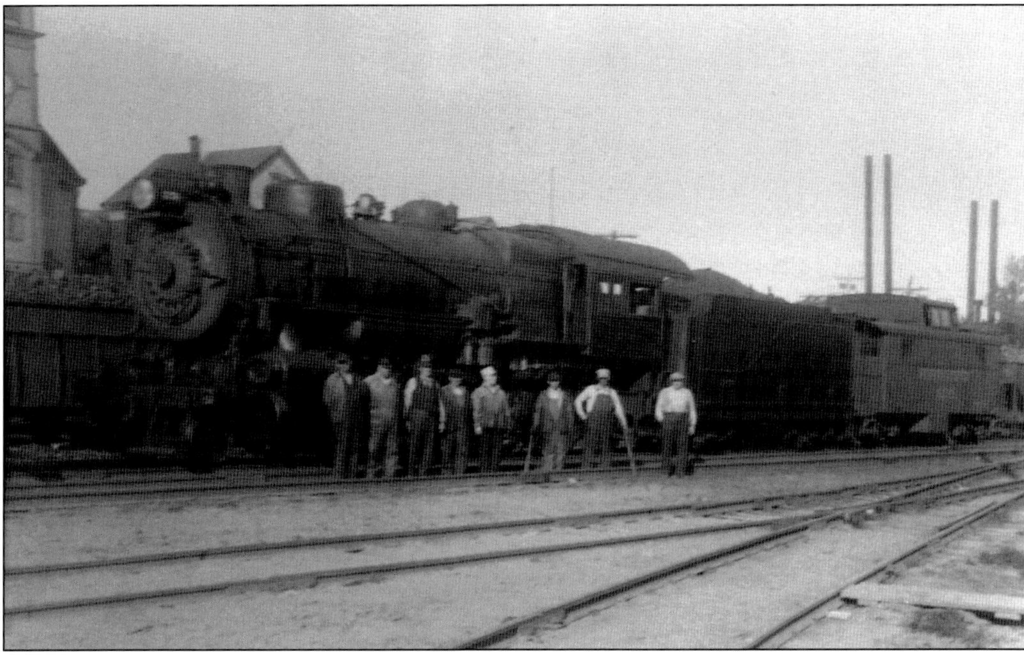

This is a crew of the Pennsylvania Railroad train after traveling through Murrysville and Export. Schoolboys who rode the Turtle Creek Branch of this railroad a mile or so between Export and Murrysville sometimes became mischievous and even actively tampered with exterior brakes. Elsewhere in the area, students rode on electric doodlebugs (small trams) to attend school.

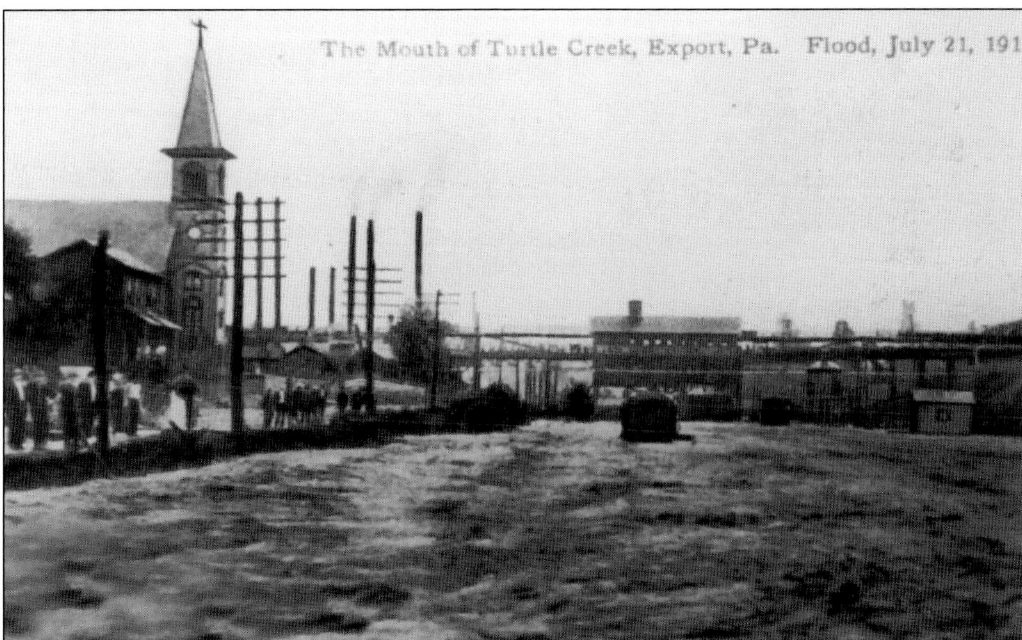

This postcard dated July 21, 1912, shows a derailed boxcar floating in Turtle Creek, which had a history of flooding. St. Mary's Catholic Church is on the left. Although the postcard indicates the view is at the mouth of Turtle Creek, it is actually near the source. This stream originates from a spring on a historic property in Delmont. Its mouth is at the Monongahela River in Braddock.

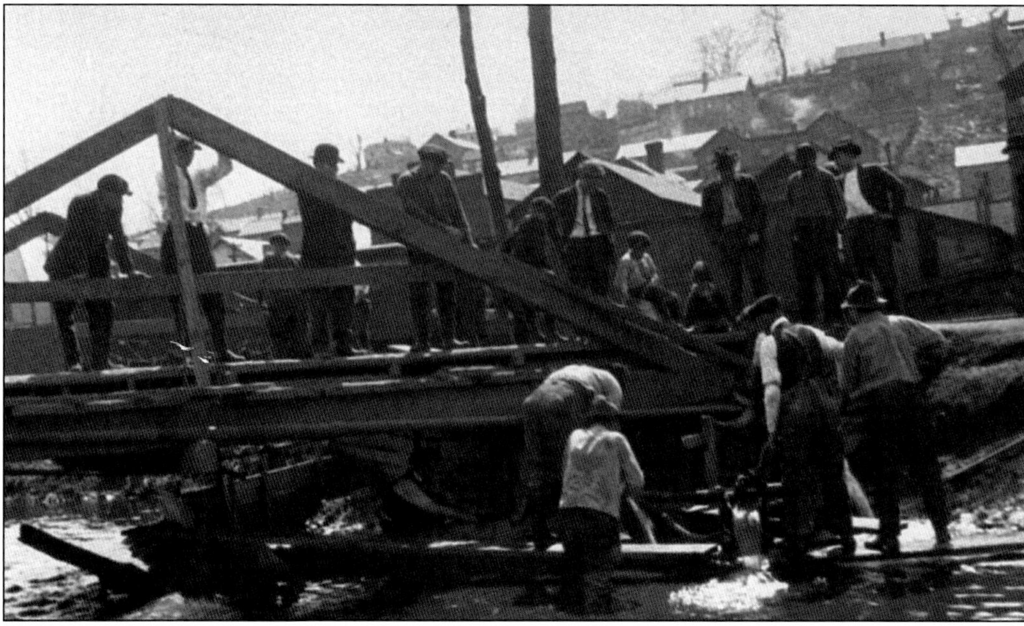

Men build a bridge over Turtle Creek at Export's Town Square. Paddling bark canoes over low or flooding water, First Americans once depended upon this creek for transportation. In September 2010, Pennsylvania governor Edward Rendell allotted $6 million to divert storm water from Turtle Creek. Export mayor Michael Calder said the two-phase project entailed an underground box culvert and construction of a dam on Puckety Drive.

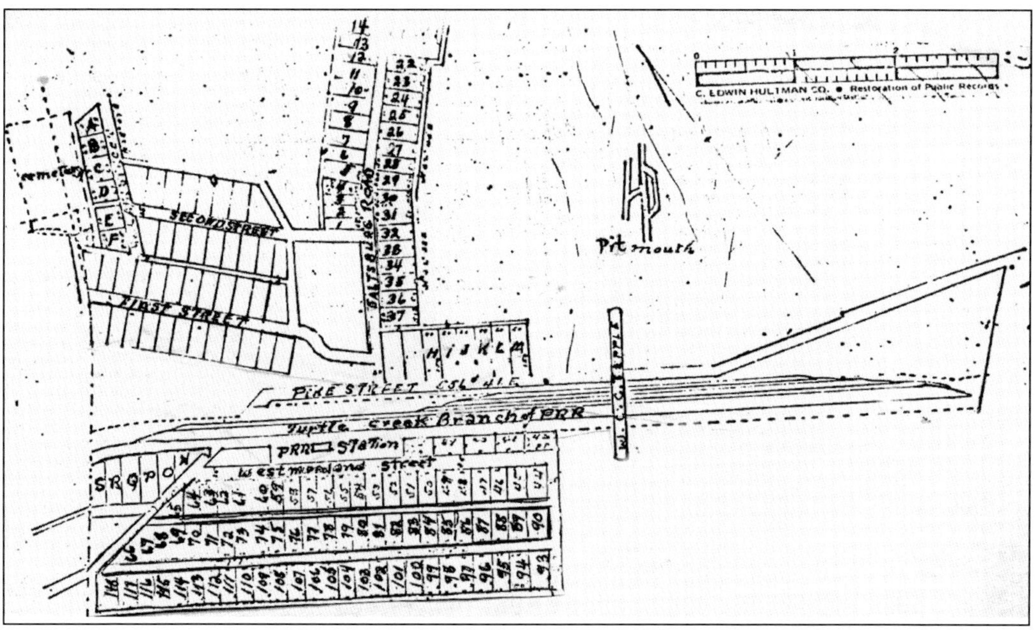

A town plan of lots shows Export prior to delivery of actual homes. Export renamed streets for presidents in 1966 when adjacent White Valley changed its street names to state names. In Turtle Creek along the Forbes Road near Export and Murrysville, George Washington reportedly saw a campfire ember drop into the water and burst into flames. One could light the ground from natural gas seepage prior to the eruption of the Haymaker well.

Two

MURRYSVILLE'S WILDCAT GAS INDUSTRY

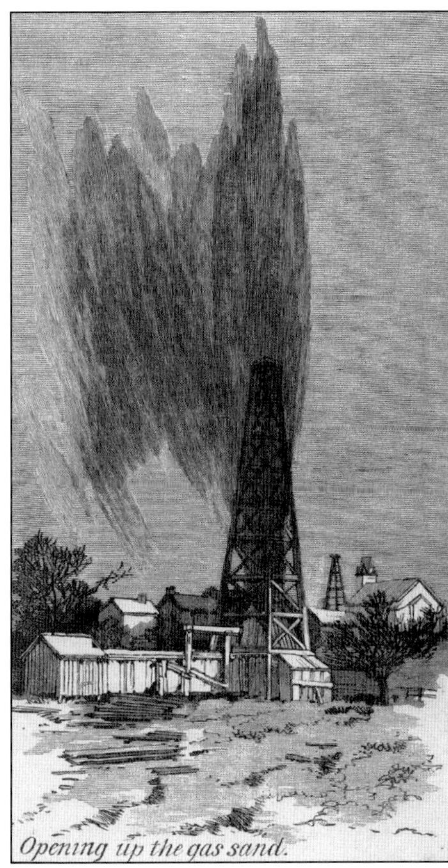

This rare woodcut, published for the first time since it appeared in *Harper's Weekly Journal of Civilization* on November 14, 1885, depicts the 1878 gas well along Turtle Creek belonging to brothers Obadiah and Michael Haymaker. Drilled at 1,400 feet through gas sandstone from the geological Devonian period (the depth is almost the same in similar deposits in Russia), the gas output was increased through additional drilling. It took a year to drill through initially. (Courtesy of Stephen Simpson.)

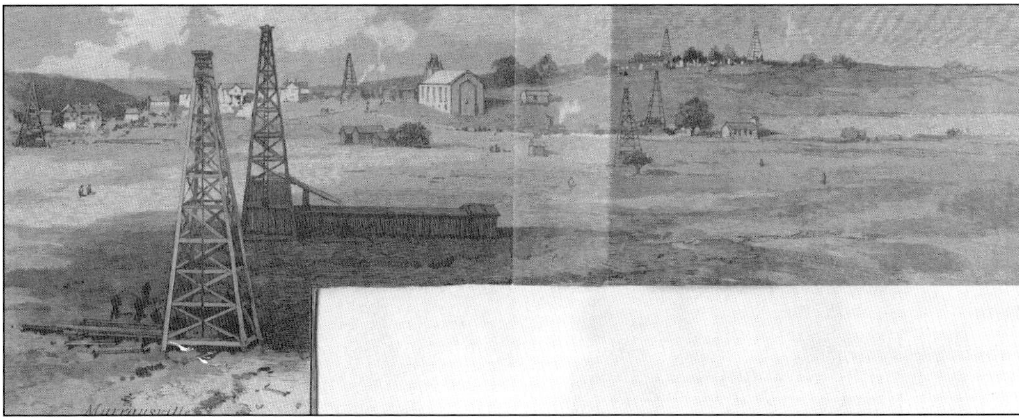

This woodcut from *Harper's Weekly* on November 14, 1885, shows the old Presbyterian church that had to cancel services because sermons could not be heard above the well roar suddenly bursting forth with gas instead of oil. The media labeled it "the eighth wonder of the modern world." G.D. Albert in his *History of Westmoreland County* says, "It was the greatest wonder of its day." (Courtesy of Stephen Simpson.)

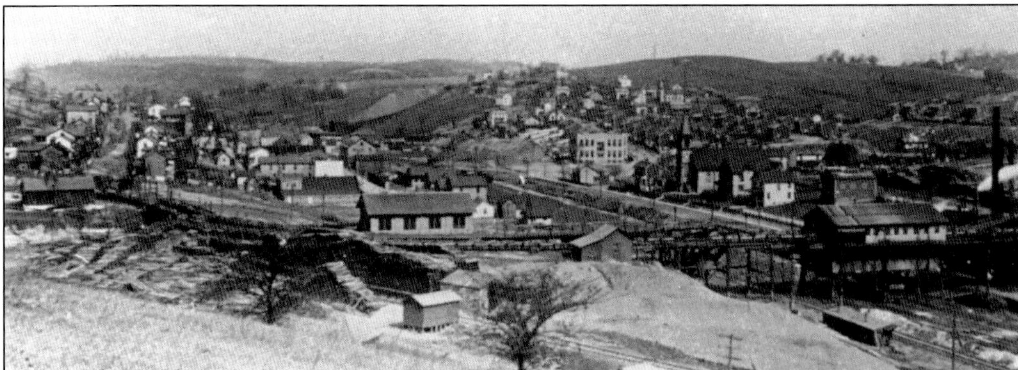

While men were drilling for gas and oil in Murrysville (in distance) in the late 1800s, next door in Export (in foreground), men were mining coal, all out of the same Pittsburgh gas-coal vein. To the right of the distant 1912 school is a Westmoreland Coal Company tipple over the William Penn Highway.

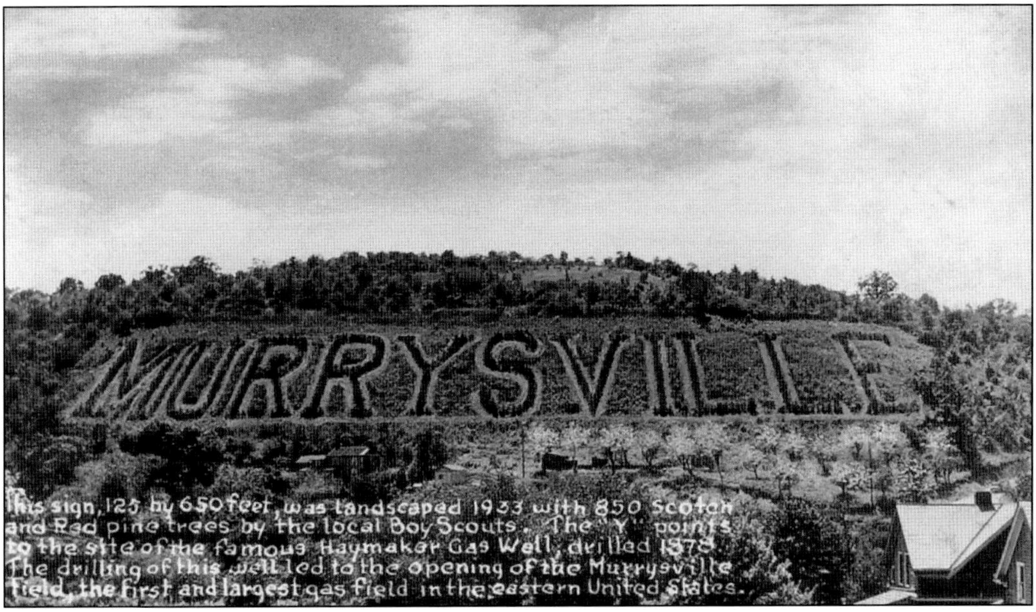

The tail of the Y in this Murrysville tree sign points to the gas monument along Turtle Creek; it was originated by Finley Morse Sloan and landscaped in 1933. Local Boy Scouts helped with the planting. This postcard shows a formal view of the unique sign overlooking the world-renowned wildcat gas site, from which gas was first piped to Pittsburgh, Greensburg, and Johnstown for industrial and domestic use in 1884.

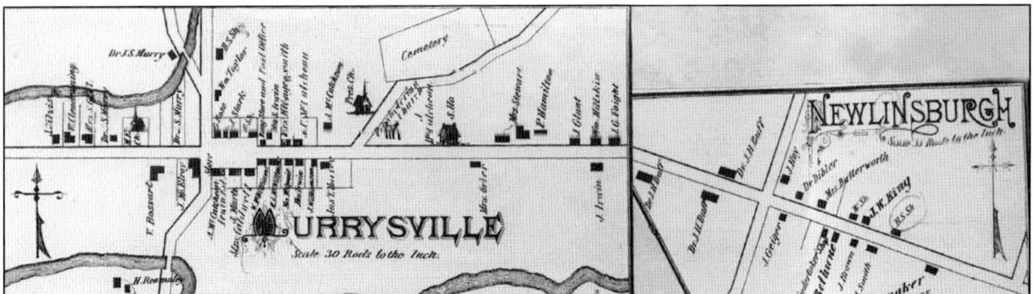

The Murrysville and Newlonsburg (Newlinsburgh) lot layout shows M.R. (Michael) Haymaker's house as 139 acres. The tapping of this great reservoir with numerous wells from the same vein inspired nationwide gas lamps, with Penn Fuel Company incorporated in 1882. Founded in 1885 by John Newton Pew and Edward Emerson (a cousin of Ralph Waldo Emerson), Peoples Gas Company operated the oldest continually producing gas well in the United States (it was still producing until several years ago) from this gas field. Peoples's other wells were located on North Hills Road.

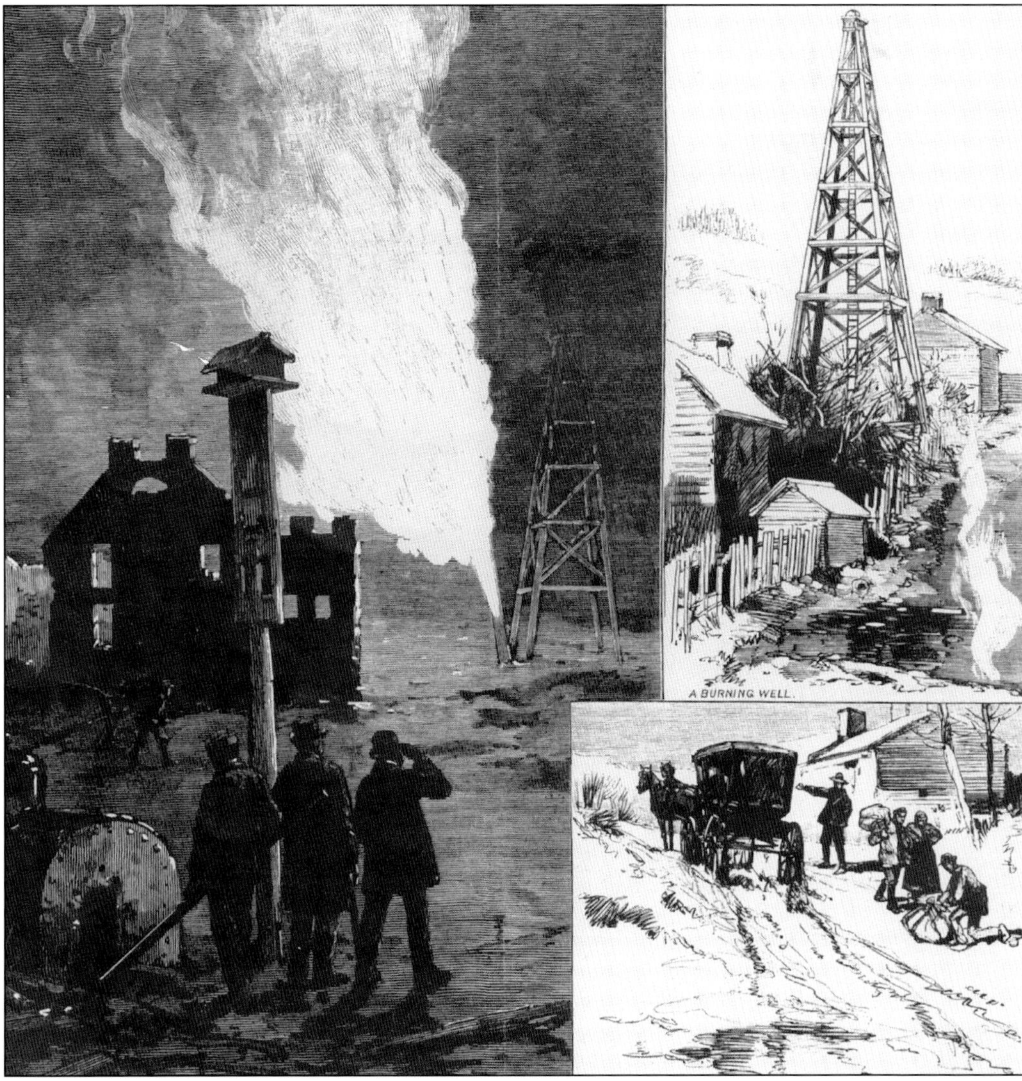

A triple woodcut in the *Harper's Weekly* from Saturday, April 3, 1886, depicts March 19, the day that Murrysville was terrorized with 34 million cubic feet of gas that burned continuously for a year and a half. Buildings were razed to stop the spread. Resident refugees fled to neighboring farmhouses. Michael Haymaker wrote, "All over the ground people were picking themselves up. Some remained motionless." (Courtesy of Stephen Simpson.)

During Murrysville's 1976 American bicentennial celebration, the *Wellspring of Power* program depicts the Haymaker well. It was about the first and largest gas field in the eastern United States and the longest producing gas well in the world. *Harper's Weekly* from Saturday, April 3, 1886, relates the story in detail. It was a disaster when the well blew up, burned for months, and scorched nature around it.

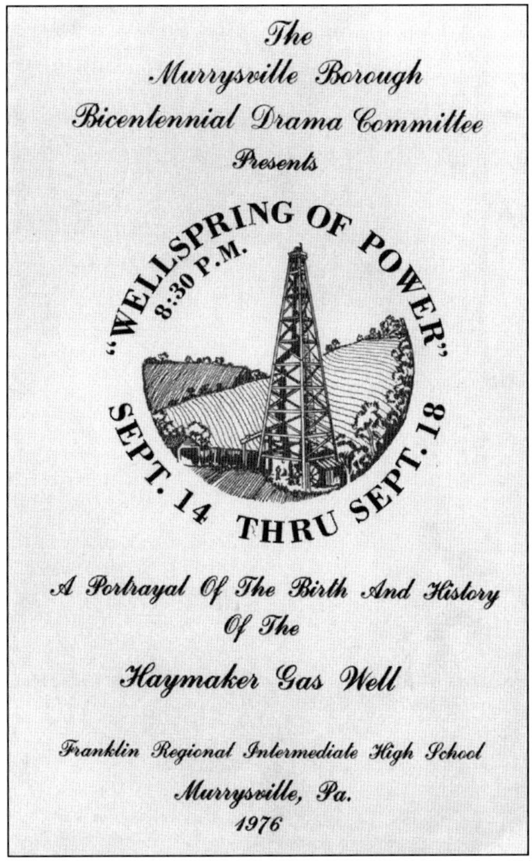
The
Murrysville Borough
Bicentennial Drama Committee
Presents
"WELLSPRING OF POWER"
8:30 P.M.
SEPT. 14 THRU SEPT. 18
A Portrayal Of The Birth And History
Of The
Haymaker Gas Well
Franklin Regional Intermediate High School
Murrysville, Pa.
1976

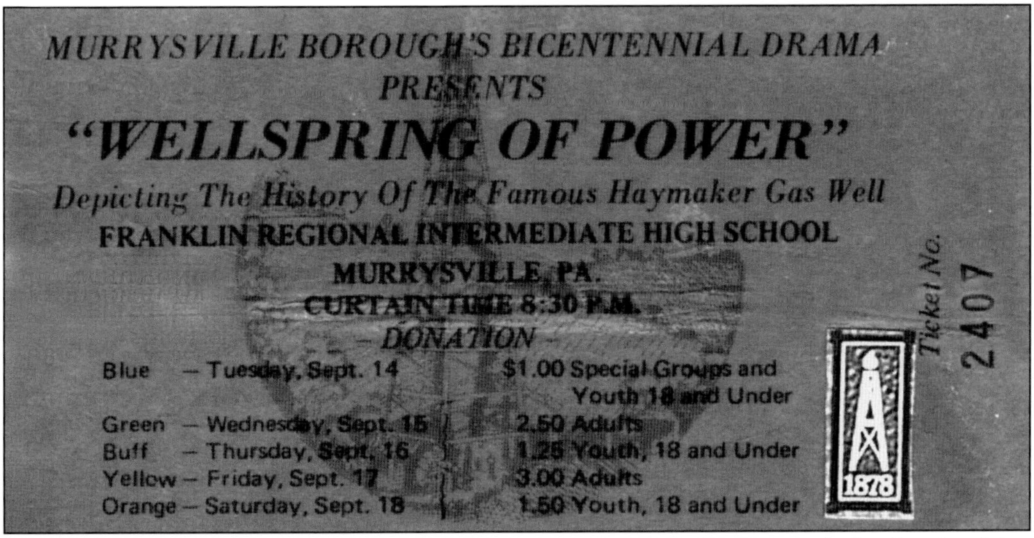
MURRYSVILLE BOROUGH'S BICENTENNIAL DRAMA
PRESENTS
"WELLSPRING OF POWER"
Depicting The History Of The Famous Haymaker Gas Well
FRANKLIN REGIONAL INTERMEDIATE HIGH SCHOOL
MURRYSVILLE, PA.
CURTAIN TIME 8:30 P.M.
DONATION

Blue	— Tuesday, Sept. 14	$1.00 Special Groups and Youth 18 and Under
Green	— Wednesday, Sept. 15	2.50 Adults
Buff	— Thursday, Sept. 16	1.25 Youth, 18 and Under
Yellow	— Friday, Sept. 17	3.00 Adults
Orange	— Saturday, Sept. 18	1.50 Youth, 18 and Under

1878
Ticket No. 2407

This is a ticket from the production. Few people in the area are familiar with the details of this phenomenal wildcat explosion, such as an investor refusing return of his down payment check as insufficient for sale terms and building an unauthorized fence around the well and insisting it was his. The logo design on the ticket is also used on the Murrysville welcome sign at the Allegheny County border. (Logo design courtesy of Wayne E. Smith Jr.)

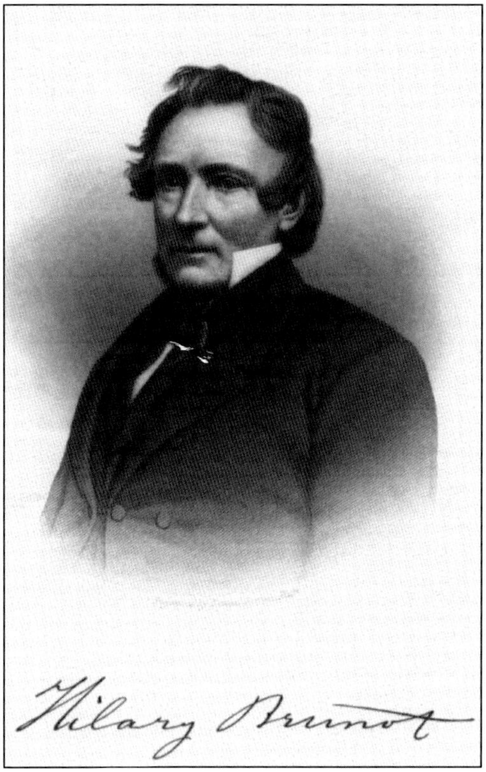

Hilary J. Brunot, an oil and coal dealer, financed Murrysville's well. His ancestor Maj. Sanson Brunot was the father of Dr. Felix Brunot, General Lafayette's foster brother. Hilary's father was a surgeon in Washington's Continental army. Brunot Island in the Ohio River near McKees Rocks has French and British officers' signatures at the base of a 100-foot cliff. Thomas Smallman, the original owner of the island, purchased it secretly in a deal signed by two Delaware chiefs.

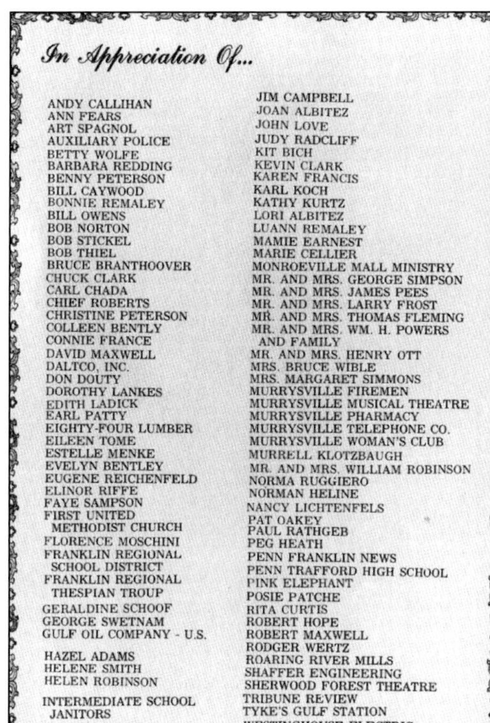

In Appreciation Of...

ANDY CALLIHAN
ANN FEARS
ART SPAGNOL
AUXILIARY POLICE
BETTY WOLFE
BARBARA REDDING
BENNY PETERSON
BILL CAYWOOD
BONNIE REMALEY
BILL OWENS
BOB NORTON
BOB STICKEL
BOB THIEL
BRUCE BRANTHOOVER
CHUCK CLARK
CARL CHADA
CHIEF ROBERTS
CHRISTINE PETERSON
COLLEEN BENTLY
CONNIE FRANCE
DAVID MAXWELL
DALTCO, INC.
DON DOUTY
DOROTHY LANKES
EDITH LADICK
EARL PATTY
EIGHTY-FOUR LUMBER
EILEEN TOME
ESTELLE MENKE
EVELYN BENTLEY
EUGENE REICHENFELD
ELINOR RIFFE
FAYE SAMPSON
FIRST UNITED METHODIST CHURCH
FLORENCE MOSCHINI
FRANKLIN REGIONAL SCHOOL DISTRICT
FRANKLIN REGIONAL THESPIAN TROUP
GERALDINE SCHOOF
GEORGE SWETNAM
GULF OIL COMPANY - U.S.
HAZEL ADAMS
HELENE SMITH
HELEN ROBINSON
INTERMEDIATE SCHOOL JANITORS
JACKIE WEIMER
JALYN PETERSON
JEANNETTE DISPATCH
JIM CAMPBELL
JOAN ALBITEZ
JOHN LOVE
JUDY RADCLIFF
KIT BICH
KEVIN CLARK
KAREN FRANCIS
KARL KOCH
KATHY KURTZ
LORI ALBITEZ
LUANN REMALEY
MAMIE EARNEST
MARIE CELLIER
MONROEVILLE MALL MINISTRY
MR. AND MRS. GEORGE SIMPSON
MR. AND MRS. JAMES PEES
MR. AND MRS. LARRY FROST
MR. AND MRS. THOMAS FLEMING
MR. AND MRS. WM. H. POWERS AND FAMILY
MR. AND MRS. HENRY OTT
MRS. BRUCE WIBLE
MRS. MARGARET SIMMONS
MURRYSVILLE FIREMEN
MURRYSVILLE MUSICAL THEATRE
MURRYSVILLE PHARMACY
MURRYSVILLE TELEPHONE CO.
MURRYSVILLE WOMAN'S CLUB
MURRELL KLOTZBAUGH
MR. AND MRS. WILLIAM ROBINSON
NORMA RUGGIERO
NORMAN HELINE
NANCY LICHTENFELS
PAT OAKEY
PAUL RATHGEB
PEG HEATH
PENN FRANKLIN NEWS
PENN TRAFFORD HIGH SCHOOL
PINK ELEPHANT
POSIE PATCHE
RITA CURTIS
ROBERT HOPE
ROBERT MAXWELL
RODGER WERTZ
ROARING RIVER MILLS
SHAFFER ENGINEERING
SHERWOOD FOREST THEATRE
TRIBUNE REVIEW
TYKE'S GULF STATION
WESTINGHOUSE ELECTRIC
WESTMORELAND STAR
WM. PENN CABLE TV

The "In Appreciation of" part of the program brings to mind millions of cubic feet of gas wasted per hour, before carbon black could be made. According to a late-1800s article in *Scientific American*, carbon black was made by "Sheriff & Hazely under contract from Pittsburgh." Carbon black is made in a factory that captures soot from burning gas and is used as pigment for ink and in other applications. The Haymaker brothers and Brunot were active in the manufacture of carbon black. They turned down the offer of Edgar Thomson Steel Works in Braddock to purchase the well and connect it to its plant.

Industrialist and philanthropist Andrew Carnegie, who funded many libraries and church organs across the nation, was portrayed in this drama. This Pittsburgh steel magnate turned down Haymaker's request for funding. According to Michael Haymaker, Carnegie said, "Turning down your well was the worst mistake of his life. The Banker's Panic of 1873 brought financial difficulties, and the Haymakers' 3,000 acres lost its backing. Thomas McCoy and John Berry of Butler helped the brothers buy equipment. (Courtesy of Carnegie Library, Pittsburgh.)

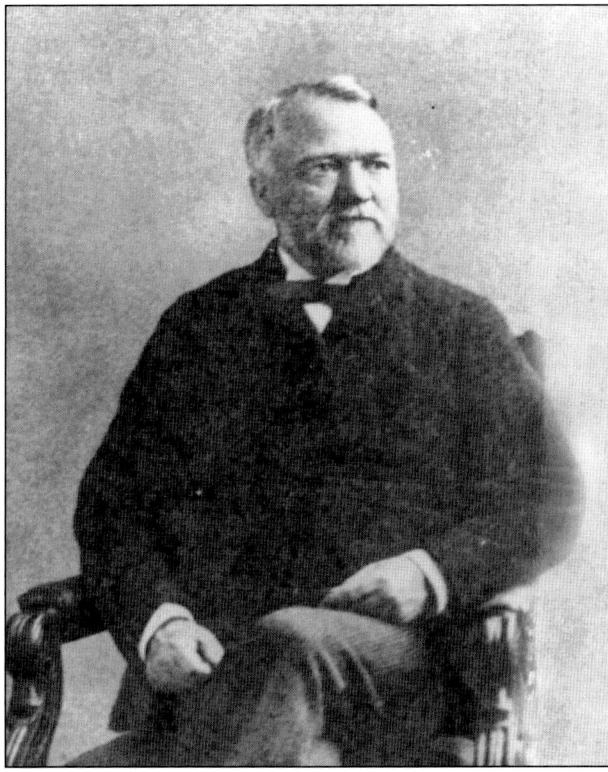

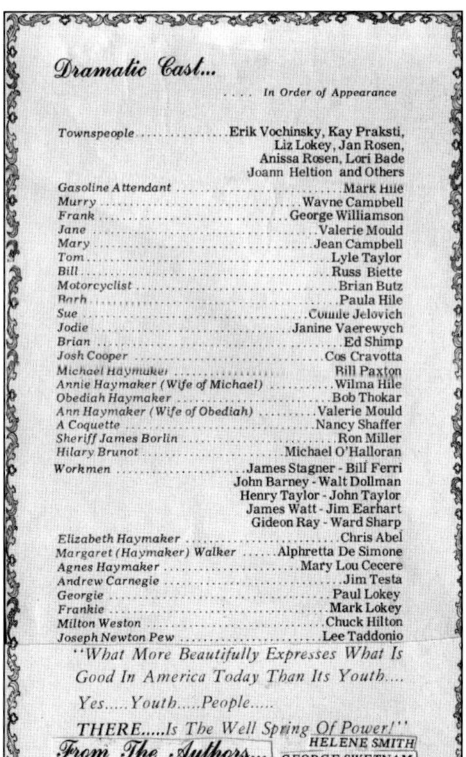

Dramatic Cast...

.... *In Order of Appearance*

Townspeople .... Erik Vochinsky, Kay Praksti, Liz Lokey, Jan Rosen, Anissa Rosen, Lori Bade, Joann Heltion and Others
Gasoline Attendant .... Mark Hile
Murry .... Wayne Campbell
Frank .... George Williamson
Jane .... Valerie Mould
Mary .... Jean Campbell
Tom .... Lyle Taylor
Bill .... Russ Biette
Motorcyclist .... Brian Butz
Barb .... Paula Hile
Sue .... Connie Jelovich
Jodie .... Janine Vaerewych
Brian .... Ed Shimp
Josh Cooper .... Cos Cravotta
Michael Haymaker .... Bill Paxton
Annie Haymaker (Wife of Michael) .... Wilma Hile
Obediah Haymaker .... Bob Thokar
Ann Haymaker (Wife of Obediah) .... Valerie Mould
A Coquette .... Nancy Shaffer
Sheriff James Borlin .... Ron Miller
Hilary Brunot .... Michael O'Halloran
Workmen .... James Stagner - Bill Ferri, John Barney - Walt Dollman, Henry Taylor - John Taylor, James Watt - Jim Earhart, Gideon Ray - Ward Sharp
Elizabeth Haymaker .... Chris Abel
Margaret (Haymaker) Walker .... Alphretta De Simone
Agnes Haymaker .... Mary Lou Cecere
Andrew Carnegie .... Jim Testa
Georgie .... Paul Lokey
Frankie .... Mark Lokey
Milton Weston .... Chuck Hilton
Joseph Newton Pew .... Lee Taddonio

"What More Beautifully Expresses What Is Good In America Today Than Its Youth....

Yes.....Youth.....People.....

THERE.....Is The Well Spring Of Power!"

From The Authors... HELENE SMITH, GEORGE SWETNAM

The cast listed in the play program includes names of descendants of both early and later immigrants to Murrysville and Manordale (Export). Those who took part in this historic play are noted throughout the program, an appropriate remembrance of what they contributed to the history of this famous site, now documented on record in the annals of America's remarkable past.

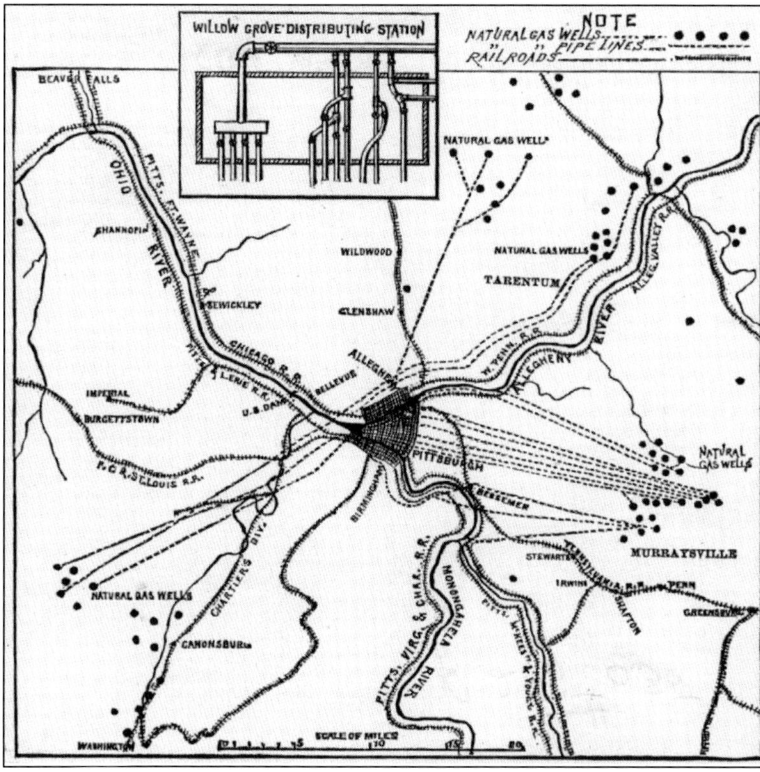

This map of natural gas wells in the Pittsburgh-Murrysville area appears in the February 27, 1886, *Scientific American*, with an article about natural gas. While the well burned for over a year, the Haymaker brothers and Greensburg resident Hilary Brunot got Joseph Newton Pew interested in buying the well. At times, an entrance fee was charged to see this fenced-in landmark site. (Courtesy of Stephen Simpson.)

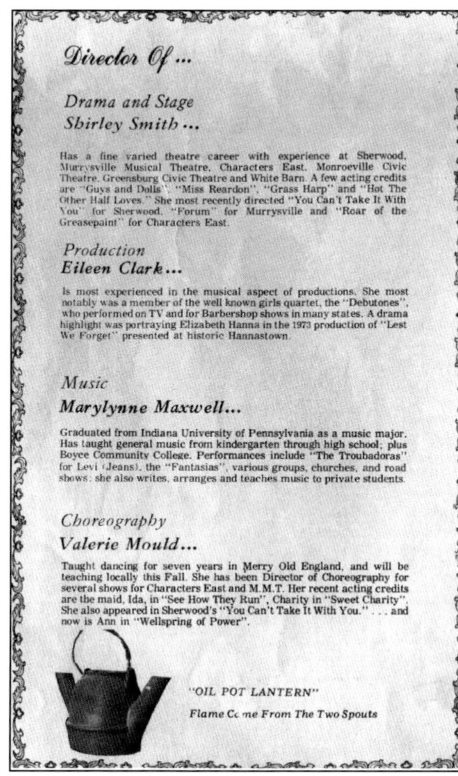

Director Of ...

Drama and Stage
Shirley Smith ...

Has a fine varied theatre career with experience at Sherwood, Murrysville Musical Theatre, Characters East, Monroeville Civic Theatre, Greensburg Civic Theatre and White Barn. A few acting credits are "Guys and Dolls", "Miss Reardon", "Grass Harp" and "Hot The Other Half Loves." She most recently directed "You Can't Take It With You" for Sherwood, "Forum" for Murrysville and "Roar of the Greasepaint" for Characters East.

Production
Eileen Clark ...

Is most experienced in the musical aspect of productions. She most notably was a member of the well known girls quartet, the "Debutones", who performed on TV and for Barbershop shows in many states. A drama highlight was portraying Elizabeth Hanna in the 1973 production of "Lest We Forget" presented at historic Hannastown.

Music
Marylynne Maxwell...

Graduated from Indiana University of Pennsylvania as a music major. Has taught general music from kindergarten through high school; plus Boyce Community College. Performances include "The Troubadoras" for Levi (Jeans), the "Fantasias", various groups, churches, and road shows; she also writes, arranges and teaches music to private students.

Choreography
Valerie Mould...

Taught dancing for seven years in Merry Old England, and will be teaching locally this Fall. She has been Director of Choreography for several shows for Characters East and M.M.T. Her recent acting credits are the maid, Ida, in "See How They Run", Charity in "Sweet Charity". She also appeared in Sherwood's "You Can't Take It With You." . . . and now is Ann in "Wellspring of Power".

"OIL POT LANTERN"

Flame Come From The Two Spouts

The program expresses gratitude to some of the many who worked to portray the early history of the village of Murrysville, now a municipality surrounding Export. One story tells how Josh Cooper boiled maple syrup along Turtle Creek by lighting gas coming from the ground. When gas exploded, tools and rigging blew sky-high as enormous pressure shook the ground and rattled windows with a constant roar.

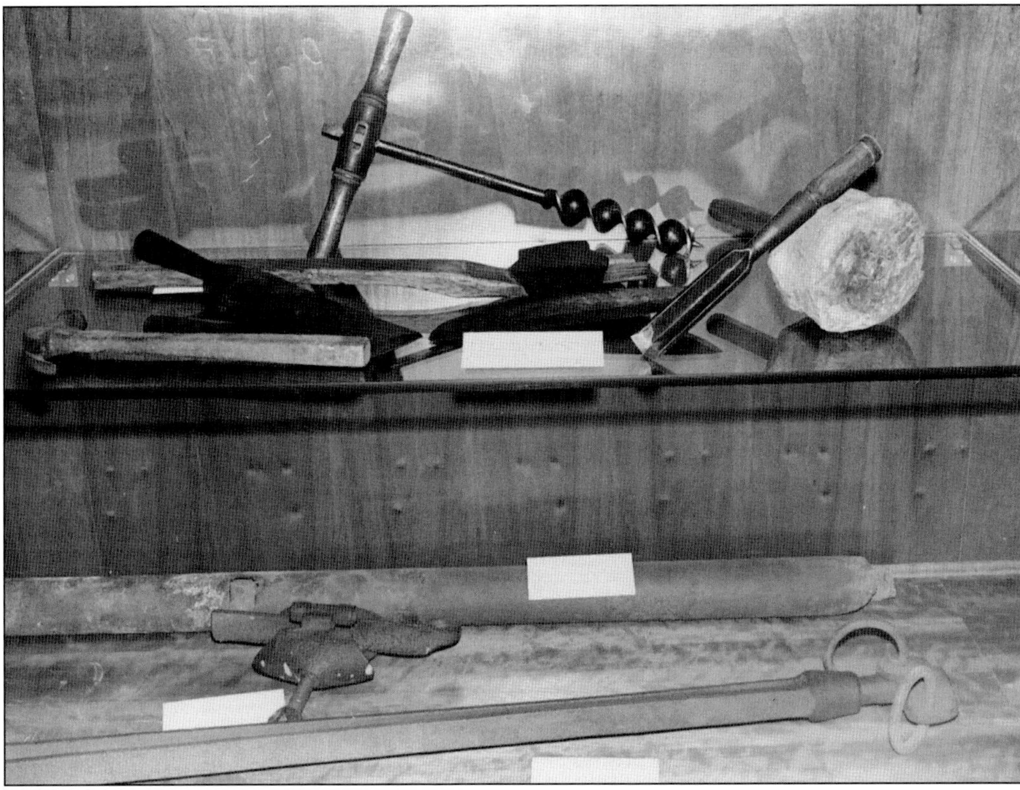

Tools used in drilling the Haymaker well are displayed at Murrysville Library. The tools, found in a Remaley mill, were donated by William J. Rose. Drills and wooden pipes always needed to be replaced, and quality steel was not available. Murrysville Historical Preservation Society Inc. owns these items. Michael Haymaker said, "My eardrums were ringing. Flames, it seemed, were everywhere." Years ago, Quay Shannon remarked, "The standpipe to the well is still visible." This exchange took place at the well site years after the eruption.

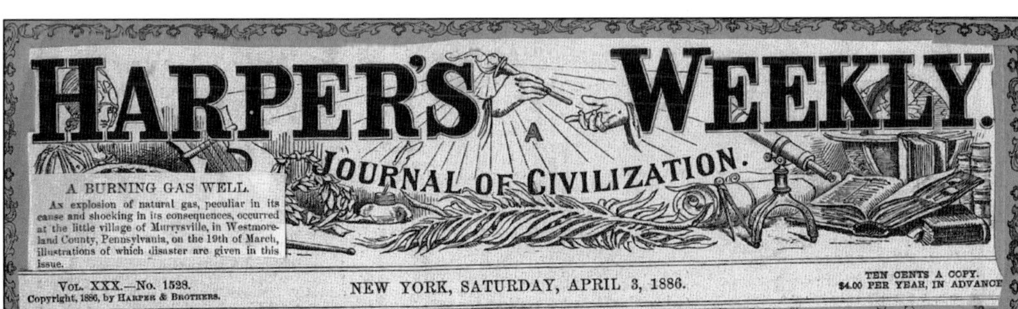

HARPER'S WEEKLY.

A JOURNAL OF CIVILIZATION.

A BURNING GAS WELL.

An explosion of natural gas, peculiar in its cause and shocking in its consequences, occurred at the little village of Murrysville, in Westmoreland County, Pennsylvania, on the 19th of March, illustrations of which disaster are given in this issue.

Vol. XXX.—No. 1528.
Copyright, 1886, by Harper & Brothers.

NEW YORK, SATURDAY, APRIL 3, 1886.

TEN CENTS A COPY.
$4.00 PER YEAR, IN ADVANCE.

Harper's Weekly carried the story: "Previously, November 26, 1883, 50 ruffians had galloped into town on horses in a cloud of dust, sent by Chicago investor, Weston, claiming ownership. Twelve employees fought with pick-handle defense. A pine tree at Paul Barnett's home marked the site where Obadiah was shot in arm—stabbed with four bayonet wounds."

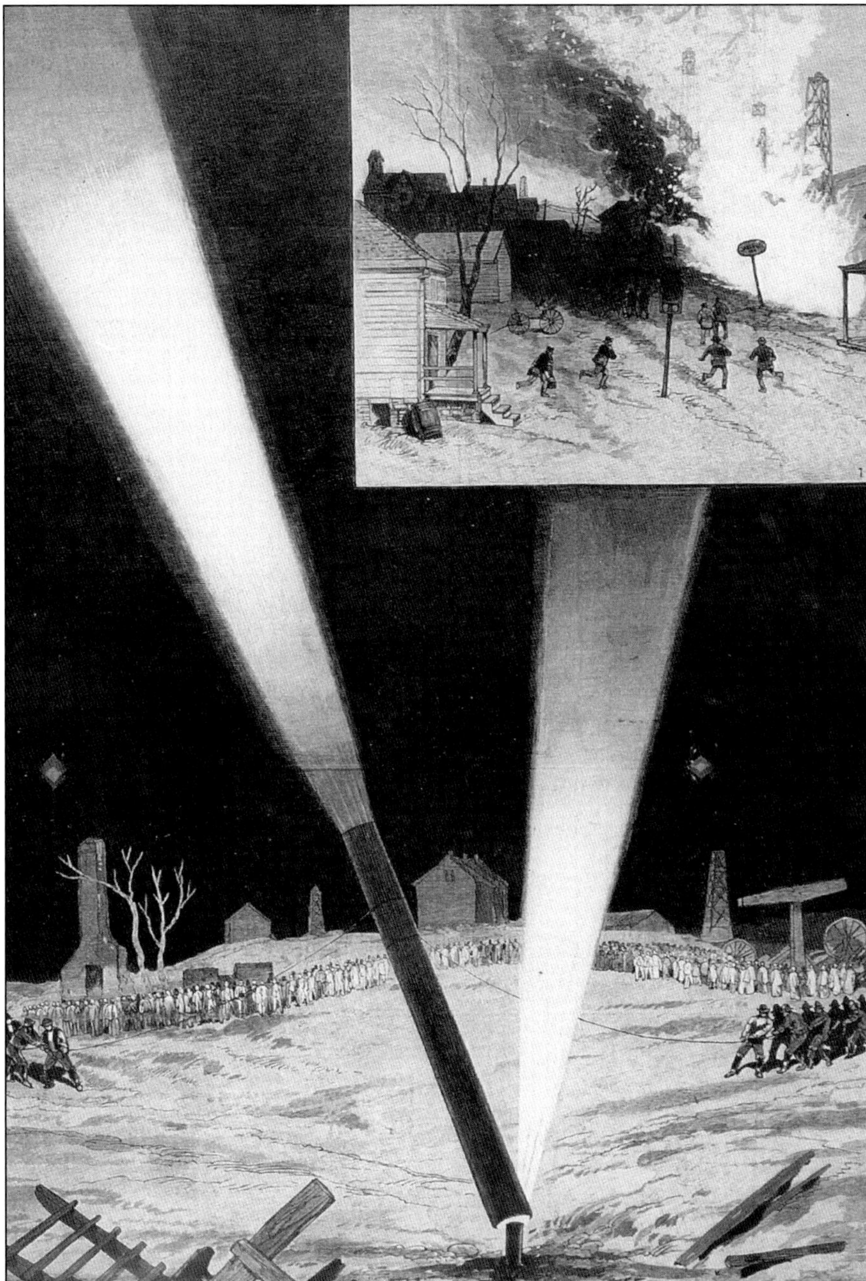

Along with this dual woodcut of Murrysville's famous well in *Frank Leslie's Illustrated Magazine*, on April 3, 1886, a journalist wrote, "Battery H of National Guard planned to shoot a hole in the gas main above the leakage. Through 20 miles of mud in drenching rain, a cannon from the battery was dragged to the fire." Instead, men used a smokestack and guy wires to smother the fire. (Courtesy of Stephen Simpson.)

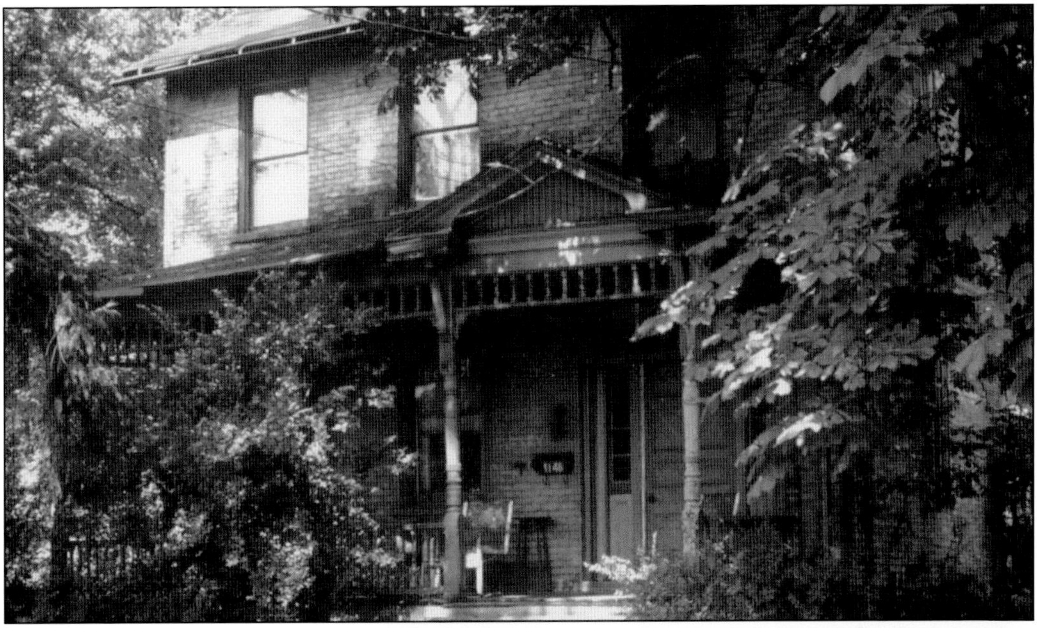

During the battle over the gas well, a bullet from one gangster crippled employee Lytle for life. Charlie Steager was hit in the back, and Gid Ray was the target of buckshot to the back of his head. Michael Haymaker and his employee, Henry Taylor, carried brother Obadiah from the murder scene to his house half a mile from Town Square where he collapsed on his porch as he entered his house and died.

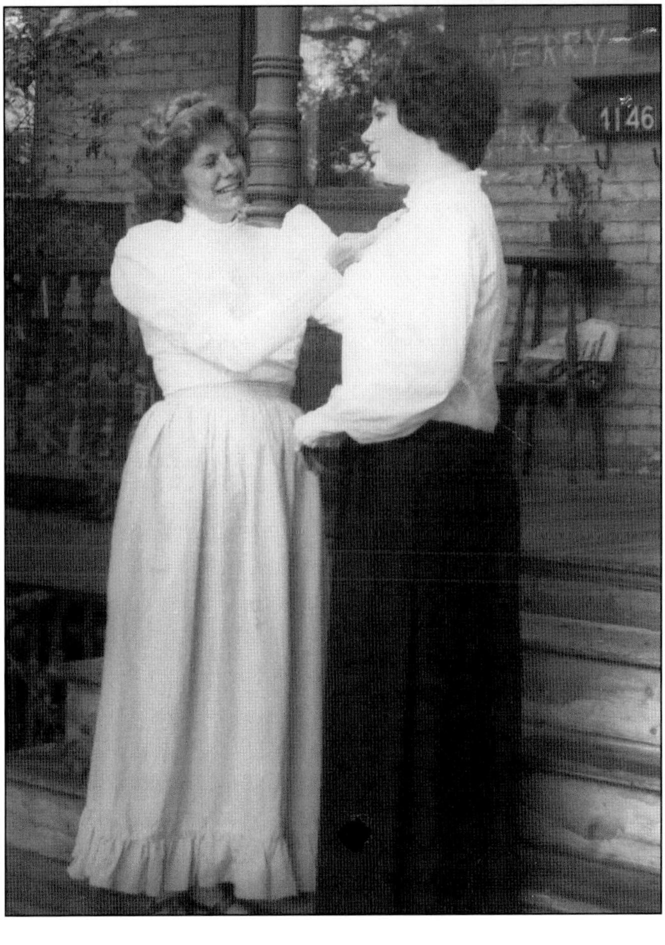

Michael's life was saved when a gun misfired. Wilma Hile (left) and Valerie Mould play the Haymaker wives in this scene from the 1976 drama. Obadiah's house was demolished several years after he collapsed on his porch. The lieutenant leader of the criminal gang received 10 years for second-degree murder but served only five. The Chicago investor was imprisoned for a year and a half. Other culprits never came to trial.

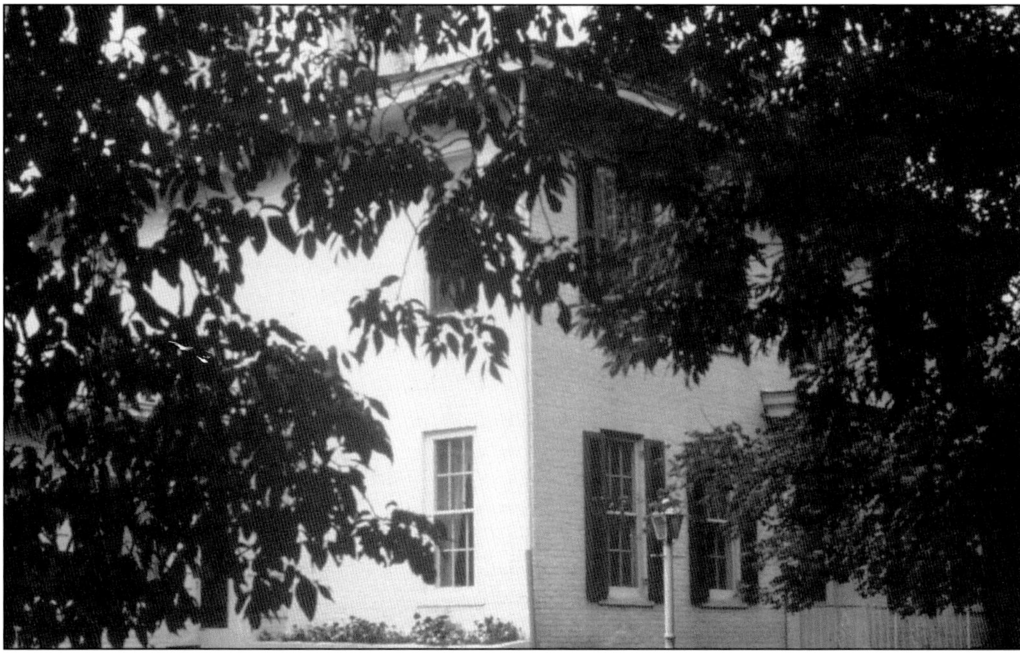

This is an exterior view of George Haymaker's estate located at Marlee Acres, pictured in 1994. George, father of Obadiah and Michael Haymaker, was the son of justice Jacob Haymaker (1771–1834), who married Mary Rugh (see page 101). The mansion was finished in 1860. It was restored by the Simmons family. Peggy (Margaret) Simmons, the great-granddaughter of Margaret Walker Haymaker, married Lee Powers.

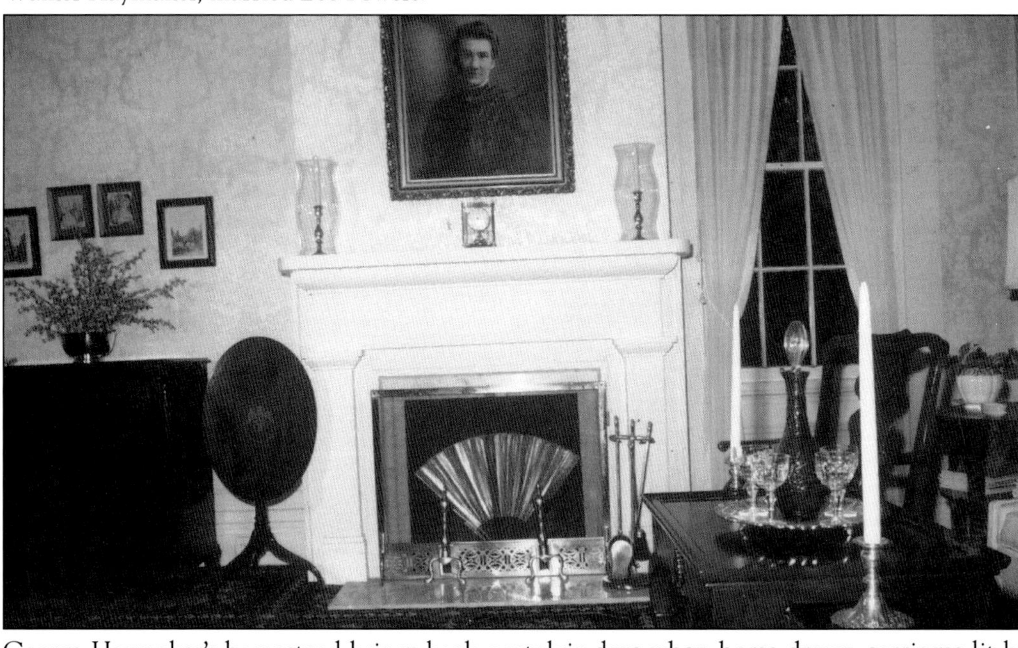

George Haymaker's homestead brings back nostalgic days when horse-drawn carriages lit by lanterns passed by, quite different from the rush of travel familiar in today's fast-paced life. The interior conjures up a genteel life of the past, when people sat by the fire and enjoyed the warmth and soft light. A Walker family portrait is prominent in the parlor.

The Music and Dance Personnel page of the program includes Murrysville's Franklin Regional High School marching band. In regard to music, the timeless song *Oil on the Brain*, with music by and lyrics by Eastburn (the pseudonym of composer Joseph Eastburn Winner), brings to mind oil-boom times, apropos for the Haymakers, who were initially drilling for oil.

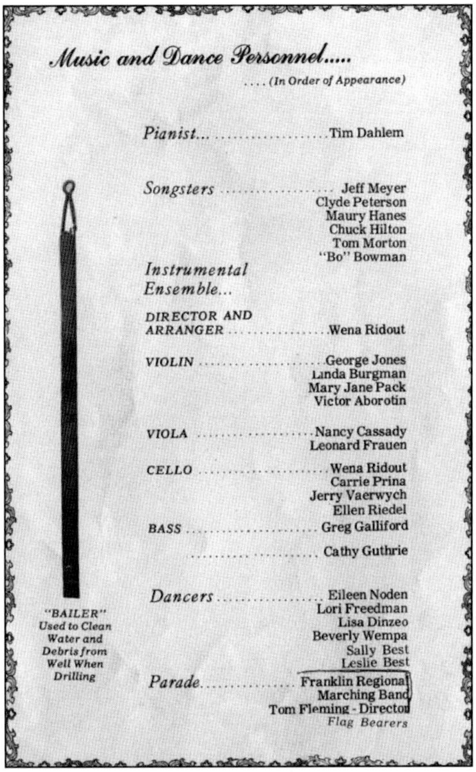

Music and Dance Personnel.....

.... (In Order of Appearance)

Pianist... Tim Dahlem

Songsters ... Jeff Meyer
Clyde Peterson
Maury Hanes
Chuck Hilton
Tom Morton
"Bo" Bowman

Instrumental Ensemble...

DIRECTOR AND ARRANGER ... Wena Ridout

VIOLIN ... George Jones
Linda Burgman
Mary Jane Pack
Victor Aborotin

VIOLA ... Nancy Cassady
Leonard Frauen

CELLO ... Wena Ridout
Carrie Prina
Jerry Vaerwych
Ellen Riedel

BASS ... Greg Galliford

... Cathy Guthrie

Dancers ... Eileen Noden
Lori Freedman
Lisa Dinzeo
Beverly Wempa
Sally Best
Leslie Best

Parade ... Franklin Regional Marching Band
Tom Fleming - Director
Flag Bearers

"BAILER" Used to Clean Water and Debris from Well When Drilling

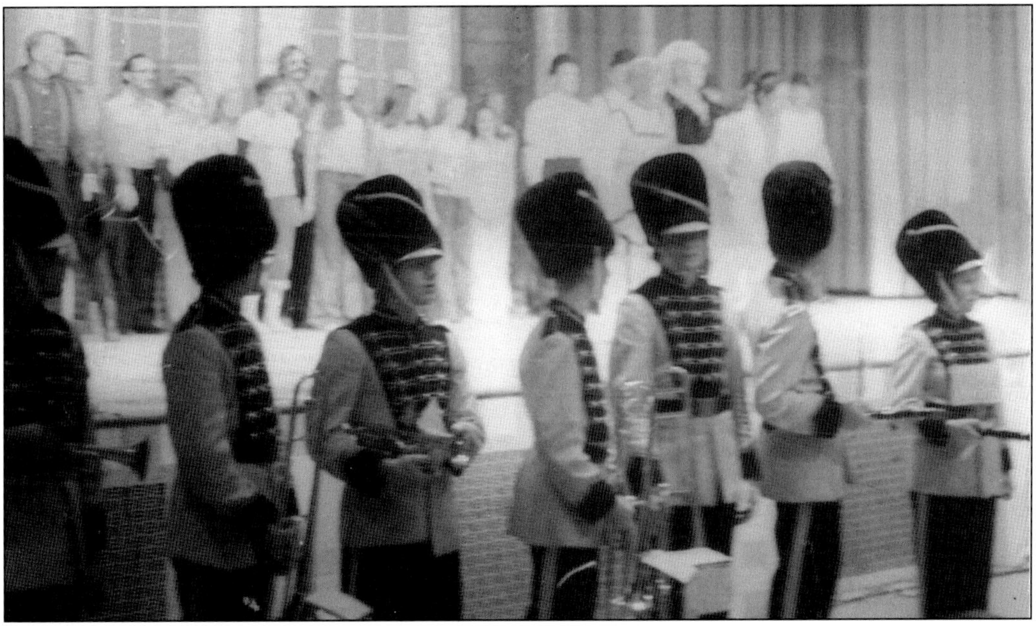

This band scene is part of the grand finale of the Haymaker flashback story that began in modern times when a gasoline shortage caused line-ups of cars—before Murrysville had its present-day welcome sign. As the performance closed and returned to the present, the Murrysville High School Band marched down the isle playing a rousing march as the gas-well history came to an end on stage but not in the minds and memories of its residents.

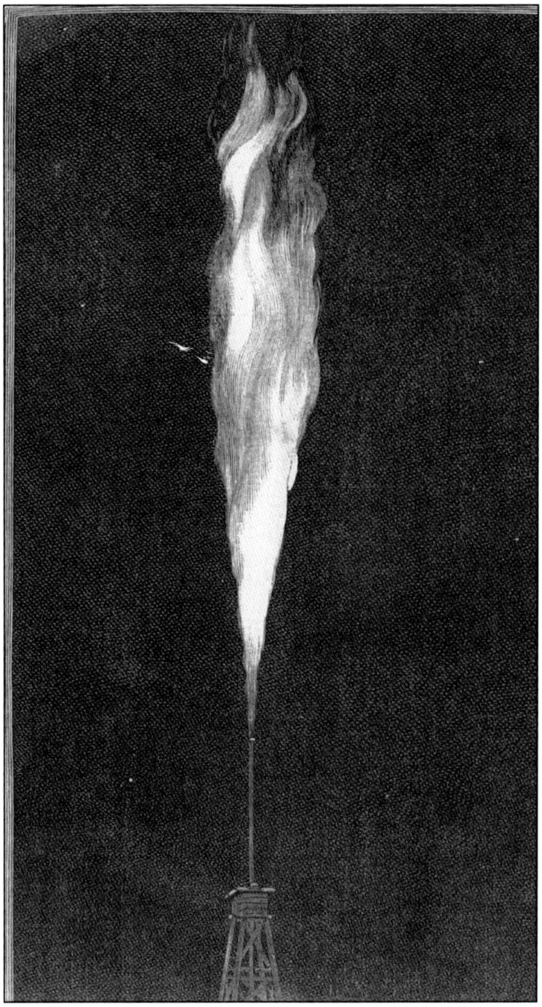

Harper's Weekly from November 14, 1885, shows an improvisation of the well that illuminated the surrounding area after it set the land on fire. The Haymakers had tried to get funding from Colonel Painter, Dan Shupe, and James Wade, Clarion County drillers interested in drilling for oil. They advised them to lease the land and they would finance the project, but money was not available until Hilary Brunot entered the scene.

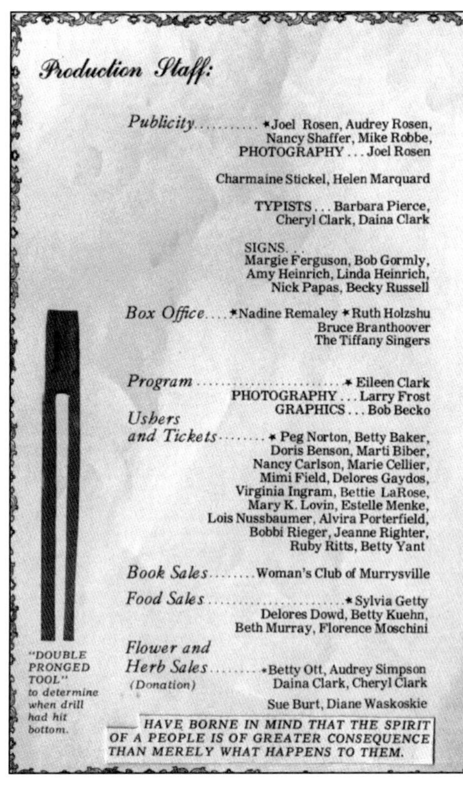

Production Staff:

Publicity.......... *Joel Rosen, Audrey Rosen, Nancy Shaffer, Mike Robbe,
PHOTOGRAPHY . . . Joel Rosen

Charmaine Stickel, Helen Marquard

TYPISTS . . . Barbara Pierce, Cheryl Clark, Daina Clark

SIGNS. . .
Margie Ferguson, Bob Gormly, Amy Heinrich, Linda Heinrich, Nick Papas, Becky Russell

Box Office.... *Nadine Remaley *Ruth Holzshu
Bruce Branthoover
The Tiffany Singers

Program .... * Eileen Clark
PHOTOGRAPHY . . . Larry Frost
GRAPHICS . . . Bob Becko

Ushers and Tickets........ * Peg Norton, Betty Baker, Doris Benson, Marti Biber, Nancy Carlson, Marie Cellier, Mimi Field, Delores Gaydos, Virginia Ingram, Bettie LaRose, Mary K. Lovin, Estelle Menke, Lois Nussbaumer, Alvira Porterfield, Bobbi Rieger, Jeanne Righter, Ruby Ritts, Betty Yant

Book Sales........ Woman's Club of Murrysville

Food Sales........................ *Sylvia Getty
Delores Dowd, Betty Kuehn, Beth Murray, Florence Moschini

Flower and Herb Sales........ *Betty Ott, Audrey Simpson
(Donation) Daina Clark, Cheryl Clark
Sue Burt, Diane Waskoskie

"DOUBLE PRONGED TOOL" to determine when drill had hit bottom.

____ HAVE BORNE IN MIND THAT THE SPIRIT OF A PEOPLE IS OF GREATER CONSEQUENCE THAN MERELY WHAT HAPPENS TO THEM.

The drama program reinforces playwrights George Swatnam and Helene Smith's words: "The spirit of people is of greater consequence than what happens. Characters in this play were real people who did the things portrayed here. We not only present happenings but promote understanding of this community. What more beautifully expresses what is good in America than its youth. There is the wellspring of power."

Another Production Staff page shows those behind the production of this depiction of the famous well story. A gas compressing station is on Old US 22 just before it crosses Haymaker Run. John Newton Pew made new strikes in Lima and Toledo, Ohio, which led to the founding of leading gas companies of the area: Peoples on June 26, 1885, the first natural gas utility to receive a charter in Pennsylvania (it was later named Dominion, but has been renamed Peoples); Philadelphia Sun Oil Company; Sunoco; and Equitable. Equitable Gas Company, started in 1878 by the Haymaker brothers, was incorporated in Pittsburgh in 1888 for the first commercial gas distribution to cities in America through Pew and Edward Emerson's Peoples Gas. Philanthropist J. Howard Pew was a descendant of J. Newton Pew and a major backer of Grove City College, in Grove City, Pennsylvania.

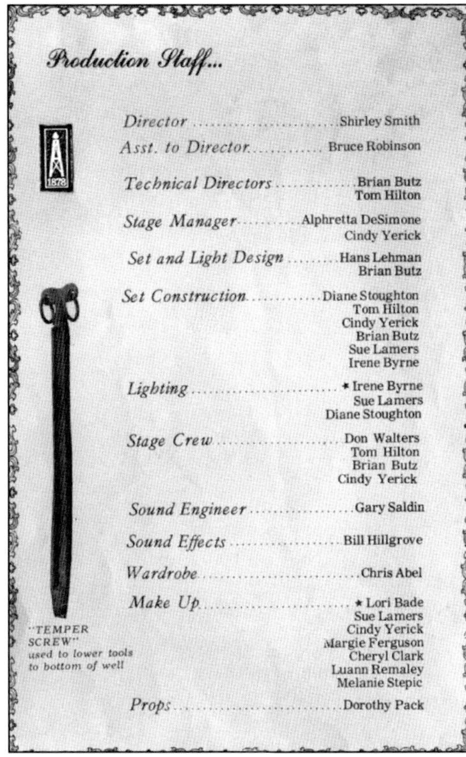

Production Staff...

Director	Shirley Smith
Asst. to Director	Bruce Robinson
Technical Directors	Brian Butz Tom Hilton
Stage Manager	Alphretta DeSimone Cindy Yerick
Set and Light Design	Hans Lehman Brian Butz
Set Construction	Diane Stoughton Tom Hilton Cindy Yerick Brian Butz Sue Lamers Irene Byrne
Lighting	* Irene Byrne Sue Lamers Diane Stoughton
Stage Crew	Don Walters Tom Hilton Brian Butz Cindy Yerick
Sound Engineer	Gary Saldin
Sound Effects	Bill Hillgrove
Wardrobe	Chris Abel
Make Up	* Lori Bade Sue Lamers Cindy Yerick Margie Ferguson Cheryl Clark Luann Remaley Melanie Stepic
Props	Dorothy Pack

"TEMPER SCREW" *used to lower tools to bottom of well*

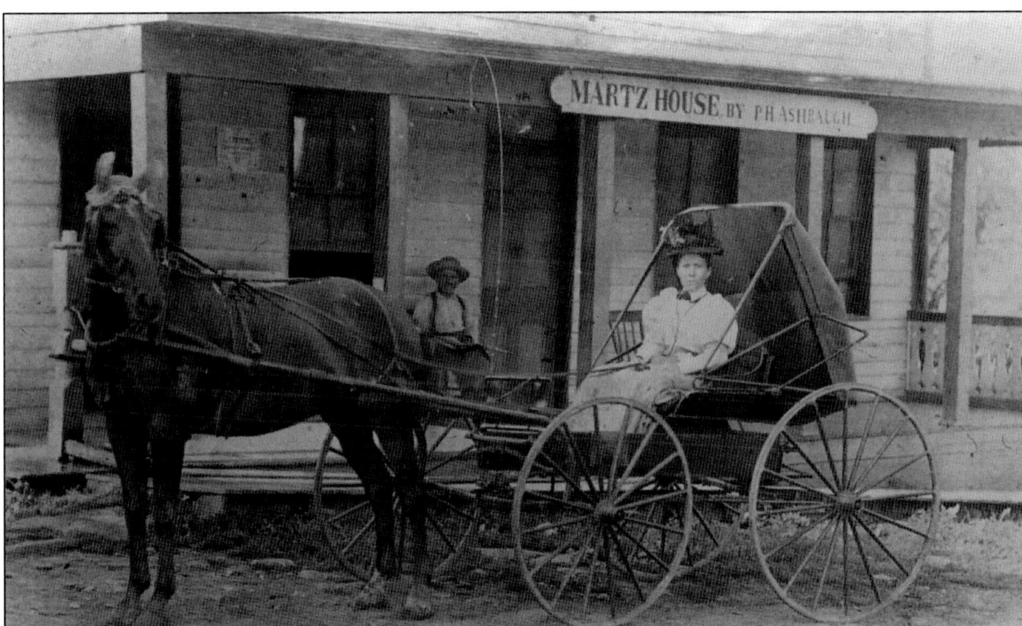

Paul Ashbaugh managed Martz's Murrysville boardinghouse, the site of Ferri's supermarket. It accommodated gas-well laborers, drillers, teamsters, and tool-dressers. German residents spelled the name Marts. Ashbaugh's wife, seated in the buggy, was the chief cook. This is a rare photograph of a boardinghouse in town. There were, no doubt, many more, as one street was known as the Poker area and contained numerous taverns. (Courtesy of Stephen Simpson.)

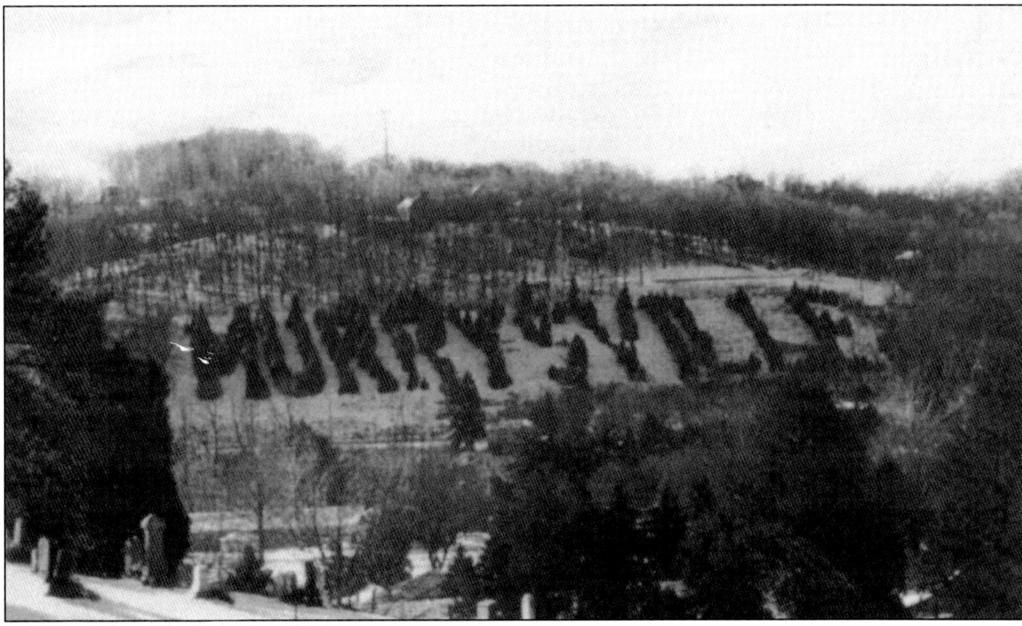

This hillside landmark, viewed from the Presbyterian Cemetery, originally encompassed 850 scotch-red pines and measured 124 by 650 feet. In 1966 and again in the 1980s, America's largest live sign was replanted by the Sportsmen and Landowners Alliance of Murrysville when overgrown trees made the name illegible and were difficult to control. The M is on former hunting grounds of First Americans. (Courtesy of Robert Stickel, volunteer for Medic One.)

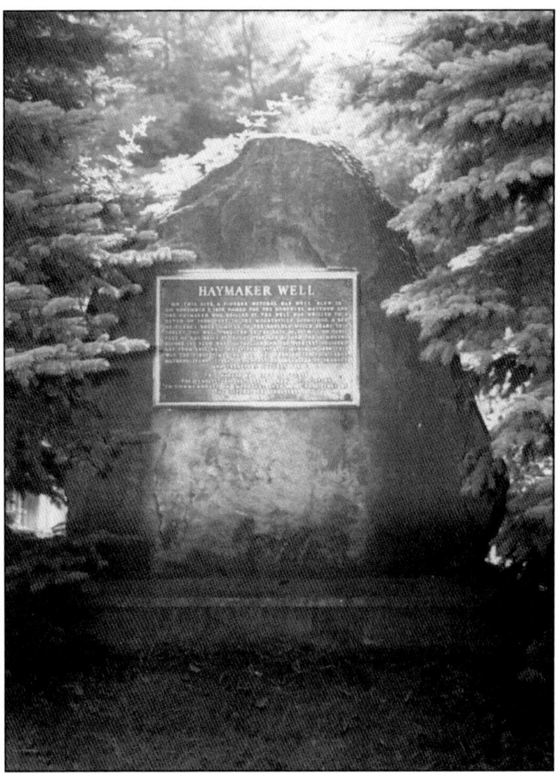

This 1961 monument at Norbatrol Court along the railroad tracks that marks the gas well is actually 200 feet north of the site, according to Quay Shannon. His grandfather helped Michael Haymaker extinguish the fire. Pipelines that recovered natural gas underground were laid to F. Morse Sloan Pumping Station. As Murrysville is world-famous for its oldest producing gas well, Export is the first site where coal was mined to be exported overseas. Both are intertwined.

Three
EXPORT'S FIRST COAL TO GO GLOBAL

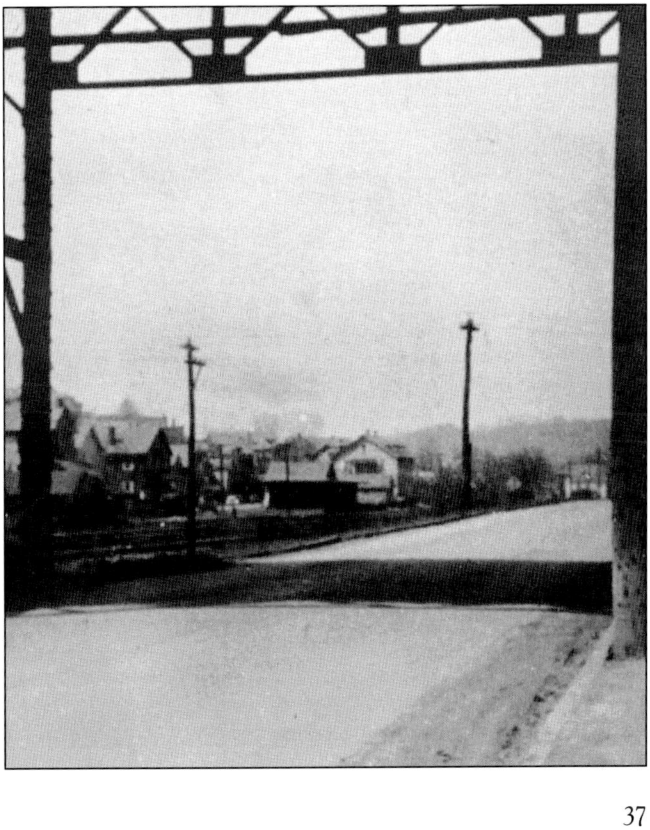

Westmoreland Coal Company's tipple became a symbol for Export, which was nicknamed "the town with the tipple over the road" and is still identified as such. Turtle Creek and the Turtle Creek Valley Railroad were parallel with the Old William Penn Highway (pictured) intertwining with the Northern Turnpike. Land was graded and streams were rerouted to make room for coal yards that took up much space.

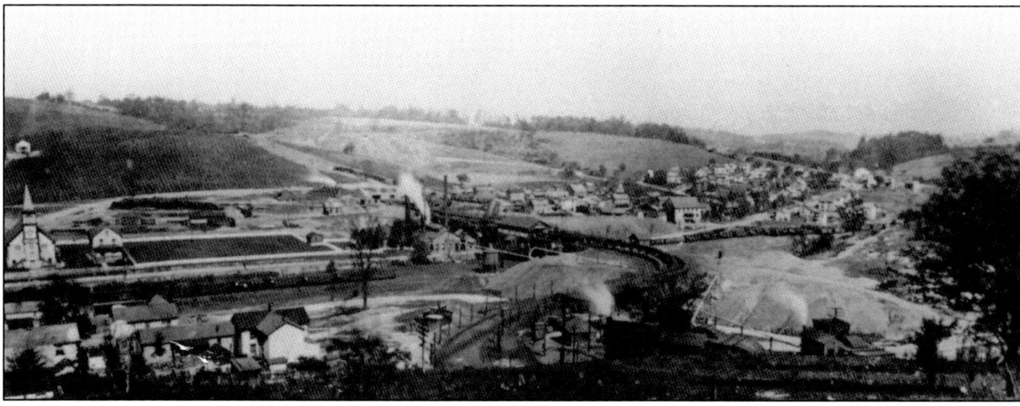

Westmoreland Coal Company's tipple over Old US 22 is in the middle of this image and to the right of St. Mary's Church and adjoining mule pasture. The old side mine entrance no. 1 north of tracks operated from 1892 to 1952 and was the source of the first coal here; side entrance no. 2 south of the tracks operated from 1904 to 1952 and was the site of the first coal exporting. From this coal seam, William Penn's heirs sold mining privileges on their private tracts of land for 30 pounds per lot and set off a primitive, private coal industry.

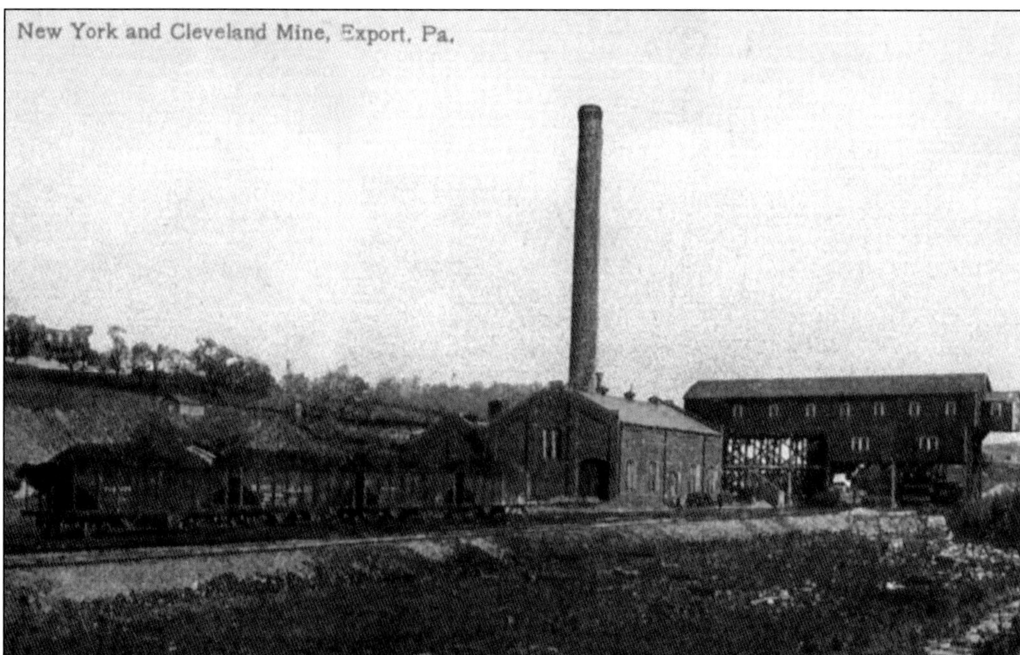

White Valley's New York–Cleveland Mine (originally named Pedora, after an Italian town) is in Murrysville as was the Pittsburgh Coal Company. Also here was the Star or Peanut Mine. This small mine was the only slope mine, as the others were drift mines. Diffenderfer, McAlister, and Gillie owned a mine nicknamed "Last Chance Mine." If a miner could not get work there, it was his last chance on the way out of town. This slope mine had its tunnel sealed at a spring on West Pike and Kistler Streets at Remaley's farm. The postcard incorrectly identifies the mine as being in Export.

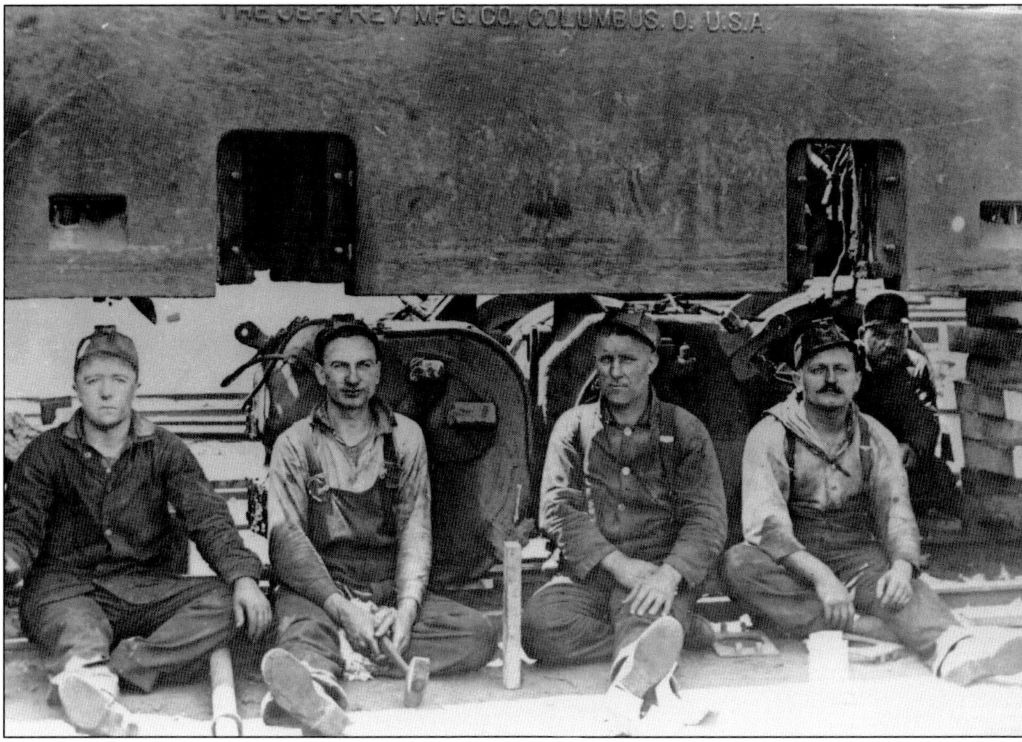

Five workers sit in front of a coal mine car-operating machine made by Jeffrey Manufacturing Company in Columbus, Ohio. From left to right are Cooper McManic, ? Deaunovich, ? Whirlow, ? Erkovich, and Paul Visnick. Motors that used coal-fired steam generators to produce electricity replaced mules in moving coal cars in and out of the mines. (Courtesy of Raymond Meehan.)

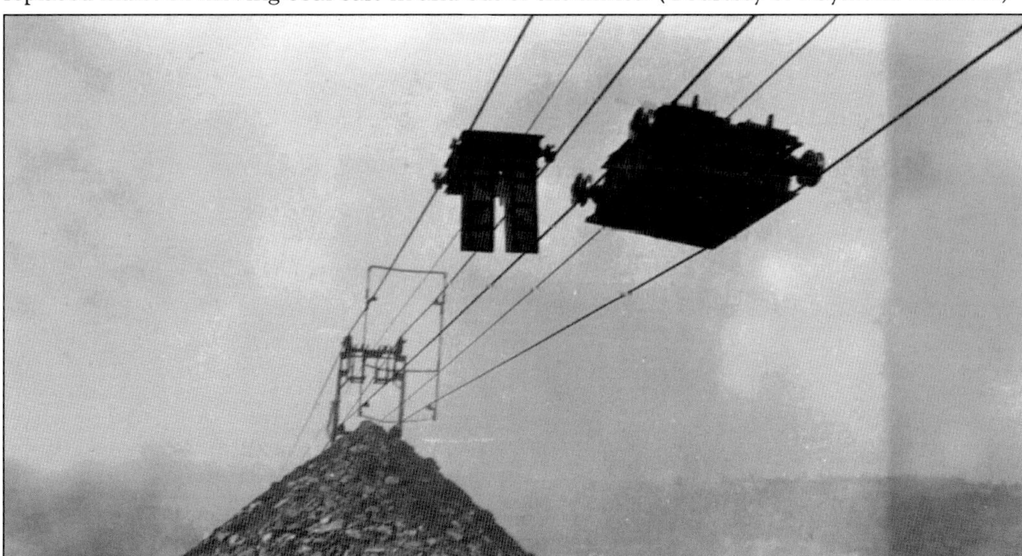

A filled aerial mine car in Export passes an empty one between the mines and the tipple and coal hills. In 1873, colliers were paid 5¢ a bushel for digging coal from the area's mines. In September 1938, this vast bed "produced a greater value of coal at mine prices than had ever been yielded by any single mineral deposit in the world's history," says a quote from *Wellspring of Power.*

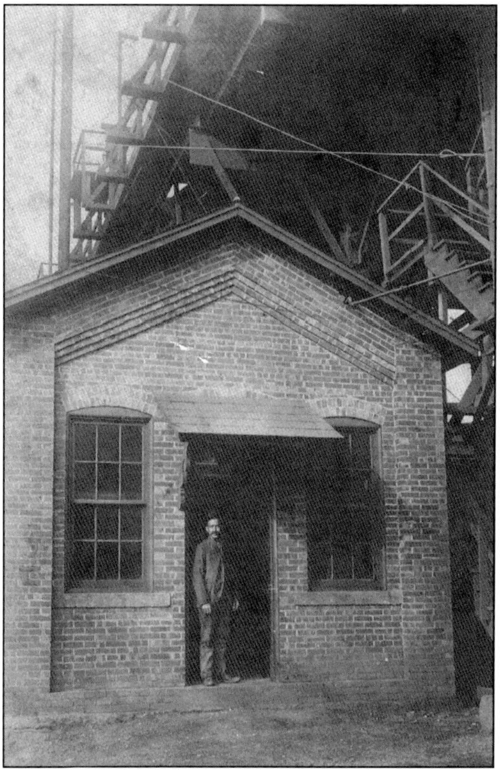

An unidentified miner is in the doorway of a building housing a communal shower in the shadow of the Westmoreland Coal Company tipple. This 1908 postcard reads, "This is a picture of Papa after he is done working and so ready to start home, as you well know." Here, a dozen boilers below the smokestacks provided steaming hot water for bathing. (Courtesy of Raymond Meehan, photograph by John "Mutt" Wuslich.)

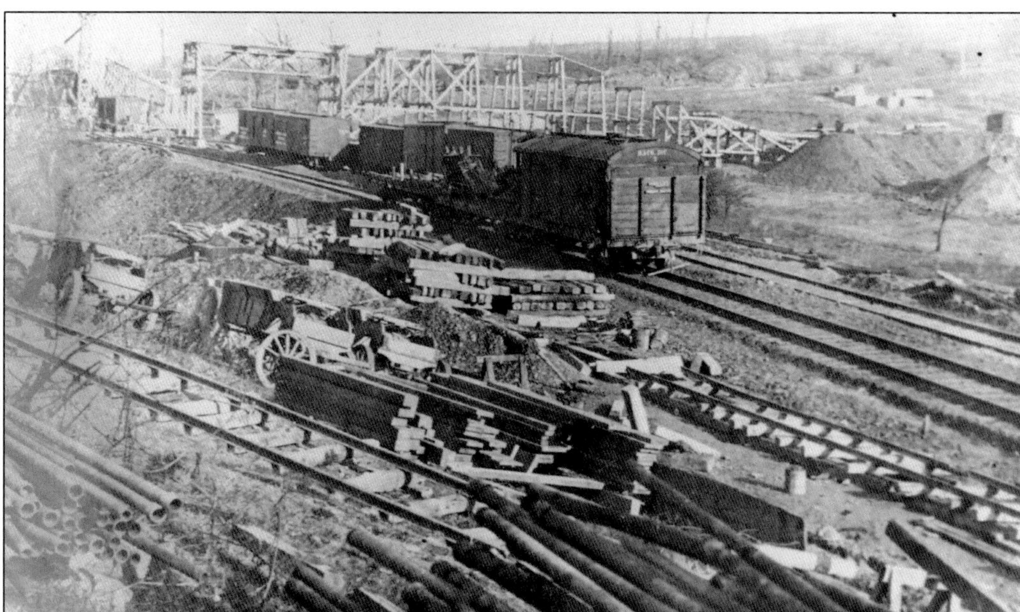

The Westmoreland Coal Company tipple is under construction. Filled wooden hop cars on tracks bring to mind George Washington's 1770 journal: "The coal seemed to be of the best kind, burning freely, and abundance of it." The great Pittsburgh seam underlying Murrysville and Export, expanded from Manordale (named for Denmark Manor, originally private land reserved for William Penn, who died in 1718).

A coal miner's daughter stands before miners who have just left Westmoreland Coal Company's colliery. Children helped mothers pack meals for miners. Each scratch and dent of a dinner pail had a story behind it, as evidenced by this poem written by Ned Harrigan: "It glistened like silver, so sparkling and bright, / I loved it, this kettle that held dear dad's bite. / In winter and summer, in rain, snow or hail, / I carried that treasure, my dad's dinner pail."

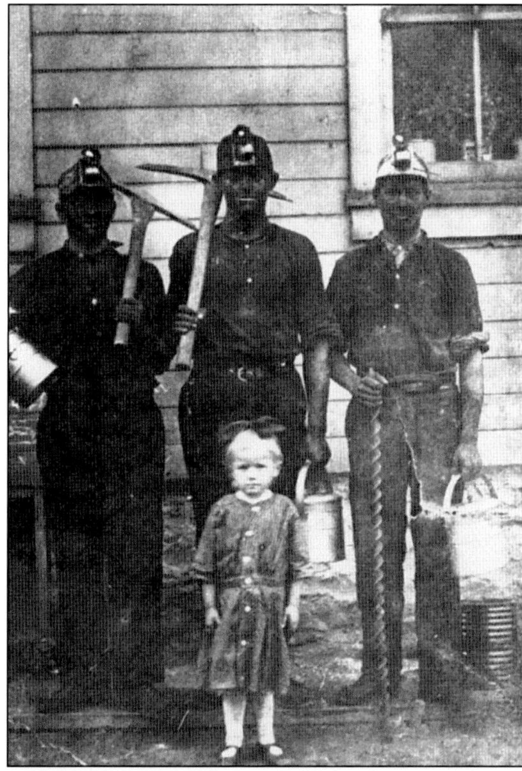

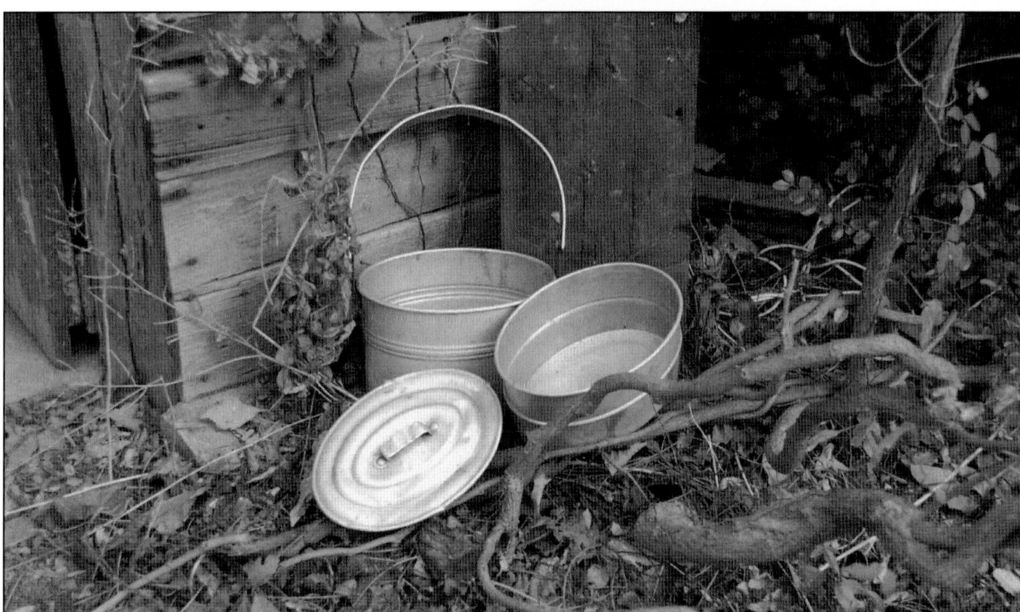

This is a dinner bucket given to the author by Bud and Mary McHugh's family, who ran a grocery store in Export. Separate containers held food with a beverage below. Women and girls packed the so-called pit buckets and greased the bottoms to prevent beer from foaming. Sadie Ayers Remaley was able to identify miners' dinner pails. George Ayers, father of twins Sadie and Sudie, operated a boardinghouse on Church Street.

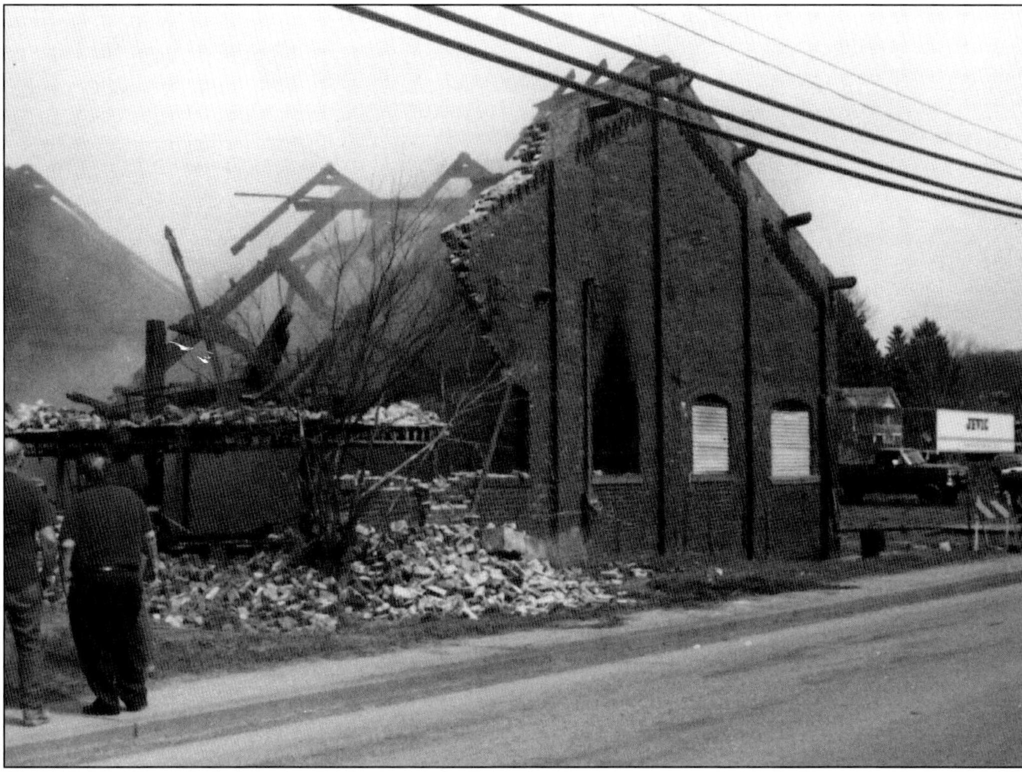

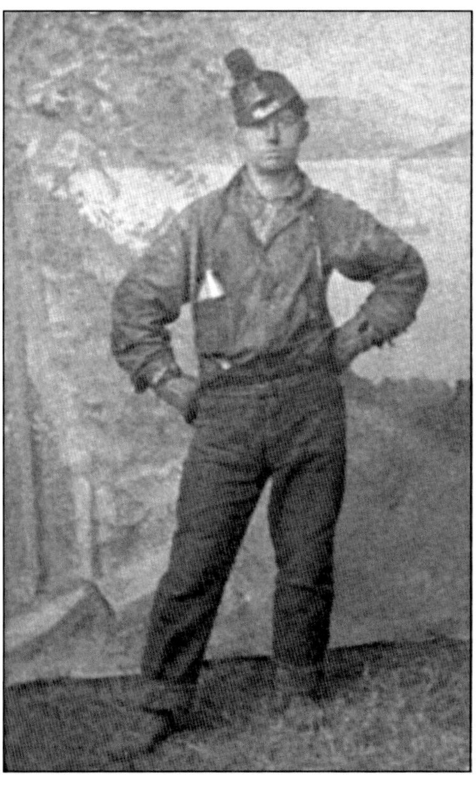

The demolished Westmoreland Coal Company boiler house on Old US 22 reflects the words of Colonel Bouquet, who advised Colonel Burd, builder of Fort Ligonier, to use coal. Export, which once had over 2,000 residents, now has around 900 people. This boomtown went through a dramatic transition from farmland to commercial center and back to farmland. As Robert Bruère wrote, "So coal wrought the Industrial Revolution, the greatest revolution in all human history."

A miner poses in front of an artist's backdrop of a lake and sailboat scene. This outdoor canvas, with grass showing underneath, was at the photographic studio of John Sartoris on Washington Avenue. The candle and oil lamps on miners' hats, which were first used in Westmoreland Coal Company No. 1 mine, were replaced by brass acetylene headlamps and later by Koehler flame safety lamps and now battery-powered lights. In the collier's pocket is his metal powder flask.

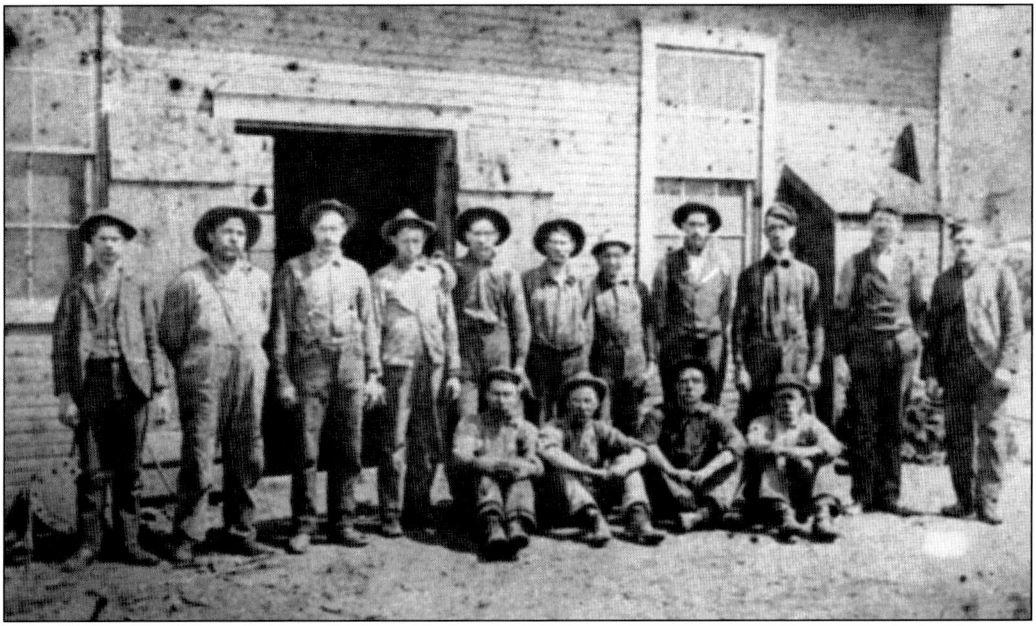

In this vintage photograph are early miners of Westmoreland County's vast coalfields. In 1870, soft bituminous coal production in America exceeded hard anthracite coal for the first time. In 1885, the tonnage of bituminous coal doubled that of anthracite, and in 1890 tripled it. George Ayers of Export, who worked for Westmoreland Coal Company, loaded the company's first coal on June 1, 1891.

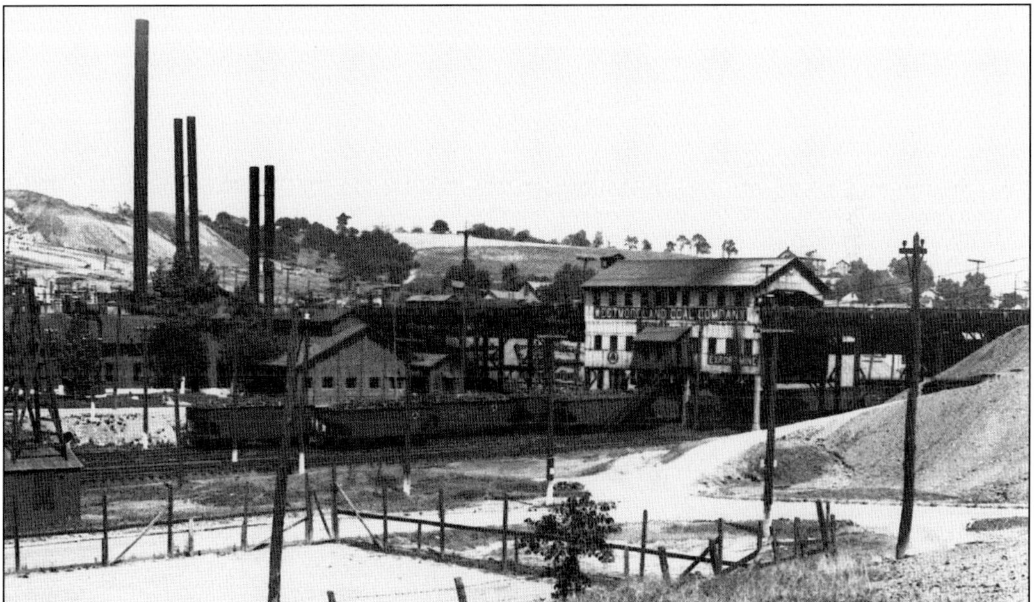

This close-up view from around 1920 shows a Westmoreland Coal Company tipple, its many smokestacks, and a tennis court that the firm provided for miners and their families. This was an unusual benefit in a mine town where the focus on making a profit kept wages and the standard of living low in the overcrowded atmosphere of company tenements.

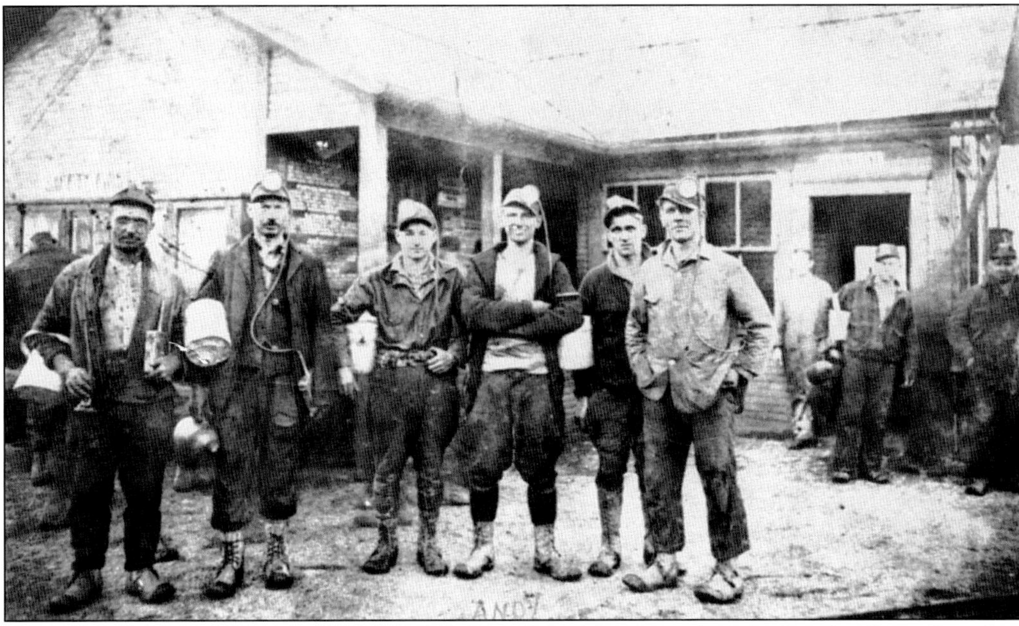

Miners stand in front of the Westmoreland Coal Company pay house. On the far right is Paul Schell, the fire boss. Other colliers are in the background in front of the lamp house. In addition to light for safety, canaries were used in cages to determine the presence of poisonous gases. Fortunately for the birds, modern methods were invented that did not take their lives; this was more pleasant for the miners, too.

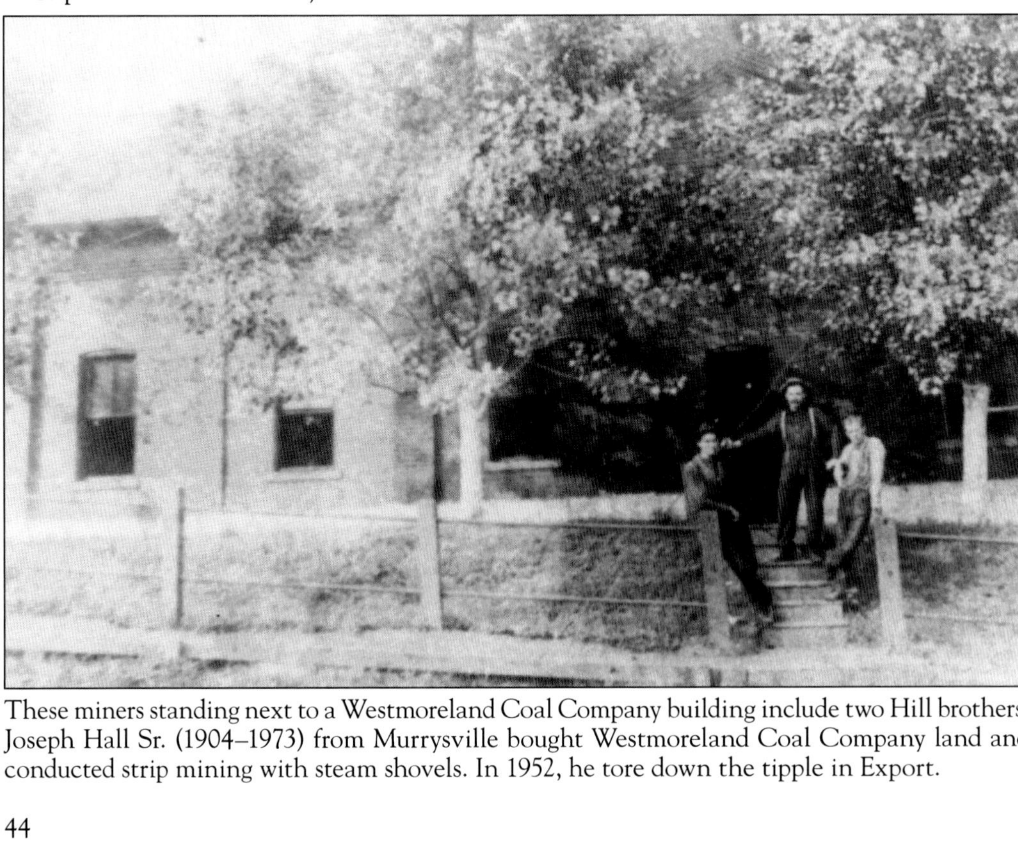

These miners standing next to a Westmoreland Coal Company building include two Hill brothers. Joseph Hall Sr. (1904–1973) from Murrysville bought Westmoreland Coal Company land and conducted strip mining with steam shovels. In 1952, he tore down the tipple in Export.

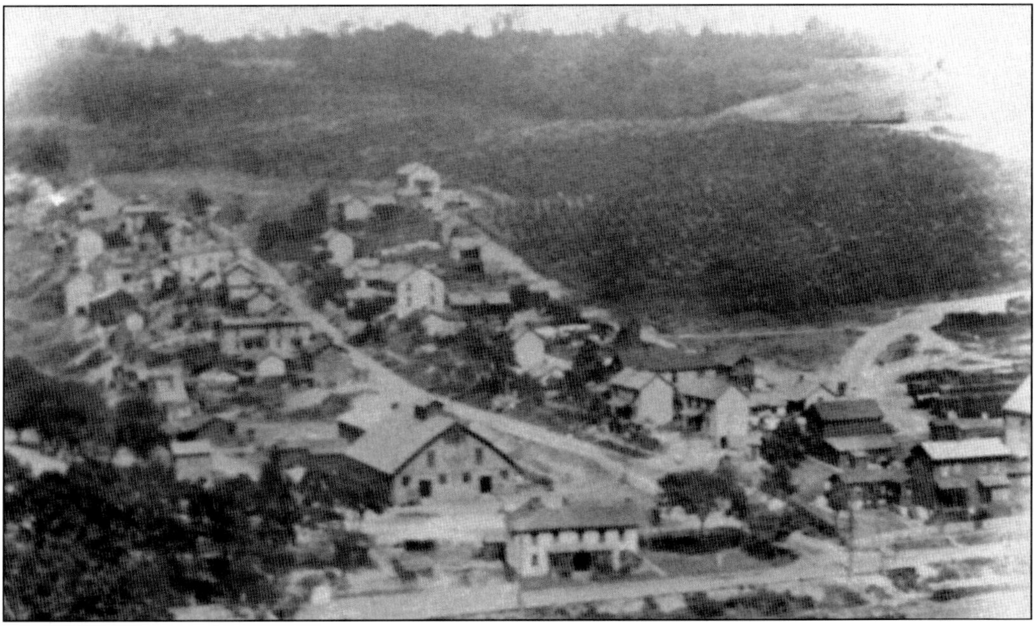

This aerial view of Export shows Westmoreland Coal's mule stable, south of Old US 22. This stable was on David Blair's cattle farm that later became a playground at the town's consolidated school. One stable boy was Tranquil Dezenet. A locust grove is seen on the right. When the trees were harvested for mine posts, white houses (referred to as blocks) were built for mine officials.

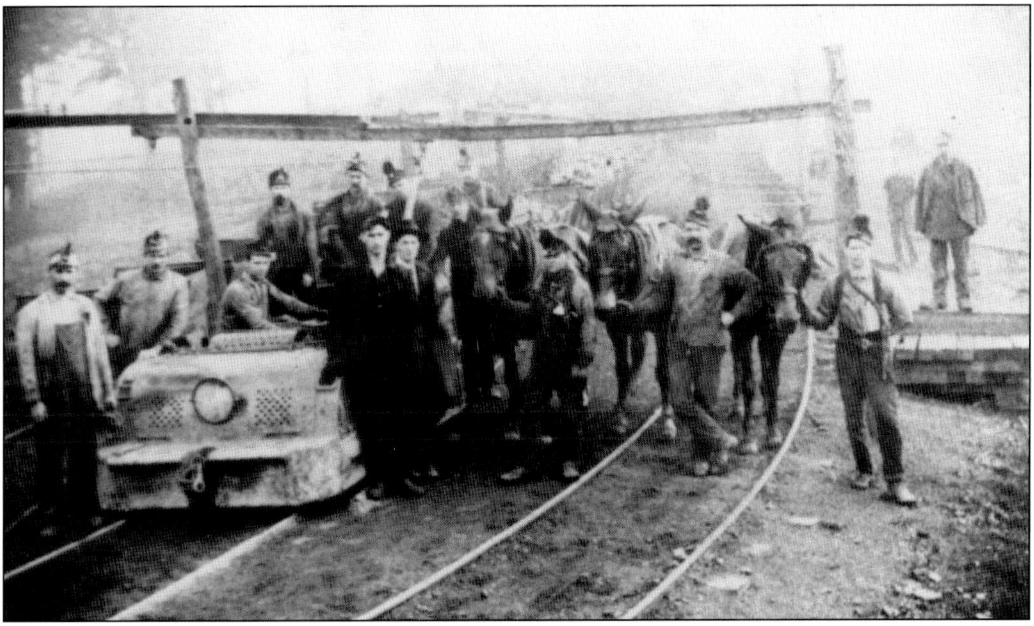

At Skelly's Mine in 1908, from left to right, are (first row) Archie Snedden, George Glunt, motorman George Kettering, Charles Stevick, George Fink with derby hat, and William McGinn. Holding the mule at right is Shorty Kemerer. Miners with both modern machines and mules—so-called beasts of burden that were once worth $200 each—reflect transition in coal business. Coalfields in Westmoreland County seemed to be inexhaustible.

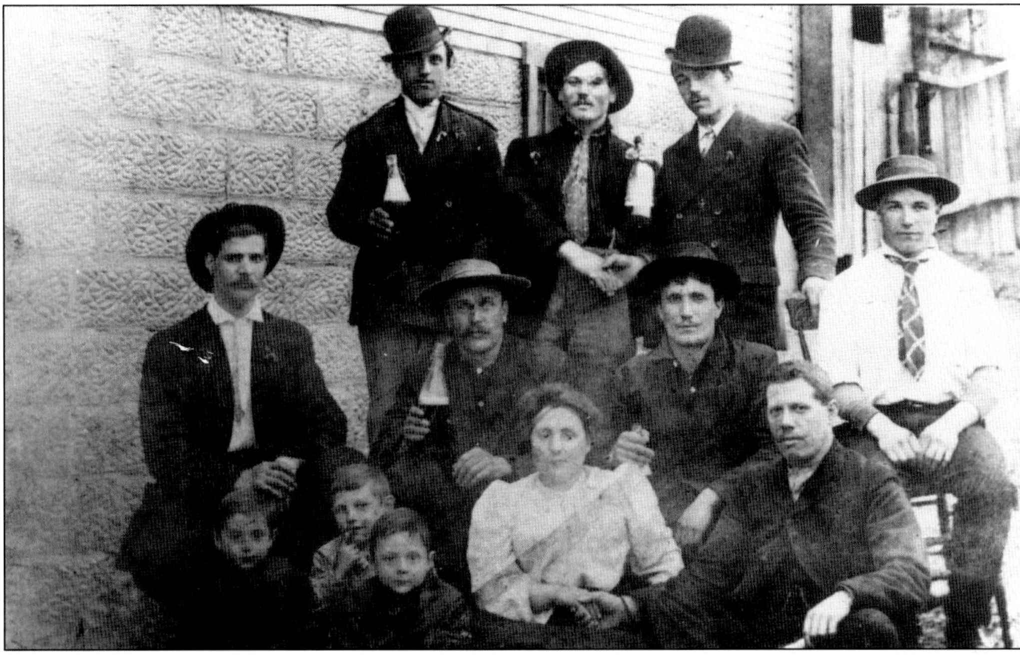

Santina Monoco Schena (Skena) Frandpol is sitting in front with her second husband, Natale, and her three children. Behind them are their brothers and boarders. Besides these boarders, Nelson Rhyberg and Oliver Leaf were renters at company houses in Export. In 1892, Leaf was the first man killed by a slate fall, a tragic occurrence in mines even today.

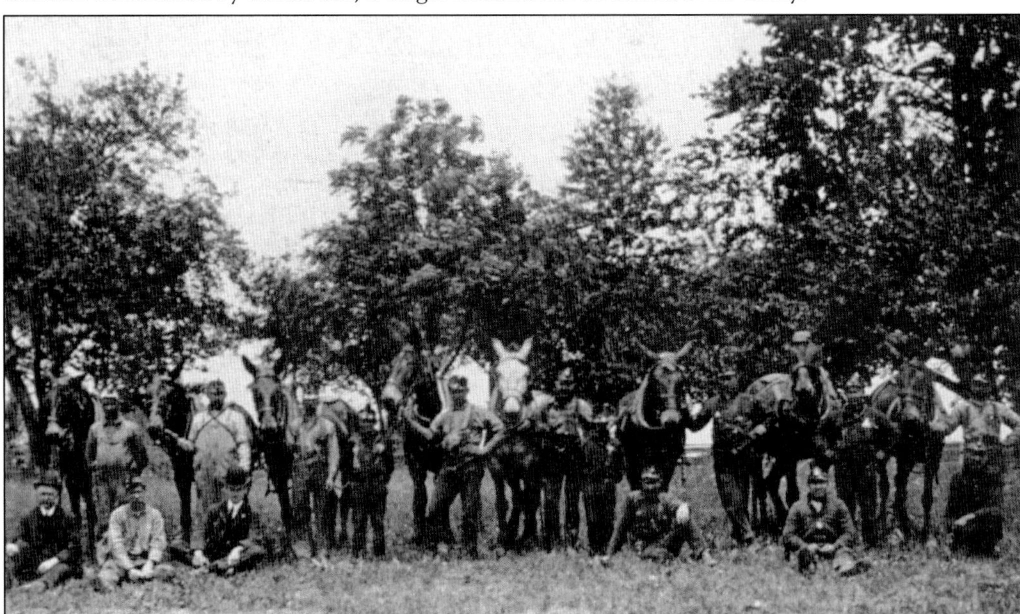

With leather bonnets to protect mules' heads against coal seams, skinners led mules into mines blindfolded. The motorized mantrip (a train-like vehicle for miner transport), nicknamed "the hobnail," transported between 50 and 60 men. Each workday, a town whistle sounded to wake miners, who left on this vehicle at 6:00 a.m. W.B. Skelly is sitting on the left in the front row with his miners, shown around 1890.

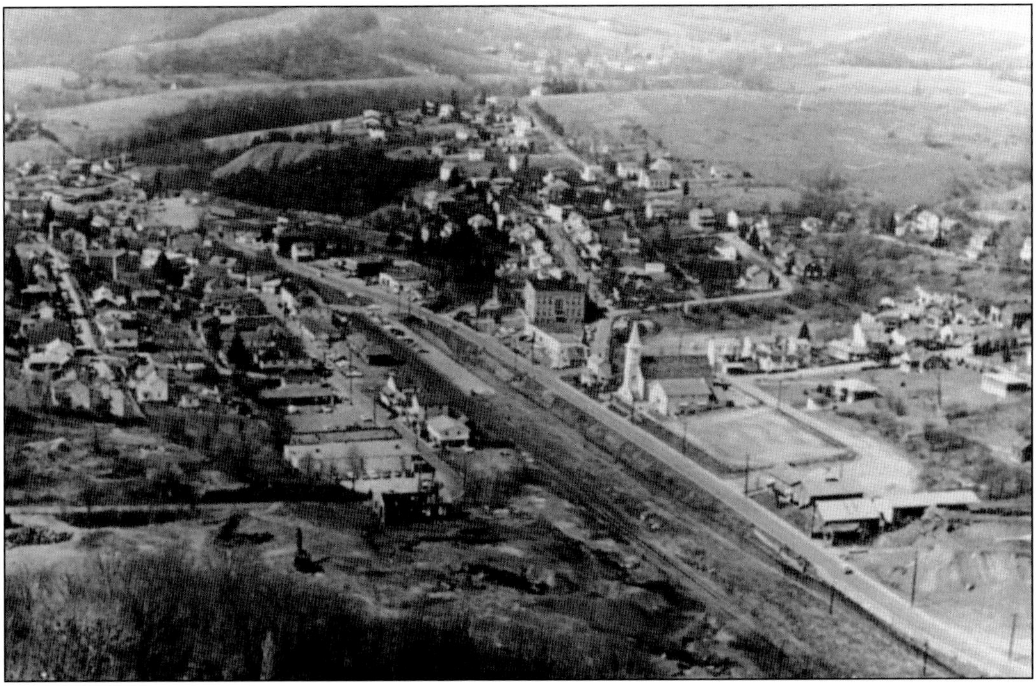

This aerial view of Export and Murrysville's hillside includes blacksmith shops that made mule shoes and supplied picks and mine wheels. Residents watched men work and learned the latest news as sparks flew and hammers banged out flaming new products. Some of the town's blacksmiths were Carl Koch, Charles Nesbitt, Adam Peanoske, and Frank LaSoto. On the right is the Westmoreland Coal Company muleyard beside St.Mary's Church.

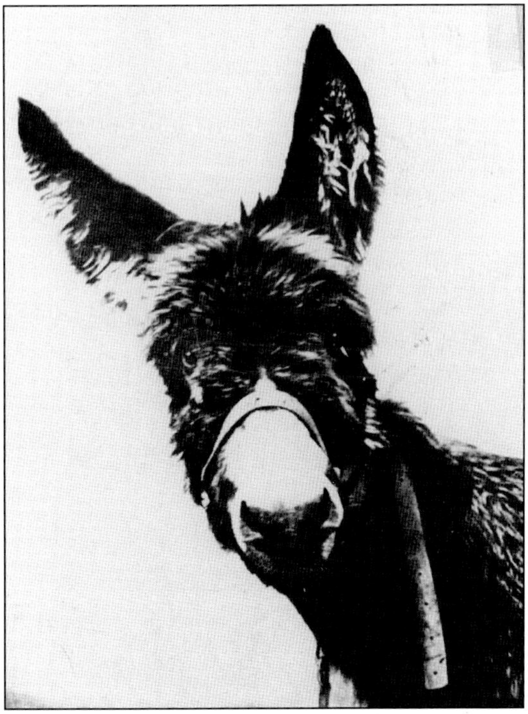

Mine Mule Molly deserves a photograph, as she brings back memories of colliers who became fond of their "pets." When motorized cars took over, mules were relieved of constant work underground. In some mines, they were only brought up to sunlight to graze during holidays and in certain mines were never brought to the surface. Mules were smaller and more sure-footed than horses, which would go blind if left in the mines.

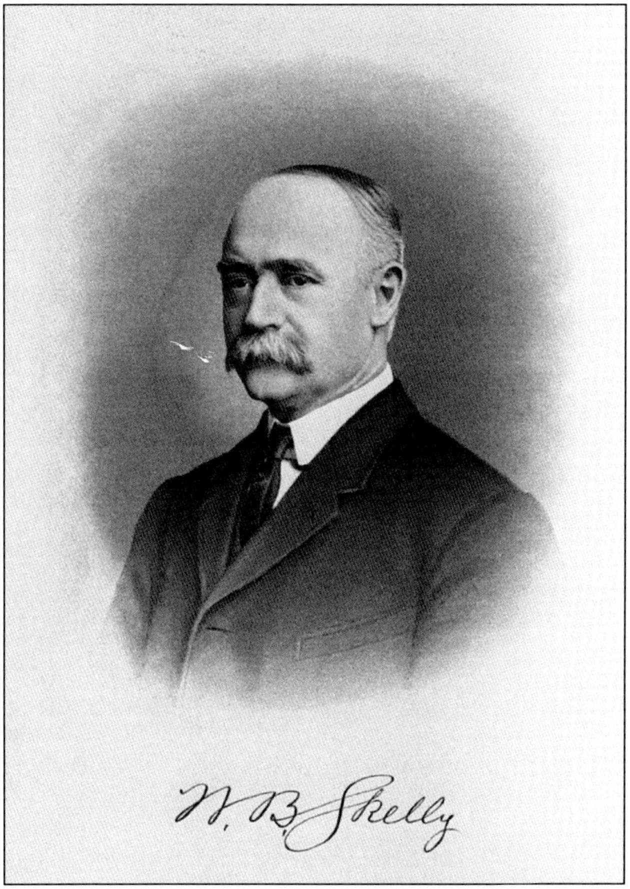

William B. (W.B.) Skelly organized his company. He was a board member of Export's First National Bank and loaded five railroad cars a day. Skelly arrived in America from Cavan, Ireland, after a 1790 voyage with one son buried at sea. Another son, William Jr., married Elizabeth Byerly, granddaughter of innkeeper Andrew Byerly and friend of Colonel Bouquet at nearby Bushy Run, a Turtle Creek tributary. W.B. Skelly died in 1929.

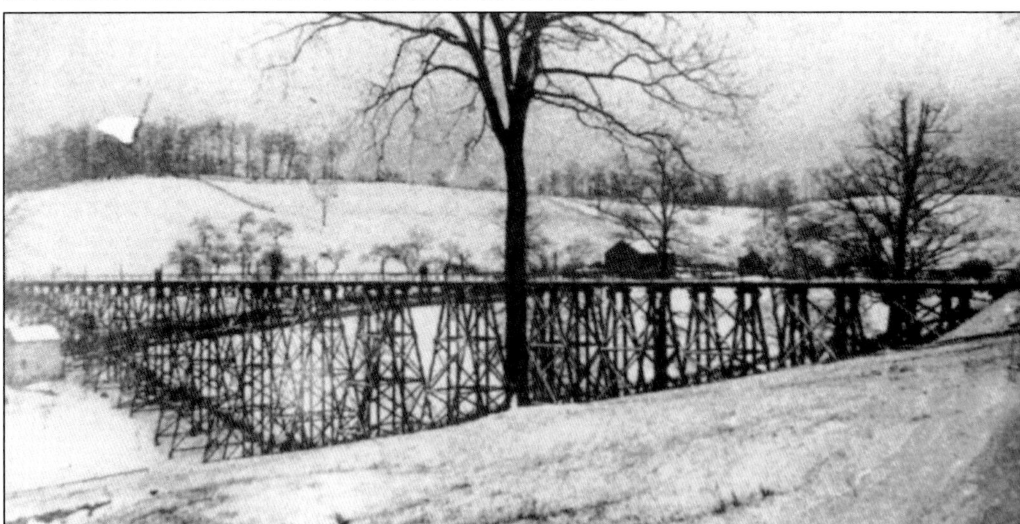

Skelly's trestle meandered through the countryside, mostly on the Silvis farm, to his tipple on Old US 22. Trestles made constant work for sawmills and lumberyards. Before the days of playgrounds and gymnastic equipment and regardless of splinters, they also made good climbing areas for children—even though they were told not to go near these frameworks.

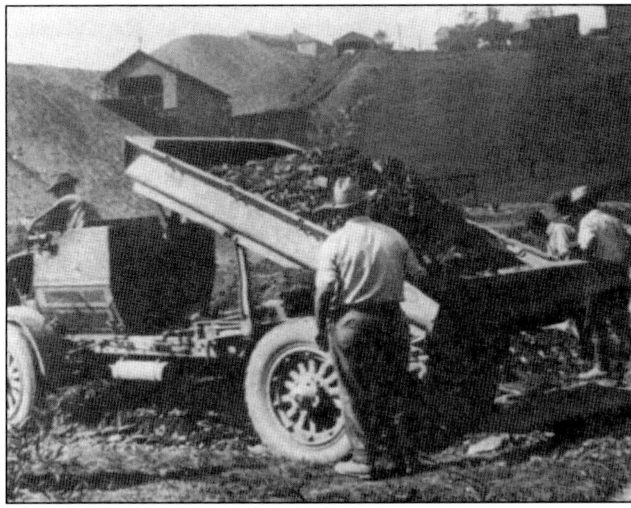

Here is Skelly's tipple with W.R. Jeffries's (of Beaver, Pennsylvania) dump truck in front. The railroad tracks for Skelly's mine crossed Turtle Creek at the junction of Duff Street and Old US 22. His company never had a fatal accident and received a certificate for safety from the Joseph A. Holmes Society. During the 1910 coal strike, part of his trestle fell, as did equipment and a mine roof. Farmers sometimes had to rescue cows from falling into mine pits.

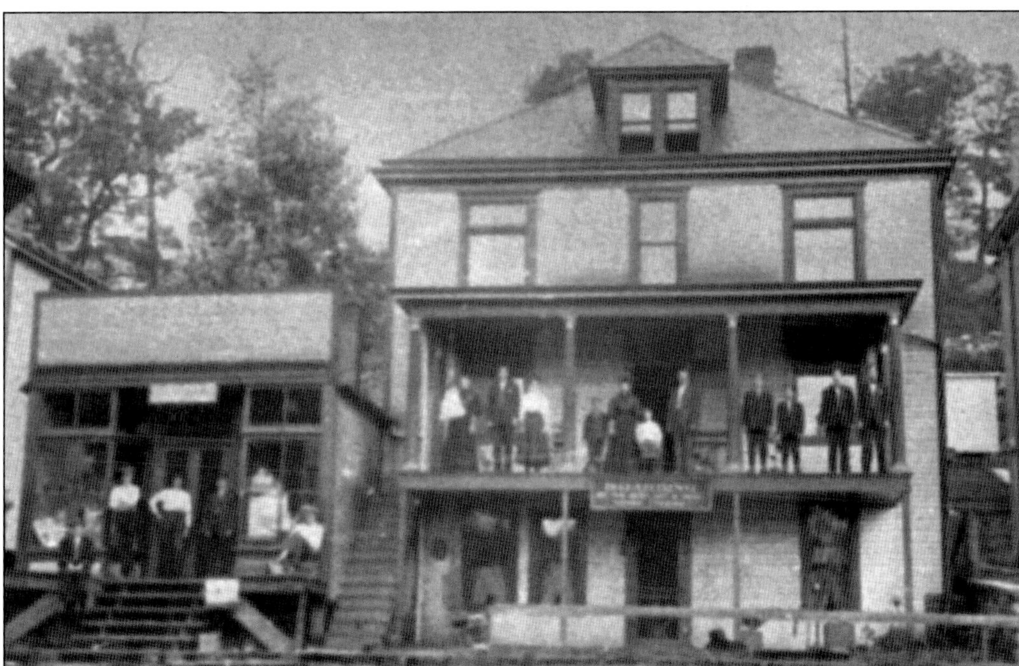

Gus Millstein's boardinghouse on Washington Avenue (formerly Westmoreland) was built for coal miners. Located next to the company store, it was always occupied. A sign over the door reads, "Boarding by the week, daily, night—horse feeding." Beds were rented double shift. The small building on the left provided a washhouse, an uncommon convenience. Those living in company houses bathed in wooden tubs with their wives washing imbedded coal dust from their backs.

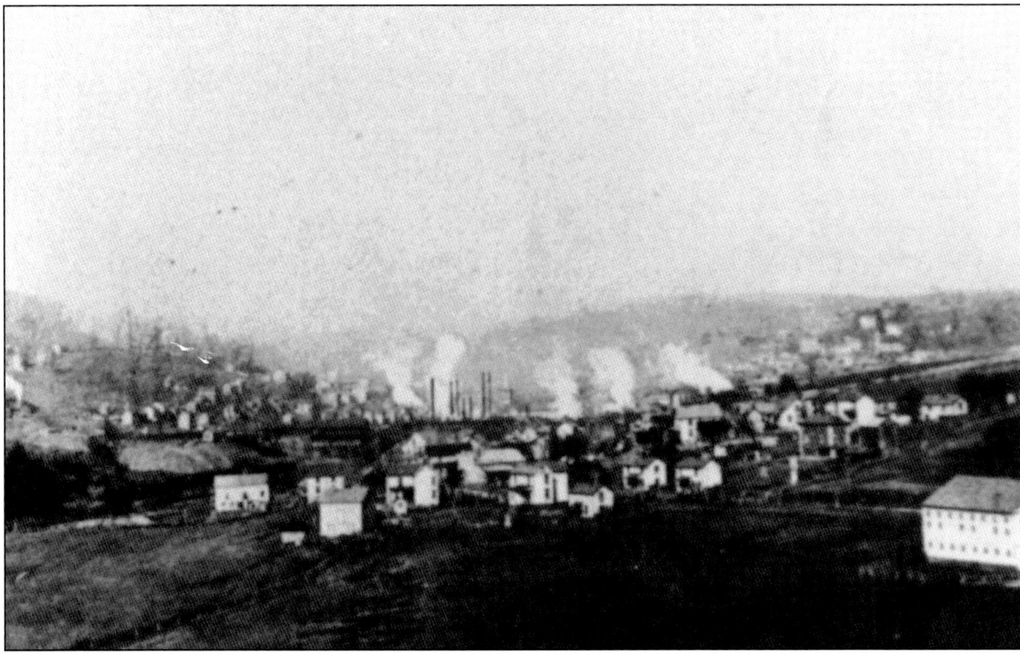

This aerial view of Export shows the so-called white blocks, houses that belonged to coal managers and the Westmoreland Coal administration. They were built after the large grove of locust trees that had been near St. Mary's Catholic Church had matured and was ready to be harvested for mine posts. The lumber business grew and thrived as one- and two-story houses were being erected.

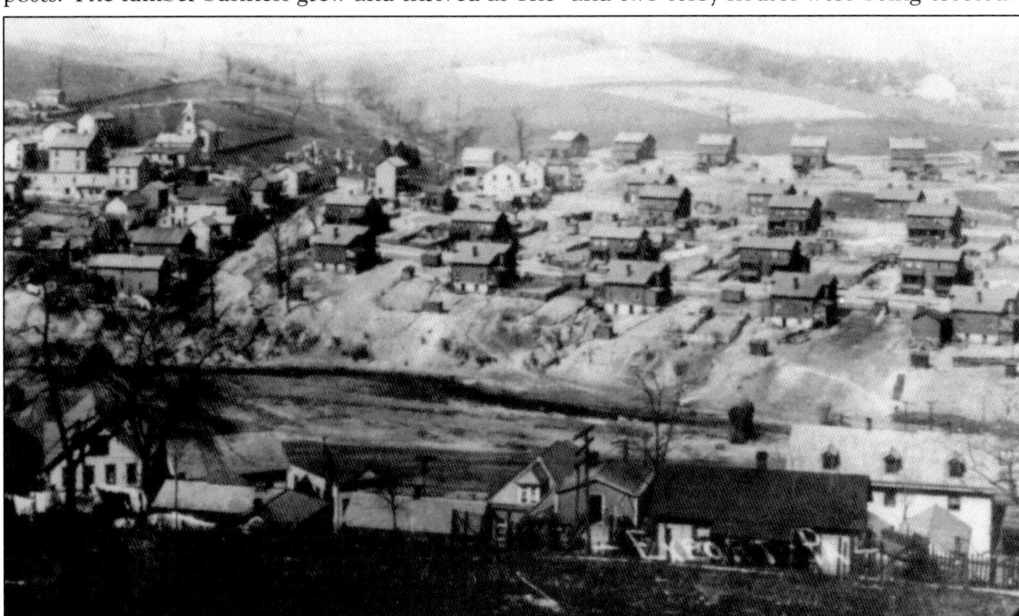

Red blocks, another type of company houses, are shown in 1914. Every third home had an outside oven. Originally, red paint was made from milk and blood from slaughterhouses and was cheaper than white. After tenants purchased these structures, they painted them other colors. They also insulated them, and sewer pipes replaced waste draining into muddy streets. (Courtesy of Raymond Meehan.)

Four

Between a Rock and a Hard Place

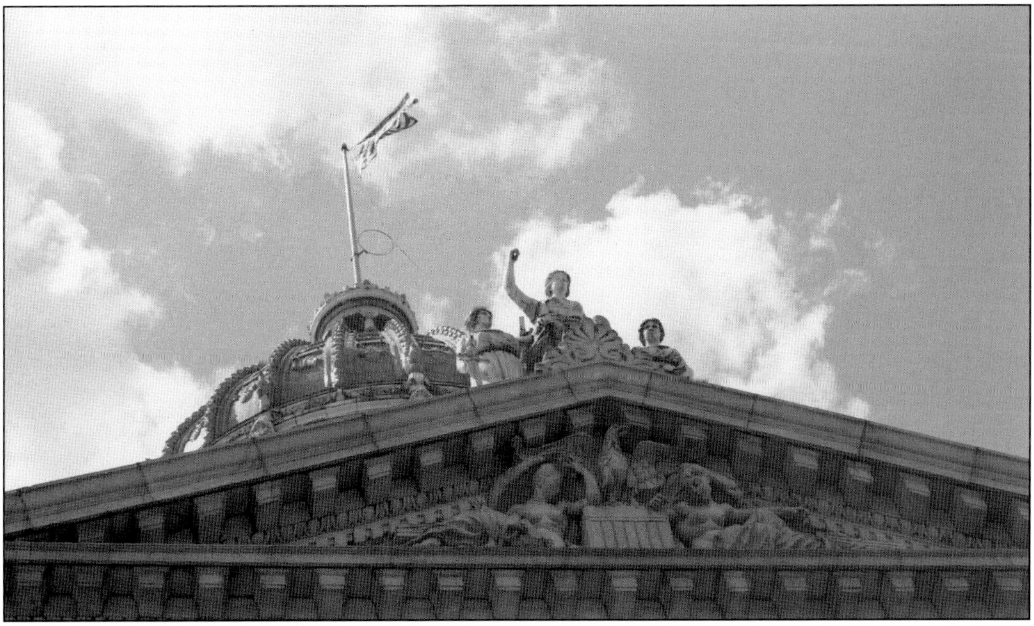

Prior to the 1910–1911 coal mine strike, Justice, on top of the Westmoreland County Courthouse's gilded dome, dropped her brass scales in view of Export miners, who believed it was an omen. Laborers received $2.07 a day for an occupation that is still perilous, even after the 1969 Mine Safety Act. The danger involved in mining is often said to be the origin of the expression "caught between a rock and a hard place."

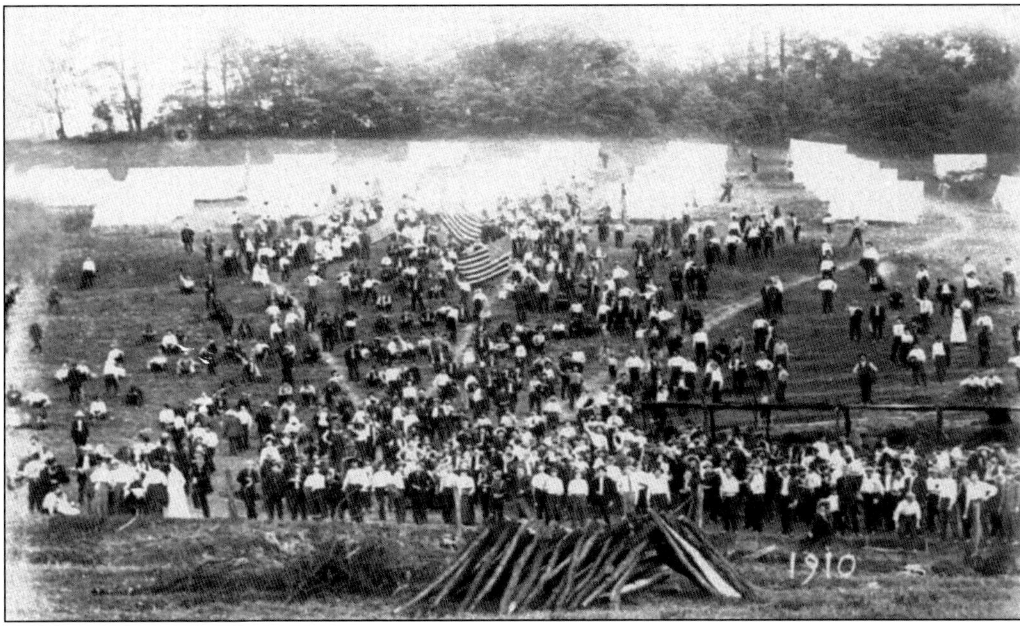

During the 1910 national coal strike, 20 tent cities served miners and families evicted from company houses they rented. The United Mine Workers (UMW) set up the damp tents on the outskirts of town on land leased from Murrysville farmers. Mother Jones (Mary Harris), champion for labor rights, said, "God Almighty, men, go down through this nation and see the damnable, infamous condition that is there." Export's tent cities were reported to be the largest.

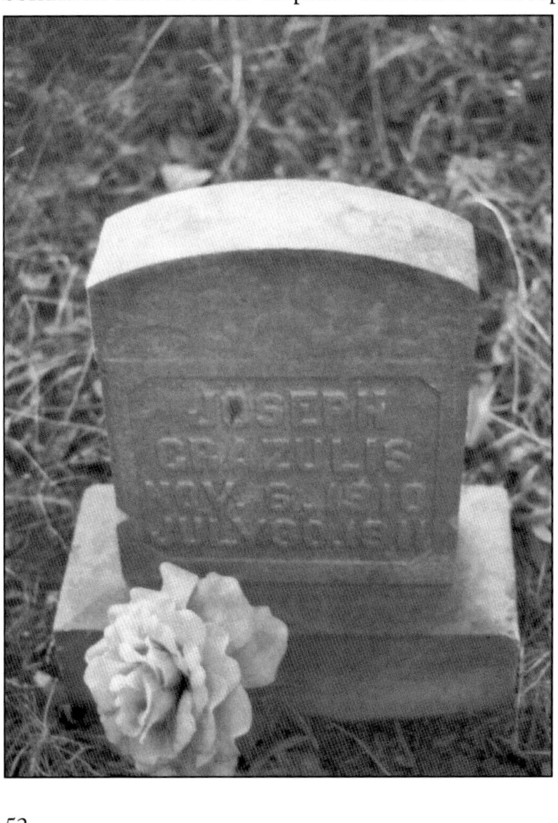

A gravestone in Grandview Cemetery (the former Humes property) in old Franklin Township reveals a baby who died during this strike. His short life was lived on the southern hillside along Puckety(a) Path, part of Sewickley Old Town Path. It was the former encampment of prehistoric Monongahela people, later owned by the Shawnee Tribe. This land was sold to Westmoreland Coal Company where its Star Park was built beside the company dam.

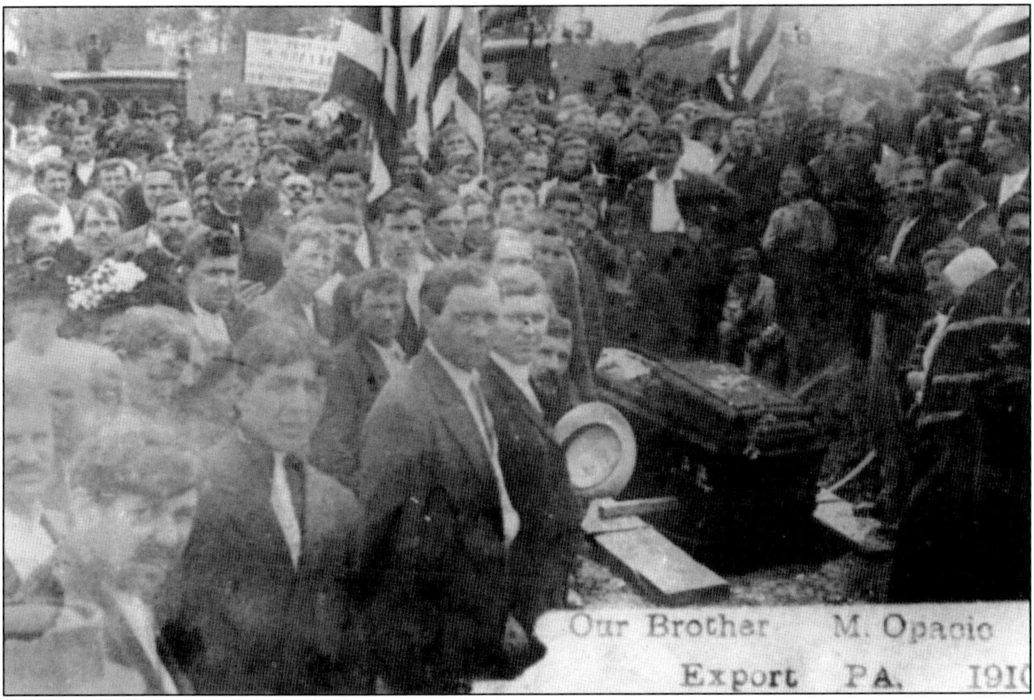

Miners gather at M. Opacic's funeral during the 1910 strike. Fearless Mother Jones, an Irish champion for miners, visited women in Greensburg jail, armed with brooms and mops. She said, "Bring your children to jail—sleep all day, sing all night." She also brought milk. Folksinger Pete Seeger is quoted in the November 22, 1974, *Greensburg-Jeannette News-Dispatch* as saying he thinks Jones was imprisoned there. She wrote, "Slowly those who create the wealth of the world are permitted to share it."

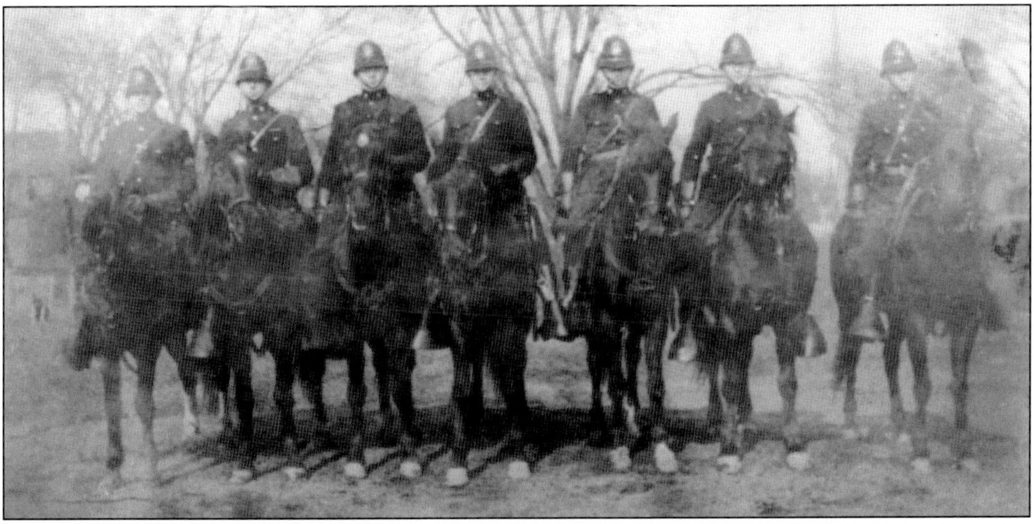

Mounted Pennsylvania State Police were called "Cossacks" due to their uniforms. Author John Guyer writes in *Pennsylvania's Cossacks and The State's Police*, "In Export, Pennsylvania, on April 8, 1922, William Haggen, organizer for Dist. 5, UMWA, called a mass meeting that 400 county men attended." Police rode horses into the crowd and beat the men who did not run. During the Depression, the UMW lost power. Wages were cut.

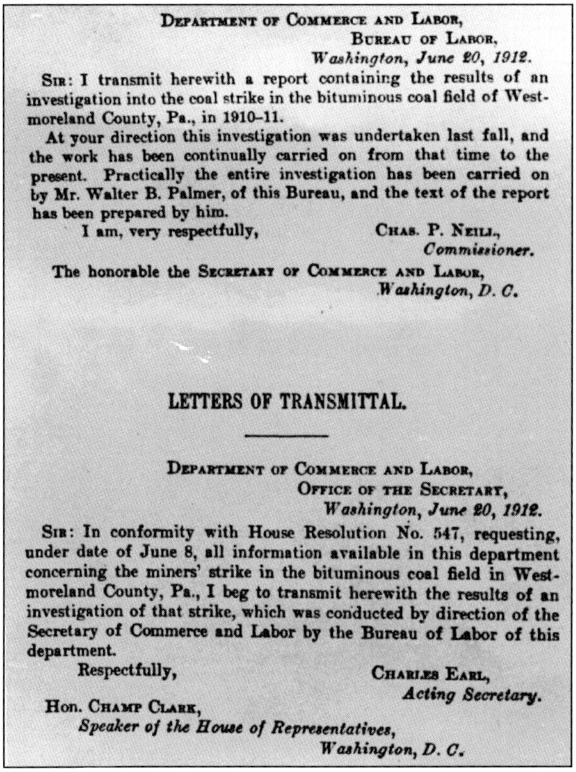

DEPARTMENT OF COMMERCE AND LABOR,
BUREAU OF LABOR,
Washington, June 20, 1912.

SIR: I transmit herewith a report containing the results of an investigation into the coal strike in the bituminous coal field of Westmoreland County, Pa., in 1910–11.

At your direction this investigation was undertaken last fall, and the work has been continually carried on from that time to the present. Practically the entire investigation has been carried on by Mr. Walter B. Palmer, of this Bureau, and the text of the report has been prepared by him.

I am, very respectfully,
CHAS. P. NEILL,
Commissioner.

The honorable the SECRETARY OF COMMERCE AND LABOR,
Washington, D. C.

LETTERS OF TRANSMITTAL.

DEPARTMENT OF COMMERCE AND LABOR,
OFFICE OF THE SECRETARY,
Washington, June 20, 1912.

SIR: In conformity with House Resolution No. 547, requesting, under date of June 8, all information available in this department concerning the miners' strike in the bituminous coal field in Westmoreland County, Pa., I beg to transmit herewith the results of an investigation of that strike, which was conducted by direction of the Secretary of Commerce and Labor by the Bureau of Labor of this department.

Respectfully,
CHARLES EARL,
Acting Secretary.

Hon. CHAMP CLARK,
Speaker of the House of Representatives,
Washington, D. C.

William Haggen said he and miners met on John Duff's 100-year-old private farm at Export, where they were banished by two mounted police for speaking Polish. Haggen and James Rosa were arrested and chained to a hot pipe. At Westmoreland Coal, policemen handcuffed Duff to a hot steam pipe in the 1922 strike. Valentine Swartz, a Polish interpreter, said, "There was no noise or disorder until police came." These documents report the investigation. (Courtesy of Department of Commerce and Labor.)

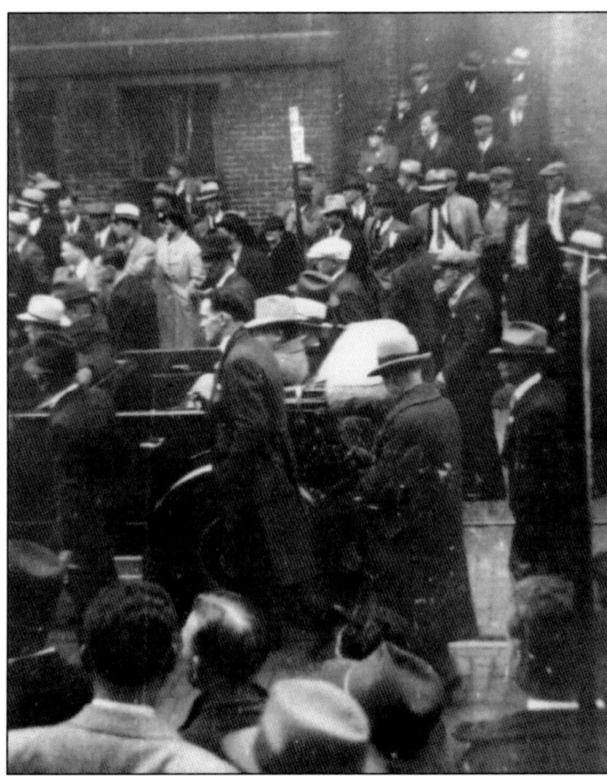

John L. Lewis (1880–1969), founder of UMW, is flanked by bodyguards in the Greensburg parade in 1920. Labor Day parades prior to speeches and during strikes were frequent, especially in the strikes in 1927–1928 and the 1950s between labor and management. Well liked by colliers, Pres. Franklin D. Roosevelt said, "Sometimes strikes are necessary, but only as last resort." Export miners marched and were told to furl their flags. They were prevented from walking together on a street during a strike.

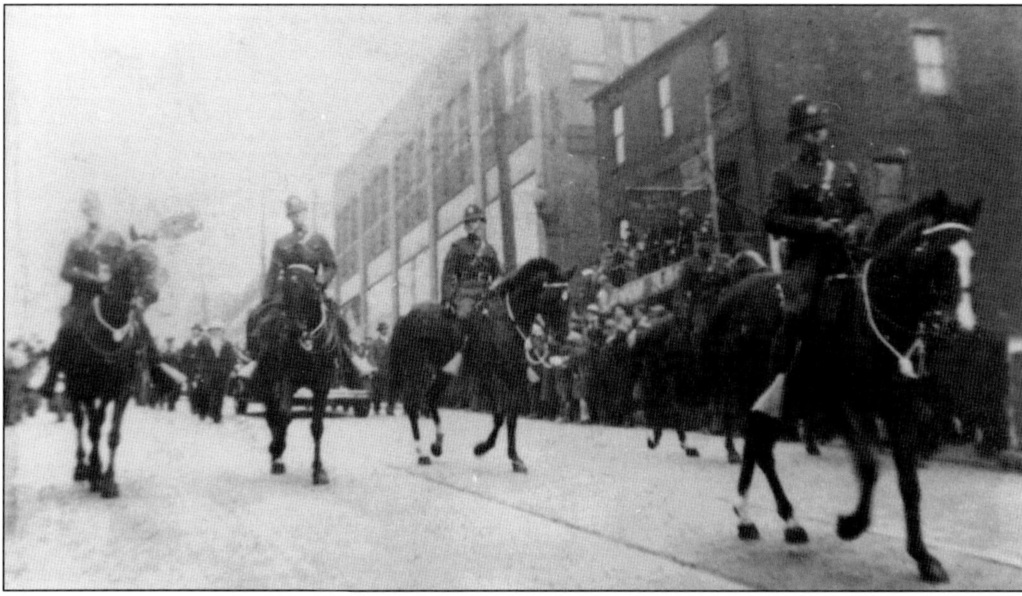

State police on horses march during the coal strike in Greensburg. Mine owners slapped badges on ex-football players, appointing them coal and iron police, and many were ruffians armed with weapons and told to go after the miners. On the tops of tipples were company searchlights flashing all night with watchmen protecting property from gunfire and explosives. Colliers often sang songs about a miner's life.

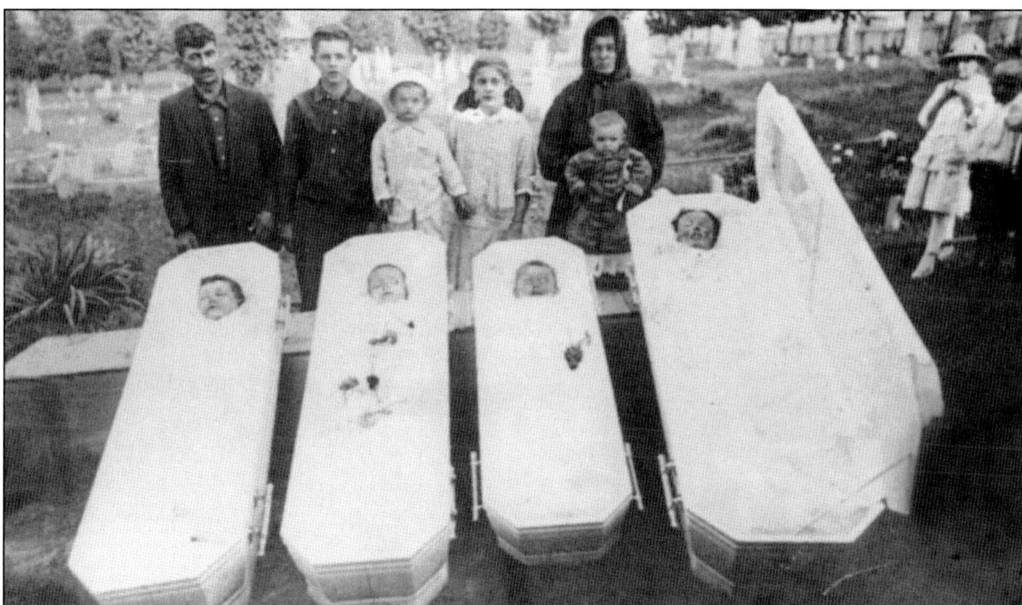

A 1917 photograph shows children who played near Export's powder house when a child with matches caused an explosion. In caskets are two children from the same family; one is named Amelia. At the far left is their father George Visnick (1881–1945) with his wife, Stoya (fifth from left), holding baby Dan (born September 1, 1914). Dan is the father of the sister and brother who graciously shared this photograph. Other people in the photograph are unidentified. (Courtesy of Barbara Geary and Dan Visnick.)

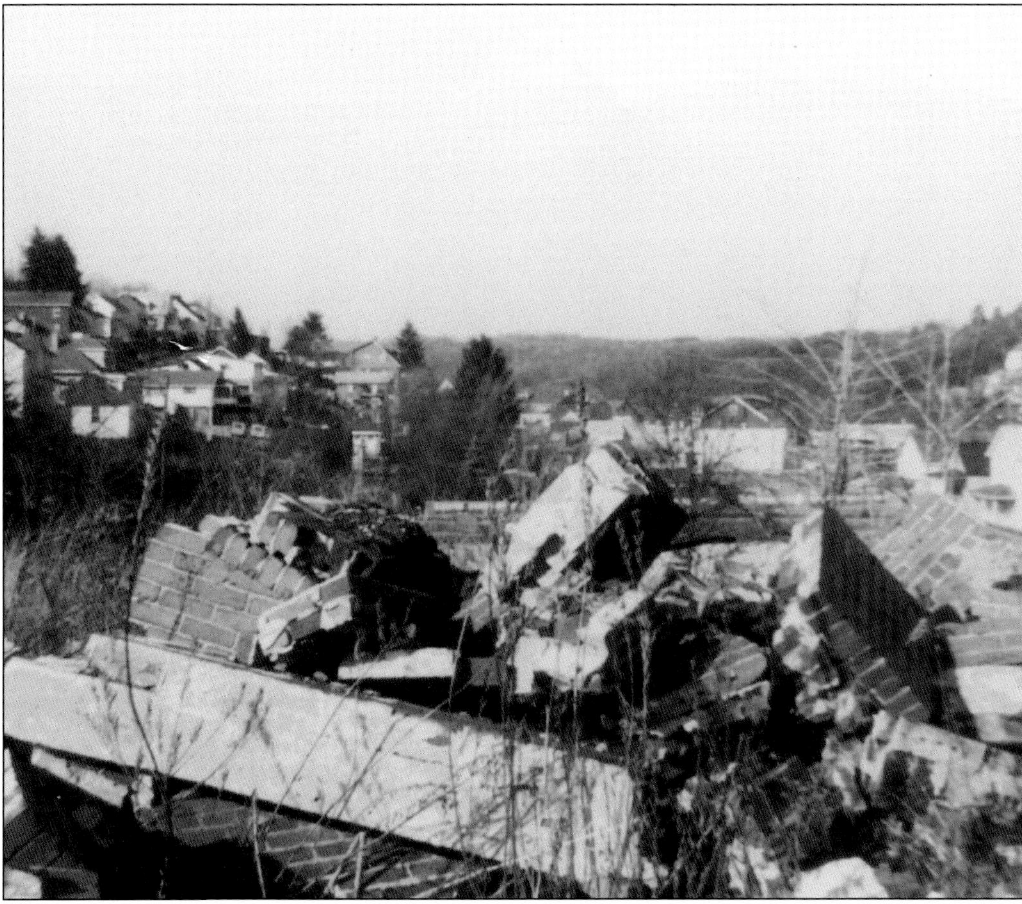

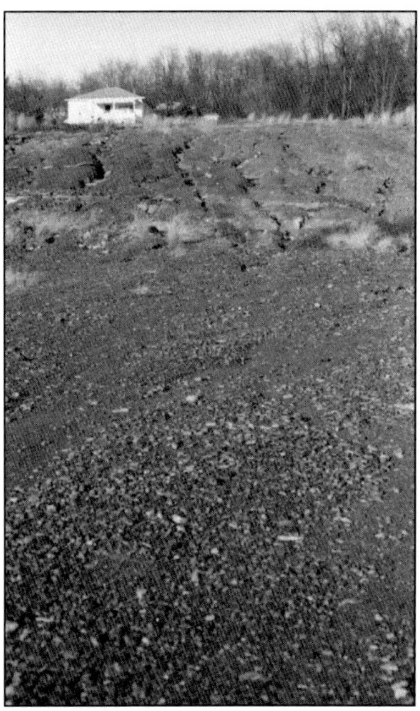

In the 1930s, White Valley's Joseph Cappa, Martin Vanovich, and Louis Revardo, on a bet, crawled into an air shaft on Biddle-Nocca farm (Pittsburgh Coal Company). Several boys and rescuers were victims of blackdamp (a choking gas). After mines closed, the landscape was marked by empty buildings, stacked wooden coal cars, sulfur water, and slag piles. Industrialized turning of the earth inside out instigated the need for reclamation with pine trees.

Children were especially vulnerable in industrial towns, with dangerous, undermined areas and cracked ground leaving deep crevices. In both towns, erosion occurred at industrial sites. In the same barren coal landscape from erosion and mine pollution, trees withered, and nothing was able to grow around the Haymaker well for years. Birds and wildlife died from the flaming gas.

Five

Children of the Gas-Coal Region

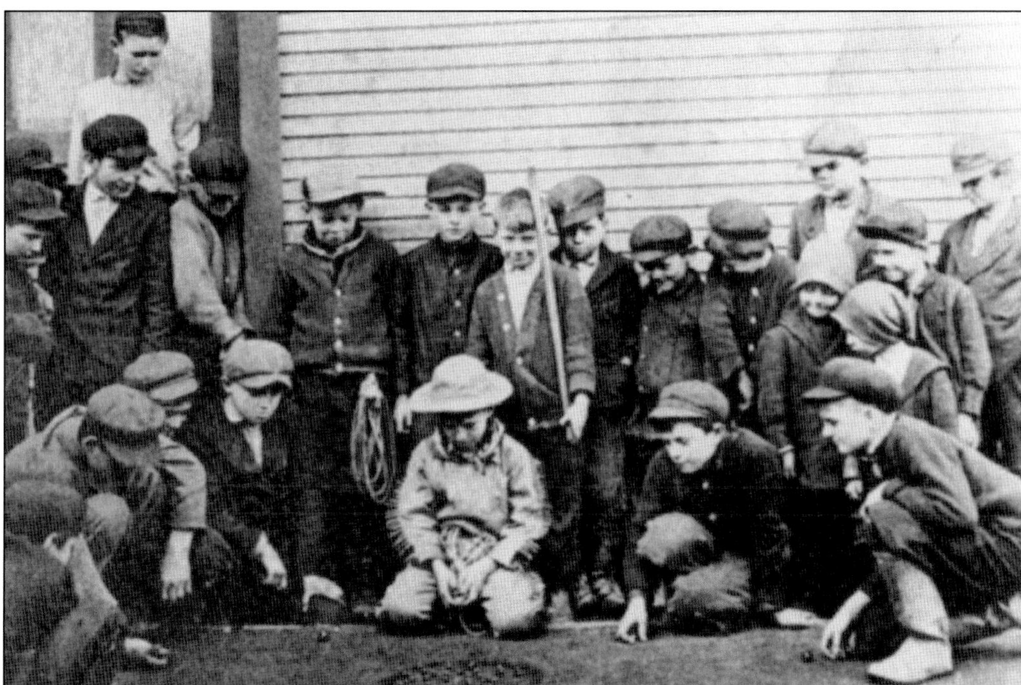

A 1912 marbles game near the Export company store porch reflects joyful childhood. All eyes—except a few peeking at the cameraman—focus on the shooter. Identified children are Adam Frescura (center), Peter McHugh (upper left), Clayton Millberg (with rope looped over his belt, front right), William Scott, M. Harold Smithgall (to right of Scott), "Cal" Cornelius Berlin (with a stick), and Steven Stugen (cap turned).

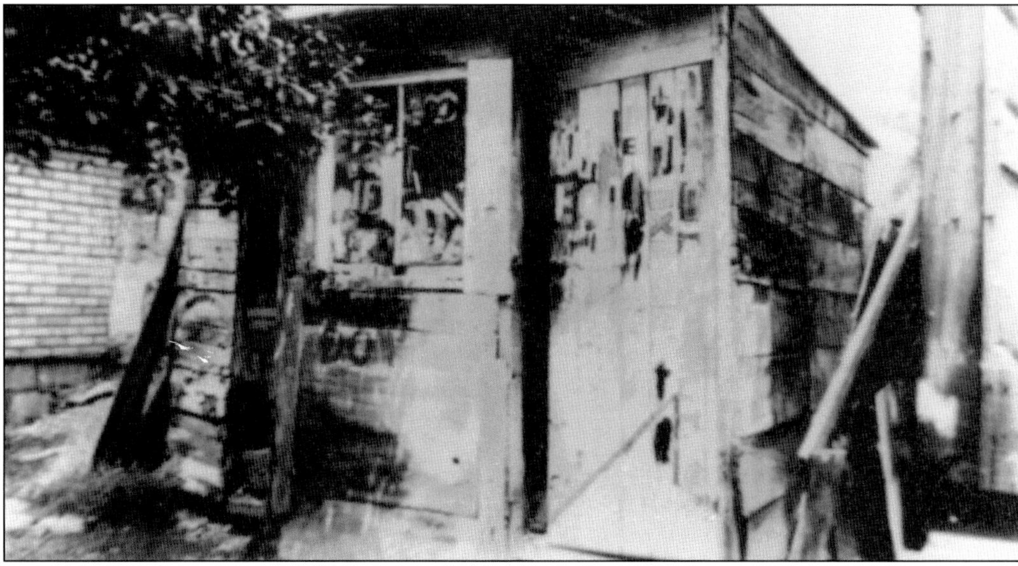

Favorite children's sites in Export were the Wuslich art shop (pictured) and Westmoreland Coal Company's dam where "Chick" Ake practiced figure and speed skating. His comedy act, *Ake (Charlie Chaplin) and Pane*, was at Madison Square Garden in the 1920s. George Karjinski became a state-champion speed skater by practicing on the Star Park Pond. Another swimming pond was across Old US 22 from John Meier's family hardware store in Murrysville, where a boy once left his shirt and pants on the railroad tracks. His companion rescued him after a train cut them in half.

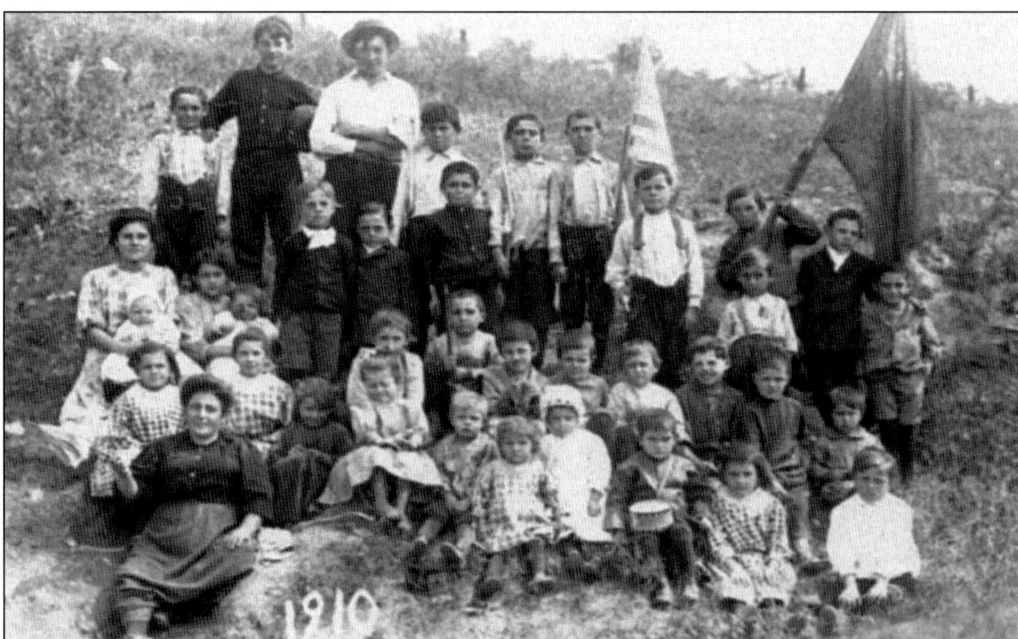

During the 1910 national coal strikes, youths joined Santina Monaco Schena's Army, an early feminist group active during the strike. Santina, with children Peter, Joseph, and Merle, married Natale Frandpol. They ran a boardinghouse in Export. In 1918, she worked in the temporary school emergency hospital during the influenza.

Camp Fire Girls were organized in 1910; Girl Scouts formed in 1912. The Scout pictured is Maxine Hamilton (Simpson), whose mother was Mayme Hamilton, the first writer for the *Penn-Franklin Newspaper.* She was also involved in the March of Dimes, American Legion Auxiliary, women's clubs, Royal Neighbors of America, and fundraising. At age 100, Mayme said, "After coming through a Great Depression, you find money isn't that important."

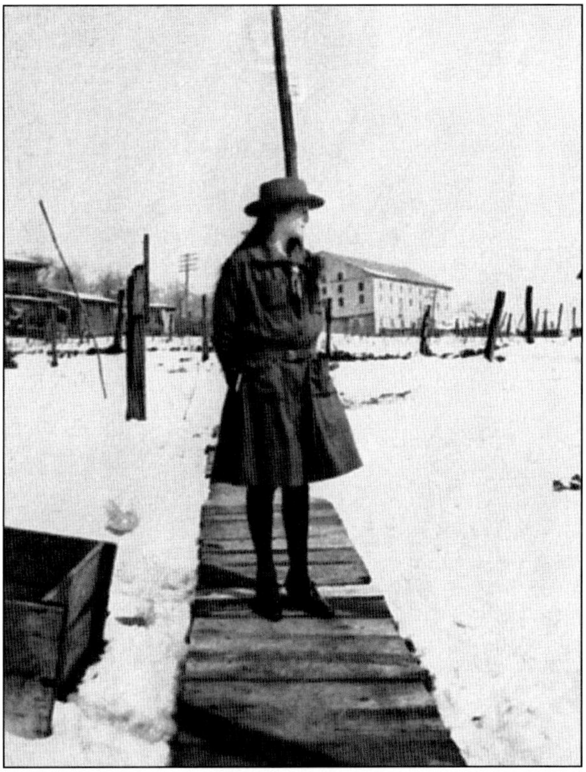

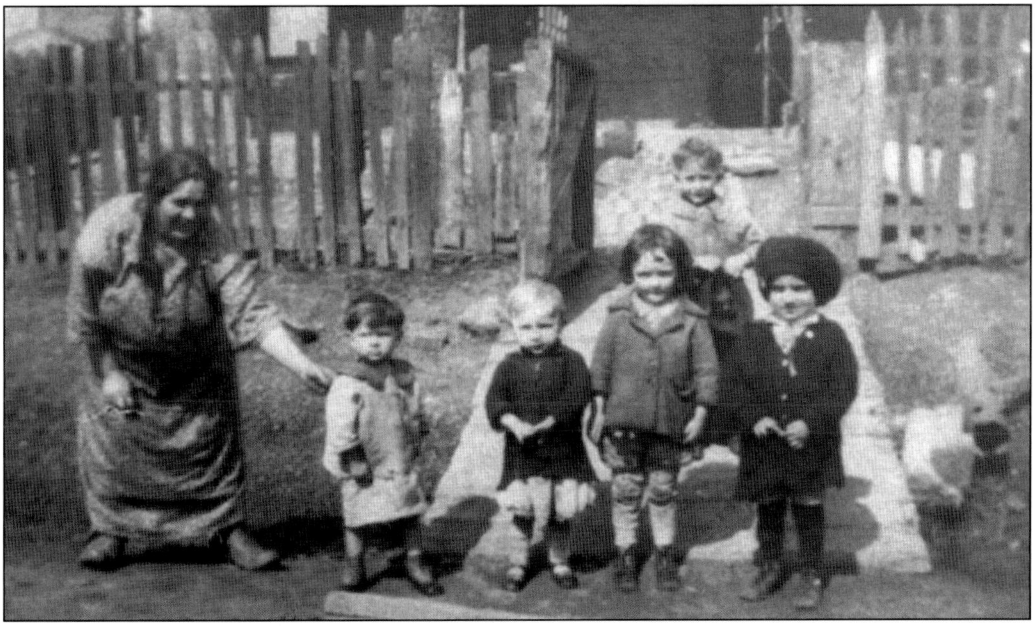

In 1929, Export's neighborhood children are at play on Berlin Street. An unidentified mother prompts Walter Delong, reluctant to join the group. Next to him, from left to right, are Walter Kurian, Elizabeth Wuslich, and George Wuslich. Andy Savitsky is in the background. Chores for little children such as these included carrying buckets of water inside from well pumps and emptying wastewater into pipe holes leading to muddy, dirt streets before the days of sewers.

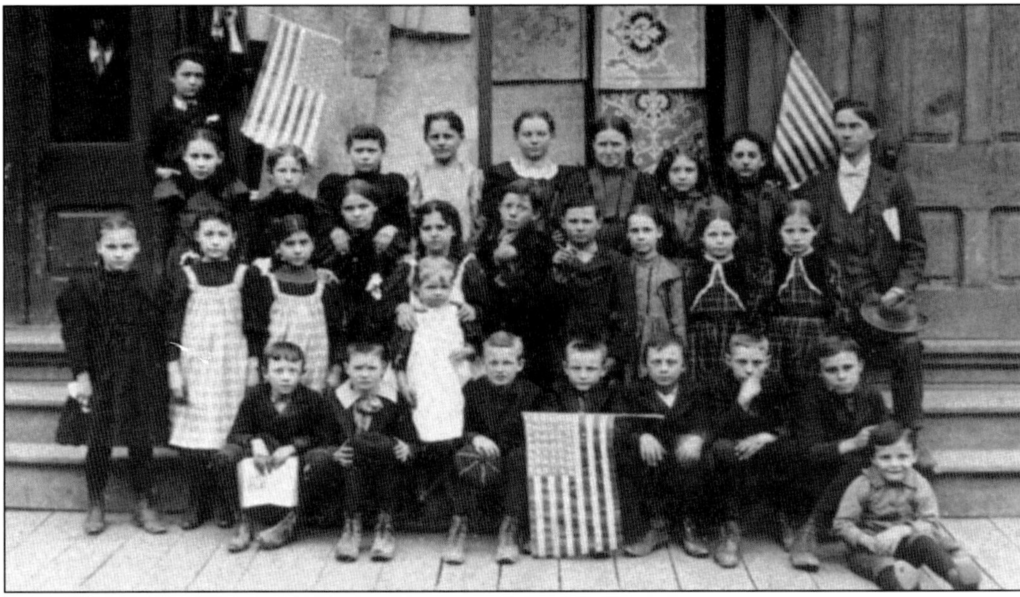

Pictured is a class at Seadler's Hall School, when classes were held in the Thomas Magram/ Max Scotten Department Store (wallpaper in windows). Pictured are, in no particular order, (first row) Hock Silvis, ? Kelly, Arnold Wigle, Albert Wigle, Glen Woods, John Sarach, and two unidentified; from left to right, (second row) Minnie Wigle, Mary Gockel, Della Darbous, Violet Millberg, Etta Hall with her sister (name unknown) in front, Bill Jones, ? Kelly, Laura Jones, and twins Katie and Maggie Wold; (third row): Bill Kistler (teacher?), Martha Painter, Rosie Kemerer, Nora Silvis, Susie Kettering, Maggie Jones, Jane Hamilton, Fannie Wilks, Zelda McCoy, and teacher James Anderson.

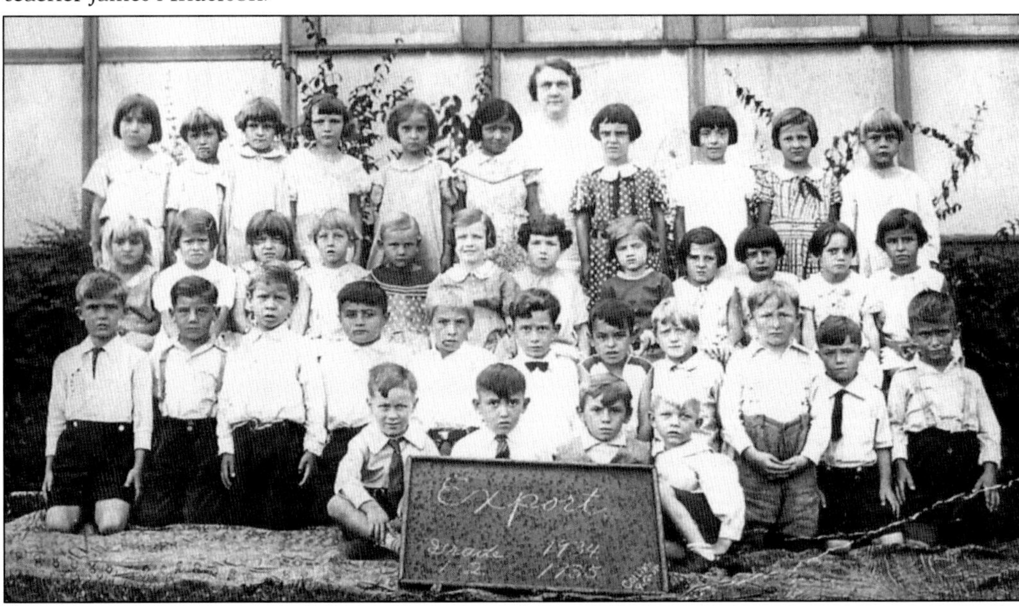

This second-grade class of 1934–1935 picture was taken in Export at the consolidated elementary school on Old US 22. Erected in 1912, the buff brick building had an annex of additional class rooms and, later, an auditorium built on to it. Since the new building resembled a barracks, the students nicknamed the modern structure the "chicken coops." (Courtesy of Nan Krushinski.)

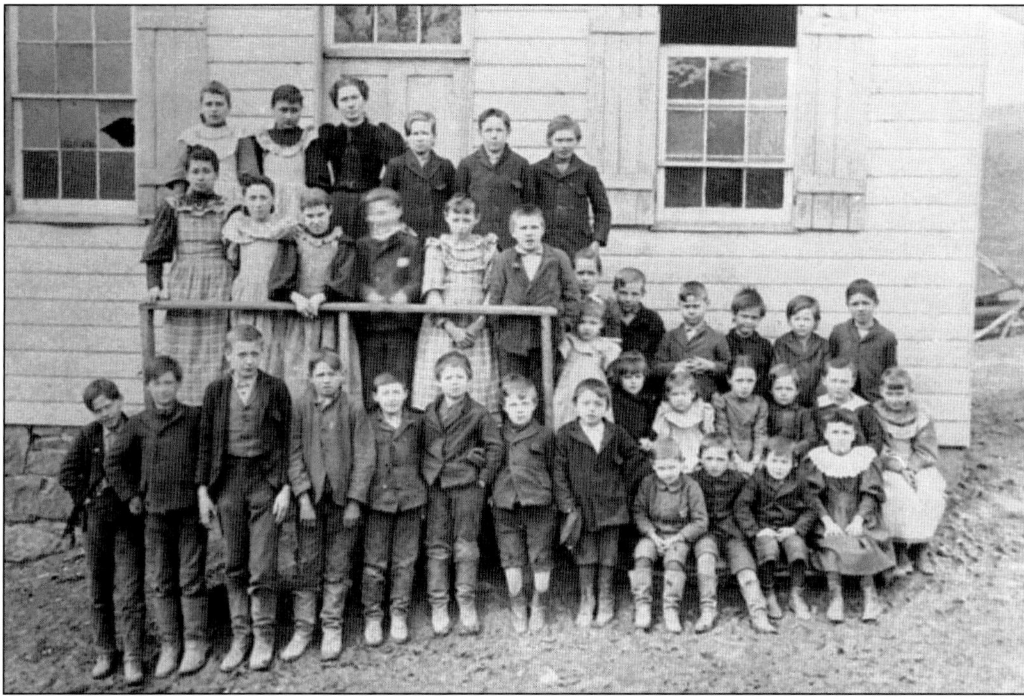

Around 1930, these students attend Murrysville's Lauffer School on the often muddy Kemerer Hollow Road. Lauffer's millstone was built into a Delmont house chimney at the New US 22 cloverleaf. A Mr. Lauffer and a Mr. Duff held classes in a one-room school at Mechanics Hall in Export.

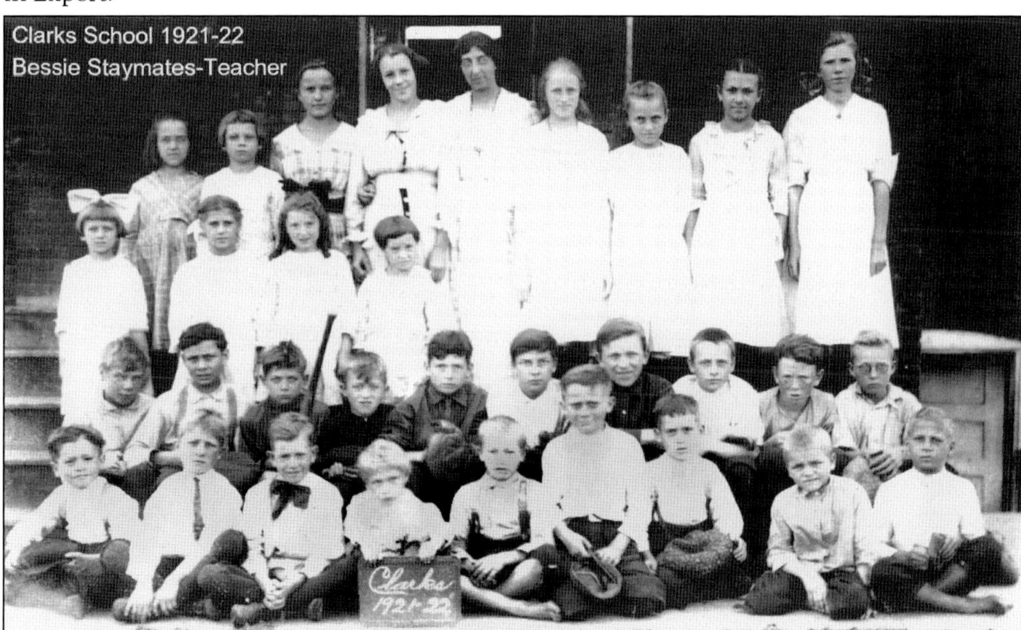

Teacher Bessie Staymates is standing in the middle of the fourth row of the Clark School elementary class of 1921–1922. The school was located near the log tollhouse in Murrysville on West Pike Street, also called the Northern Turnpike (Old US 22). (Courtesy of Carl Patty.)

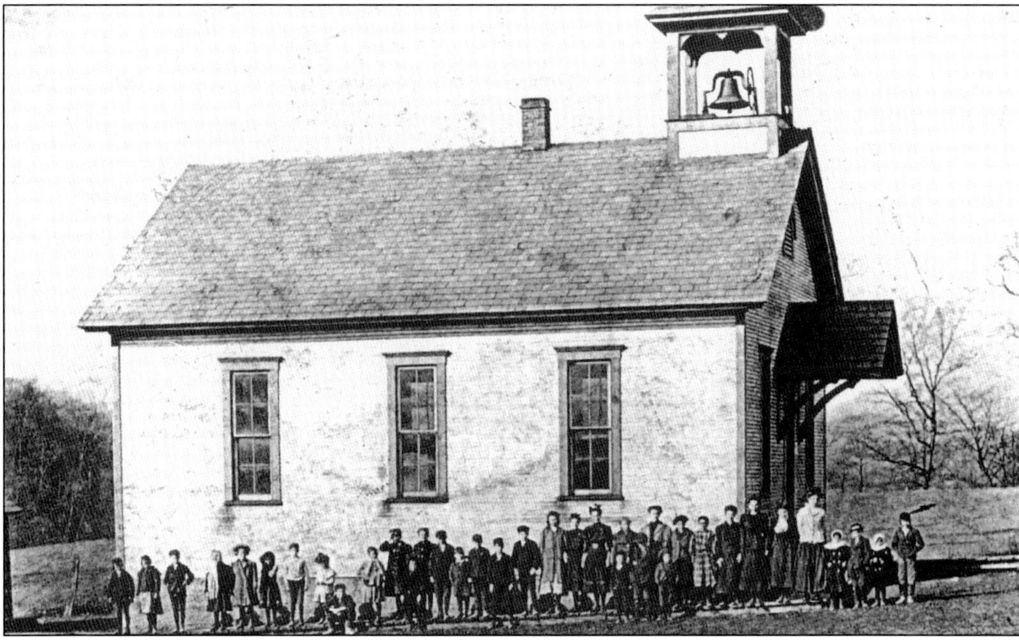

Seen here around 1913, this Murrysville one-room schoolhouse was located on Reed Boulevard. It preceded a brick school building. In those days, parents had many children—especially on farms where much help was needed. Children learned together in one common room. These schools had black, potbelly woodstoves often tended by older students. First- through eighth-grade classes were taught one at a time throughout the day. (Courtesy of Carl Patty.)

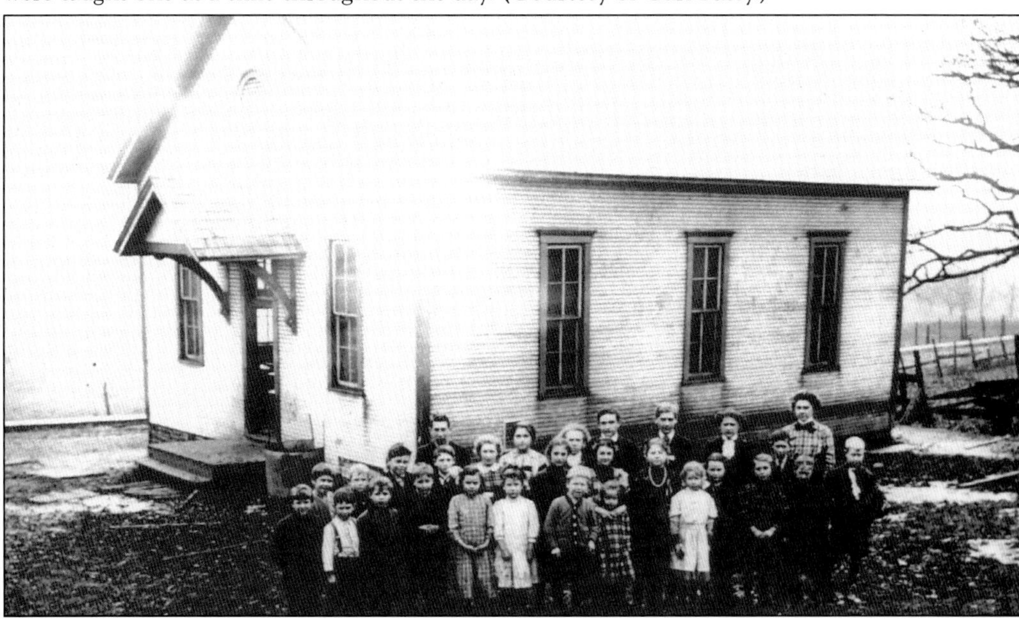

This Murrysville one-room school was located on Old William Penn Highway, the Northern Pike. When this picture was taken, wind was blowing snow off the roof. In this area are three houses that were typically brought by rail for convenient construction along tracks. One is believed to be the first of this type built by Sears, Roebuck and Company. Teacher Florence John Rings is pictured with students in 1910. (Courtesy of Carl Patty.)

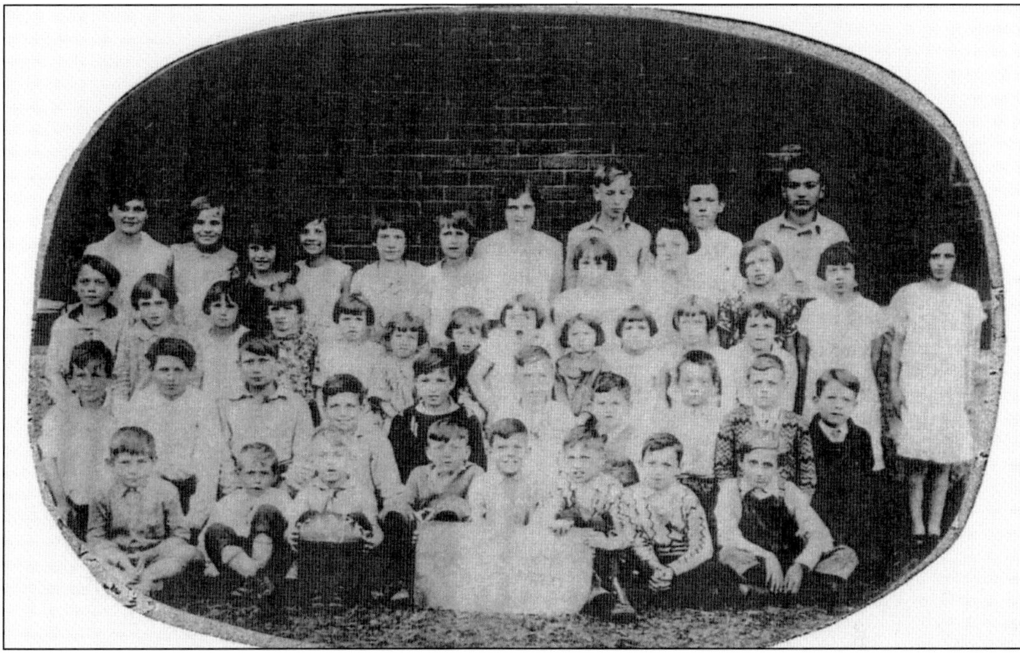

In this c. 1943 photograph taken at Clark School in Murrysville, the following Turtle Creek Valley families are represented: Stevick, Beniger, Carp, Kuzik, Geiger, Brewer, Viola, Karp, Shaffer, Eberts, Moose, Parker, Danesi, Soles, Tarr, Stump, Mika, and Stark. Often, several students from the same family attended this one-room school at the same time but in different grades. (Courtesy of Carl Patty.)

ALUMNI NEWS

Franklin Township High School was organized in 1919-20 with only 2 years High School. The following year the first class was graduated.

CLASS OF 1921
Levi Elwood—married
Florence Green—deceased
Alice Houston—married

CLASS OF 1922
Myron Elwood—married
Edith Elliott
Mary Minnis—married
Mary Shaw—married

CLASS OF 1923
Leona Cline
Marie Duff—married
Edith Elwood—Nurse
Loretta Schake—married
Orpha Whipkey—married
Mae Blanche Lintner
Lucetta Harvey—married
Mabel Branthoover—married
Clair Geiger—married
Clarence Remaley
Robert Thompson

CLASS OF 1924
Primitivo Colombo—Teacher
Olive Rugh—Teacher
Bertha Elwood—Teacher
Louise Schake—married
Violet Duff—Teacher
Gertrude Humes—Teacher
Butler Waugh—married
Carl Whipkey—married
Charles Stimmel

CLASS OF 1925
Jack Deakins
Elizabeth Fink—Teacher
Mary Greer
[illegible]
Marian Hall—Music Teacher
Marian Soady
Opal King—Teacher
Mary Young—married
Esther McAlister—deceased
James Thompson
Glen Branthoover

CLASS OF 1926
Priscella Allison—Teacher
Louise Barber—Teacher
Faye Courtright
Eva Good—Married
Sara McWilliams—married
Cecile Martz
Eleanor Speer
Emma Stout
Nelda Stump—Teacher
Eunice Wallover
Clinton Kistler
Karl Koch
Arthur Schake
James Walters
Wilda Christy—married

CLASS OF 1927
Jane Dittrich
Wilfred Eckman
Thomas Earll
Carl Fink
Alson Latshaw
James Minnis
John Pommersheim
James Sleigh—married
Ernest Shaw—married
Ruth Remaley—Nurse
Martha Christy
Martha Rugh—Nurse
Howard Tarr

CLASS OF 1928
Margaret Allison
John Ader
Ralph Bush
Andrew Demko
Violet Carr
George Eckman
Helen Fink—In school
George Hall—In school
Hazel Christy—In school
Vera Christy
Jessie Christy
Joe McCall—In school
Bert Krushinski—Married
Nick Manovich
Norman Weigle
Elmer Warner
Sybil Wardle
Anna Waugh—In school
Sadie Zimmerman—Married
Lucille Hilty—In school
Ella Mae Stout
Conrad Balest—In School
Anna Slavnick
Lawrence Thompson

CLASS OF 1929
Genevieve Atherton
Steve Ader
Louis Cornali
Dorothy Earle
Alice Kerpec
Virginia King—Married
Carl Patty
Martin Raymaky
[illegible]
Alberta Sonners
James Shaw
Eli Visnick
Olive Watt—In school
Alex Waugh
Edward Yelowchan
Hazel Young

SUMMARY

Girl Graduates	60
Boy Graduates	46
Married	20
Teachers	14
Nurses	5
College or Business Course	22
Working	16
Deceased	2
Total Graduates	106

1930-Franklin Twp. Quill

Murrysville's Franklin Regional High School alumni are listed in the yearbook, the *Quill*. Organized in 1919–1920, the school started out as a two-year institution, with ninth and tenth grades.

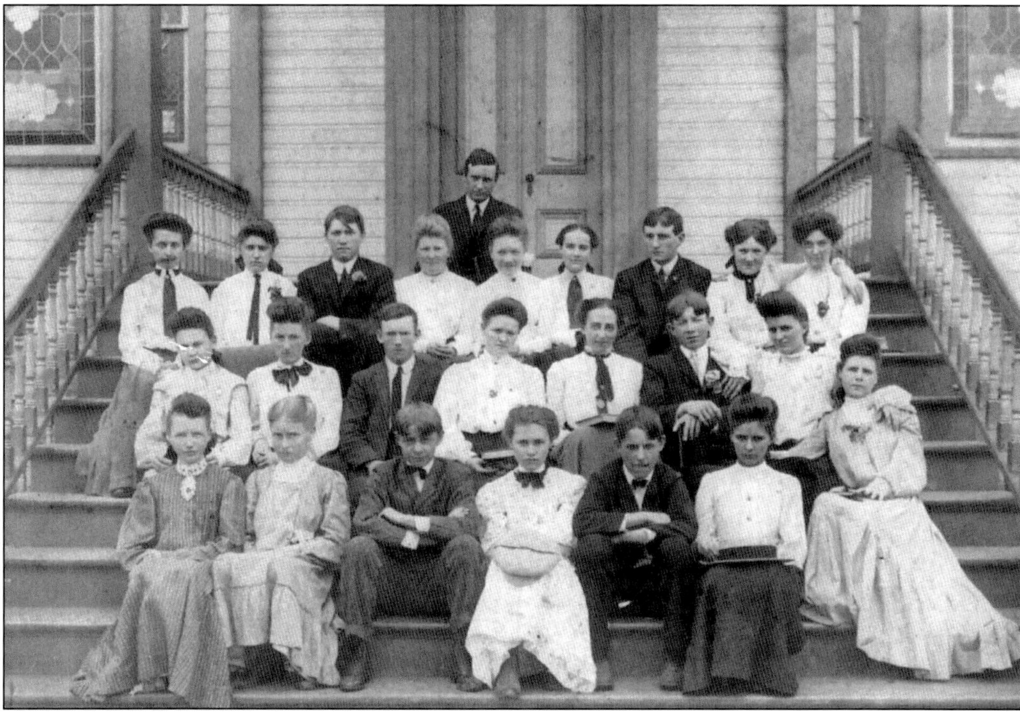

Dr. Zachariah Stewart died during a Gettysburg battle. He was the father of F.L. Stewart, Laird Institute's first principal. F.L. Stewart married Jane Laird, daughter of Francis and Mary Moore Laird. Mary's father was John Moore, the first Westmoreland County judge. Identified in this image are student Bessie Staymates (first row, middle with tie) and teacher Charles Stunkard (top). (Courtesy of Murrysville Historical Preservation Society.)

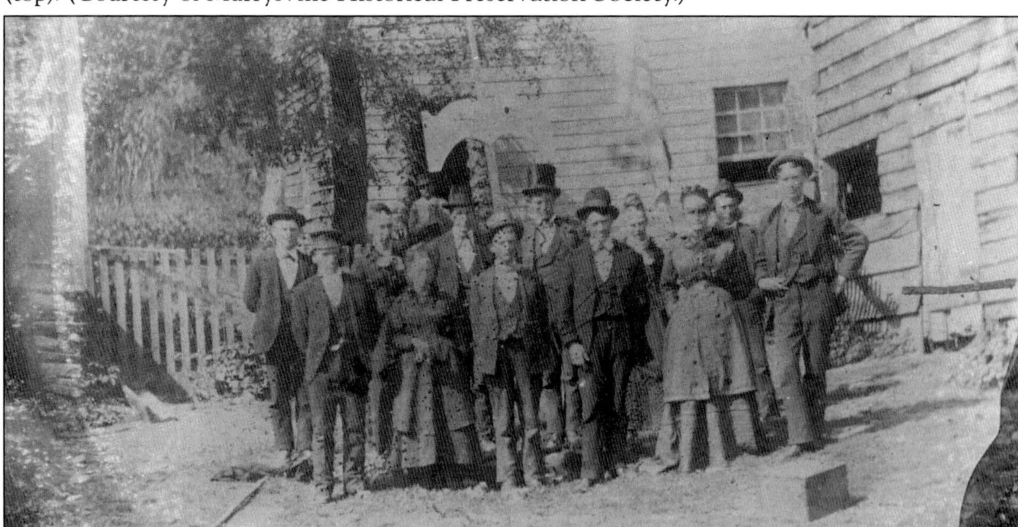

These are unidentified students at Francis Laird Stewarts's Turtle Creek Academy, known as Laird Institute when is was at the Stewart family home in Murrysville before it moved to the First Presbyterian Church. Scientist Stewart, besides inventing a way to process sugar from maize, initiated the Turtle Creek Valley Railroad and determined properties of natural gas escaping from the ground before Murrysville's famous well erupted. (Courtesy of Raymond Meehan.)

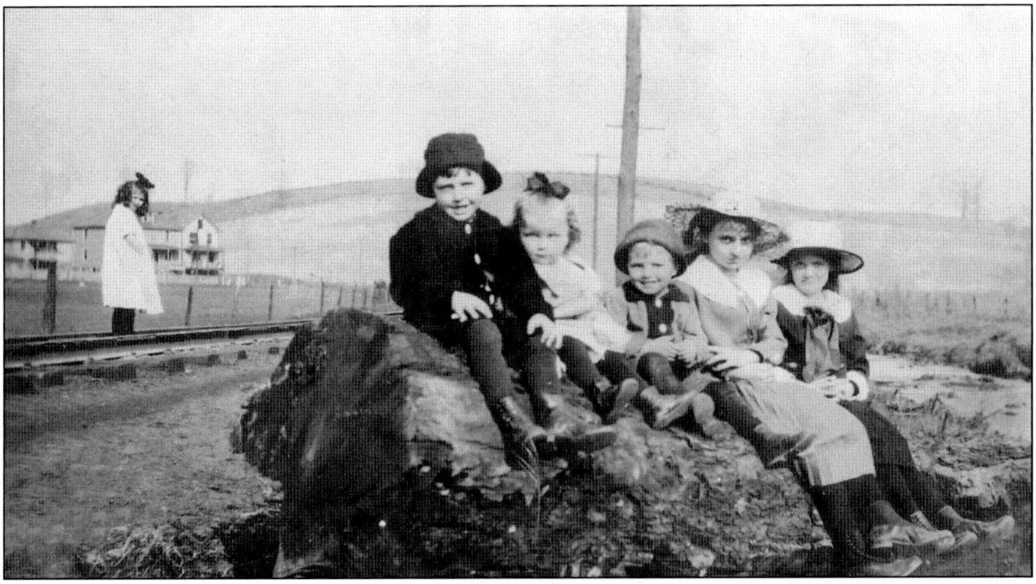

From left to right are Norman Weigle (Wigle), Nelda Good, Forest Wigle, Norma Wigle, and Vogene Humes—all sitting on a rock. In summer, children such as these often swam in the pond at the Westmoreland Coal Company dam on the outskirts of east Export. In winter, they skated there or rode sleds on the streets or slid down red-dog slate dumps on cardboard and other makeshift creations.

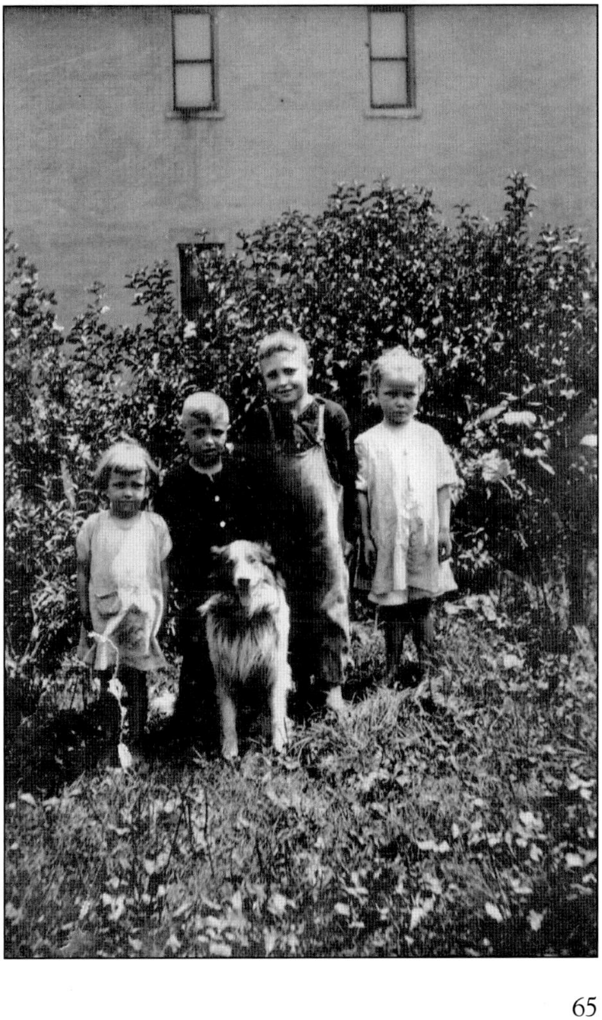

From left to right are Ethel, Forest, and Norman Wigle with Nelda Good and their dog. Dogs usually ran freely in coal company towns. In his memoirs of the Roaring Twenties, the son of Export blacksmith Karl Koch tells about his dog being run over when cars first appeared. A touring group zipped through town with passengers wearing goggles, blowing scarves, and white dusters to keep clothes clean from coal dust and dirt roads.

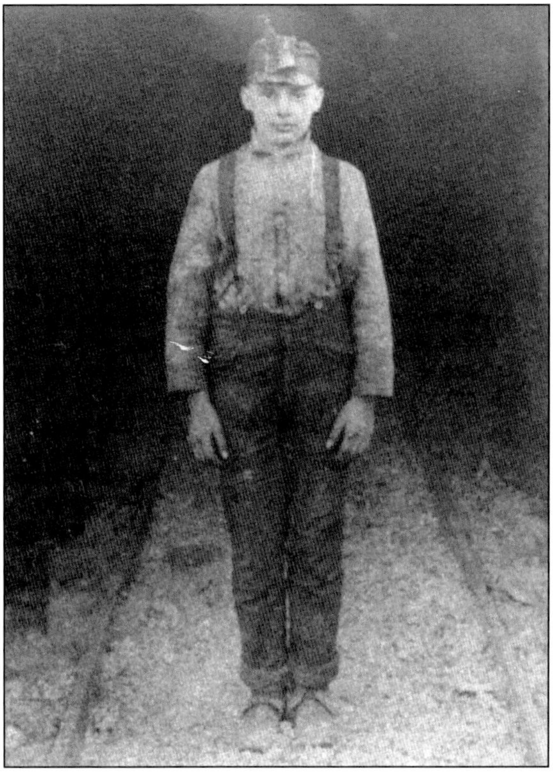

Herman Wigle was a nine-year-old trapper boy who opened and closed interior air-controlling mine flaps. He later worked for W.B. Skelly, grooming and taking care of his horses. Often, boys cried to release fears of the dark mines. One trapper boy was nicknamed Glimmer because he kept his oil lamp as bright as possible. Some youths were squeezed to death between coal cars before they had brakes.

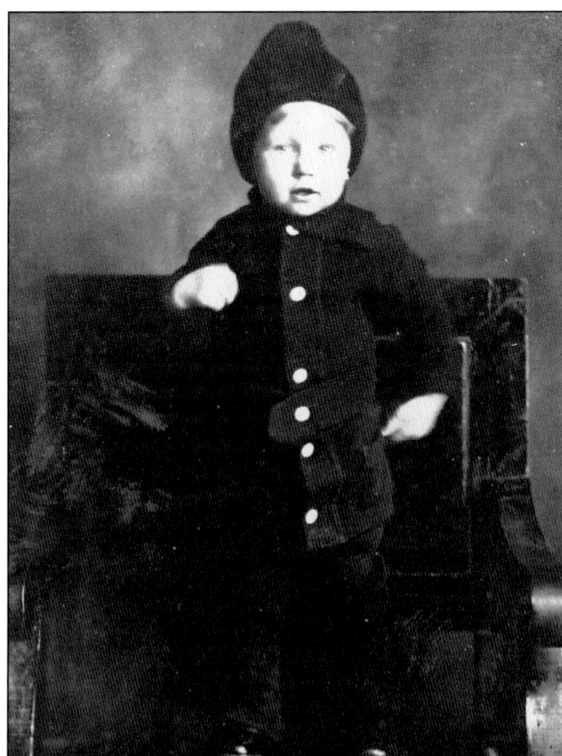

Herman's son, Robert Edwin, is pictured at 20 months old. Child labor laws enacted during the Depression of the 1930s spared him from working in perilous coal mines as a boy. Pres. Franklin D. Roosevelt signed the Fair Labor Standards Act of 1938, which banned oppressive child labor. Little boys small enough to get in tight areas of mines were often employed before then.

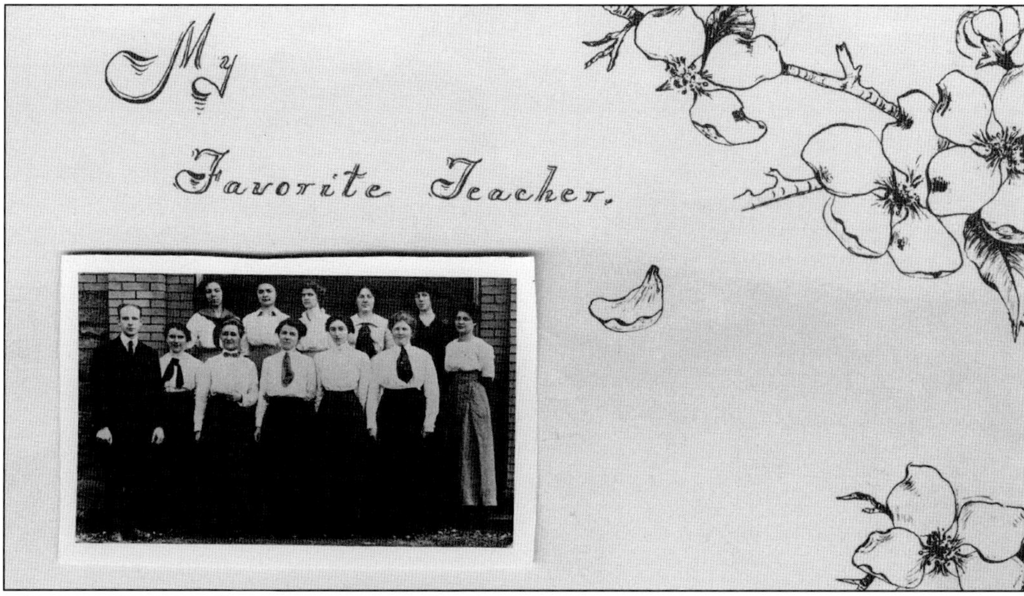

These teachers taught in Export's 1912 brick consolidated school. Women then could not have children and teach. In 1906, Franklin Township paid male and female teachers equal wages, but other county communities paid men larger salaries. Not pictured, "Professor" Hart, Roy Speer, George Fink Aber Shaw, and George Geiger were all on the administration and board. Before high schools were built in the two communities, students traveled by train to neighboring towns.

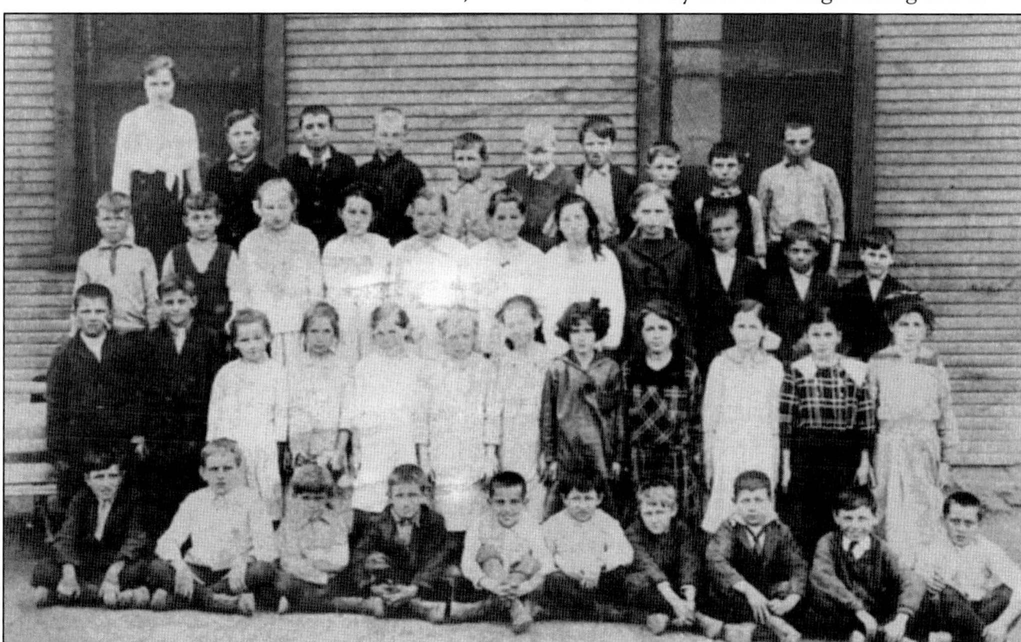

These students were enrolled in the Murrysville-Export area school system about 1930. In both communities, besides education, Boy Scouts and Girl Scout programs have always been well supported. Frank Morse Sloan was presented awards for his work with the Boy Scouts of Murrysville, as was Bessie Staymates. Other residents have their names engraved on historic millstones at Haymaker Park honoring their dedication in the area of the Haymaker Gas Well site.

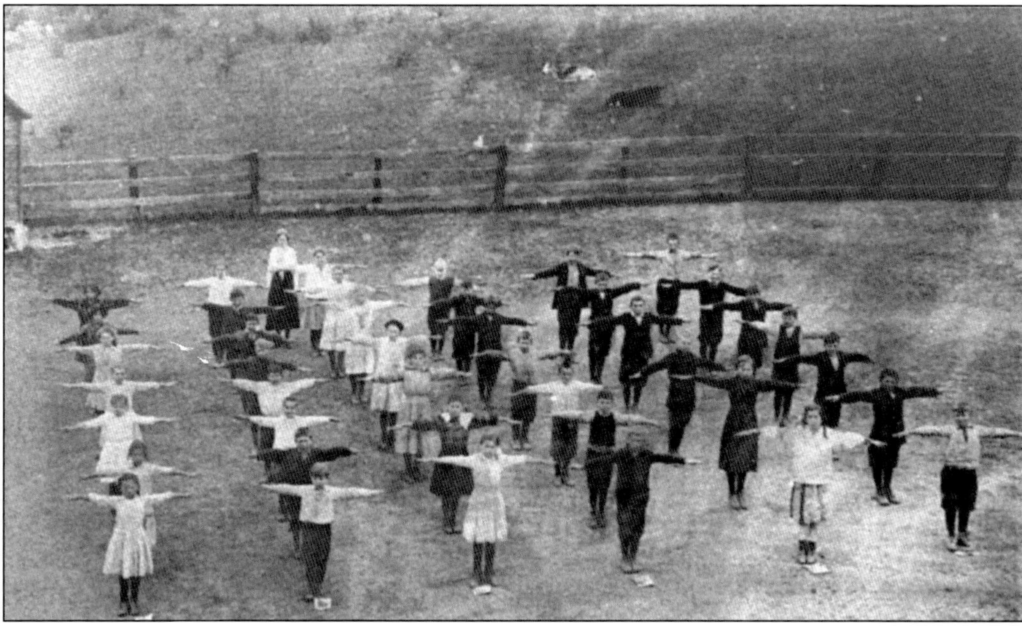

Through calisthenics and other means, children got their exercise. At St. Mary's Catholic Church in Export, when a manually operated organ was used, children were required to sit on the floor and pump it. During mass, alter boys at the church took turns playing a xylophone, while their companions played tricks on them by loosening the ball on the stick which would fly out into the congregation when the music began.

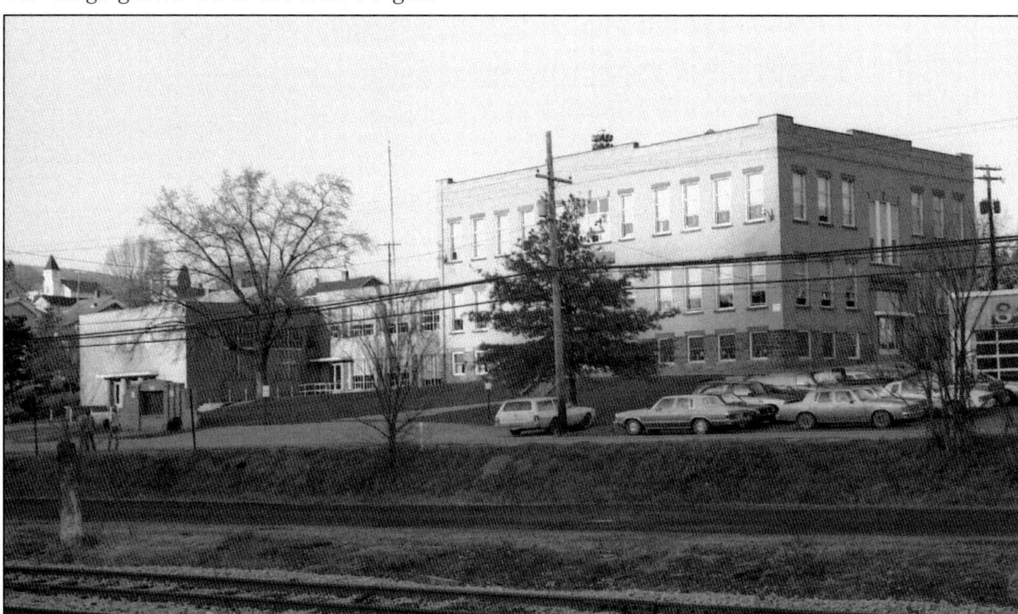

Export's brick school was built in 1912 on Westmoreland Coal land, as was the Catholic church along Old US 22 at Town Square. This building replaced five earlier ones because the school system was not centrally organized. The contractor was J.E. Myers. Construction, and the cost was $19,050. Greensburg's Dr. Peterson's Penmanship System for cursory writing was taught here. The structure now serves as housing for local residents.

Margaret Walker Haymaker's brothers George and Frankie, are seen here. They were the uncles of Obadiah and Michael Haymaker, who as adults owned the wildcat gas well of 1878. In the innocence of childhood, neither one could foresee then what would happen to them as entrepreneurs in their world-renowned business in the little village of Murrysville.

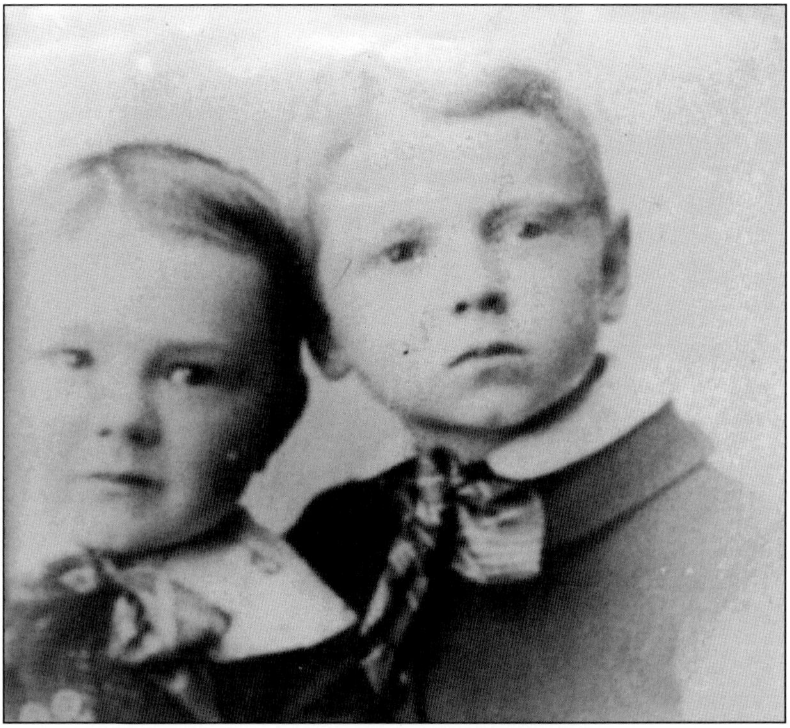

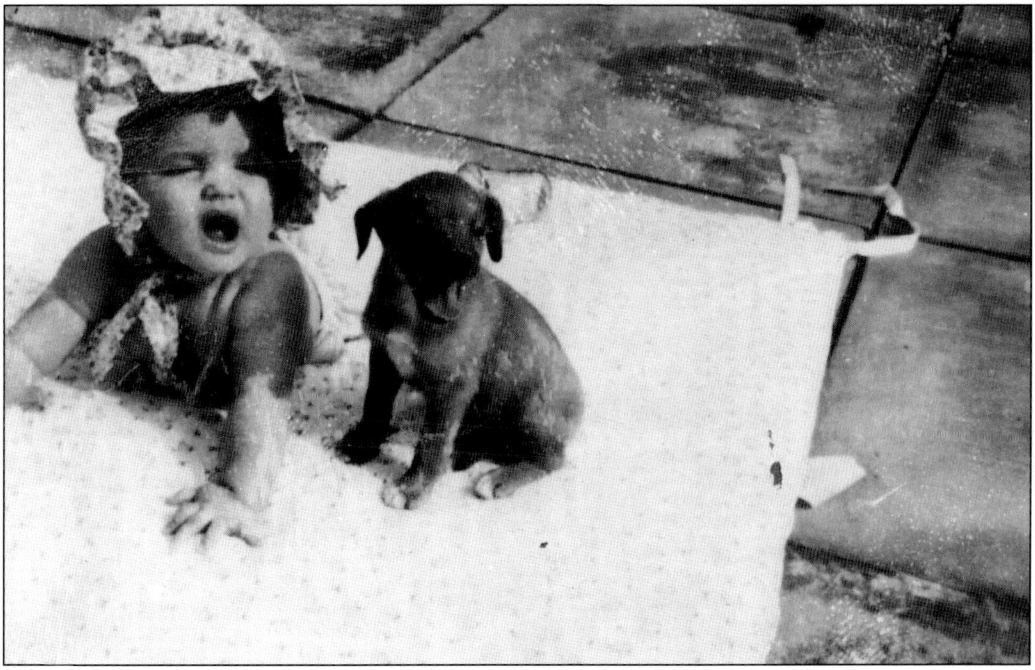

This little girl grew up in the oil and coal region. Besides Franklin Regional High School, she attended White Valley School, now gone. The photograph was taken when both baby and puppy happened to yawn at the same time. Besides excellent education at Laird Institute in Murrysville, children have been given special priority through a unique North Hills Road swimming program known for both its instruction and competitiveness, which produce outstanding athletes.

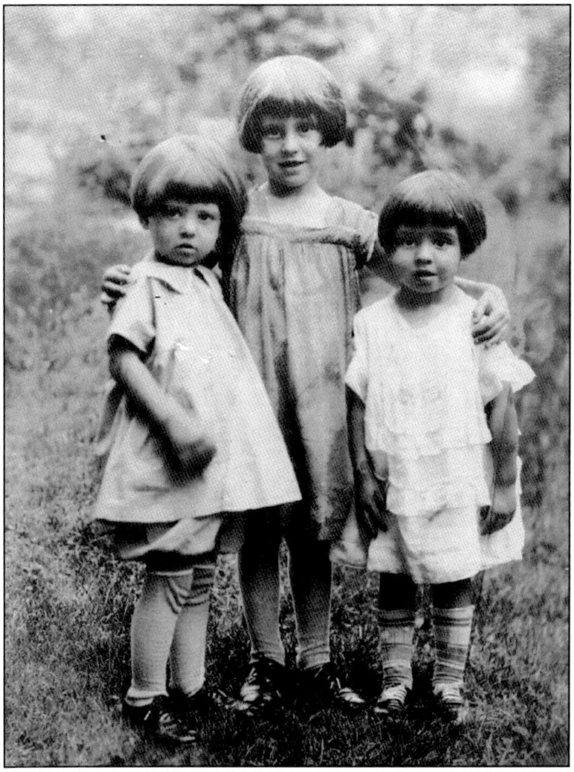

Pictured are sisters Helen (left), Gail (center), and Ruth, daughters of Arnold Wigle. This prominent family of Murrysville as well as Export operated a pharmacy in the latter town. Export residents received the special benefit of being enrolled in both school systems with outstanding teachers and instructors who have supported and inspired them to become champions in sporting events.

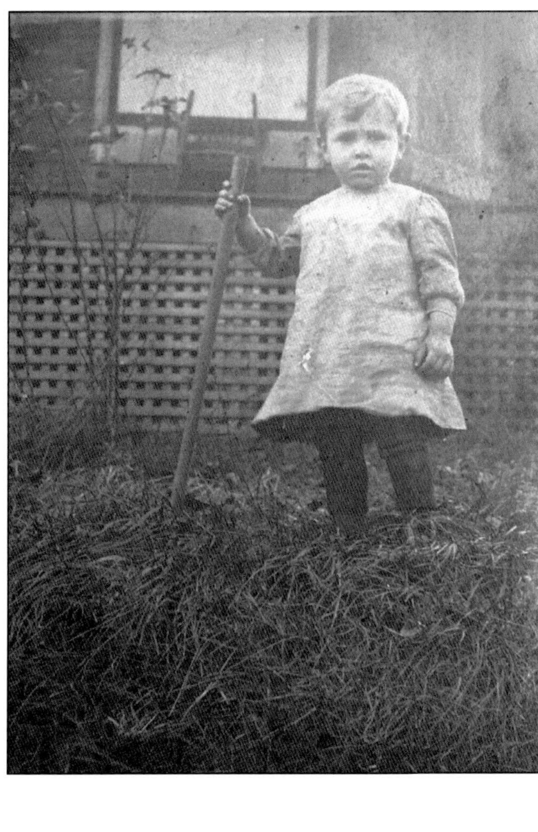

This is an unknown child of Export. Numerous homes were constructed in a unique way. Turtle Creek Valley houses were often built into hillsides. Their first-floor front doors opened on the lower entrance, with the second-story backdoors also accessible from the elevated ground. Basement levels allowed coal to be dug directly from a door leading into the coal seam and sometimes gathered by little children.

Six

For Dedication in Helping Others

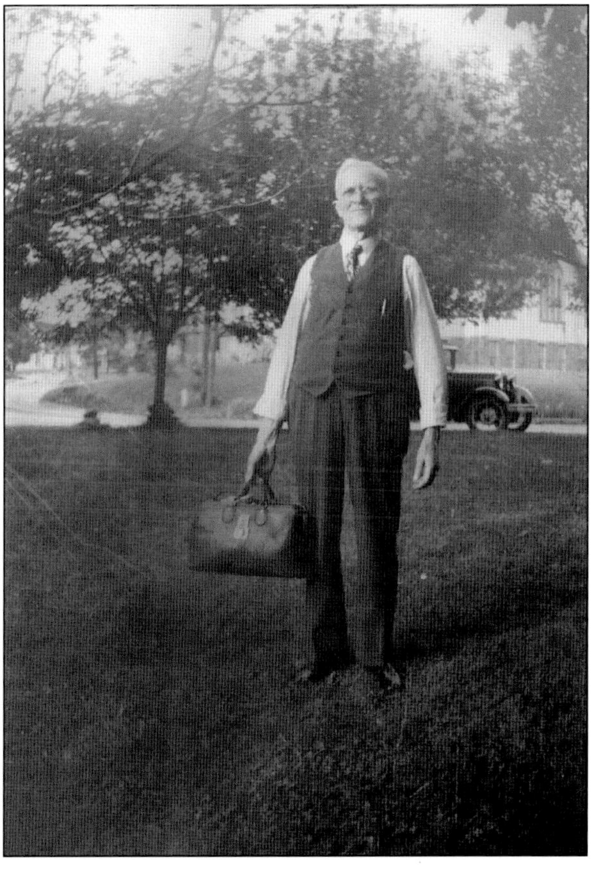

Dr. George Orbin Hall (1875–1944) wore many hats as a doctor, surgeon, pharmacist, dentist, and pastor. His grandson Charles Hall recalls a quote from his aunt Marion: "Dr. Hall did it all—pulled teeth, removed tonsils, set broken bones, mixed his own liquid medicines, passed out packets of pills, delivered babies, and read the Bible to the dying." This picture was taken around 1900. (Courtesy of Charles Hall.)

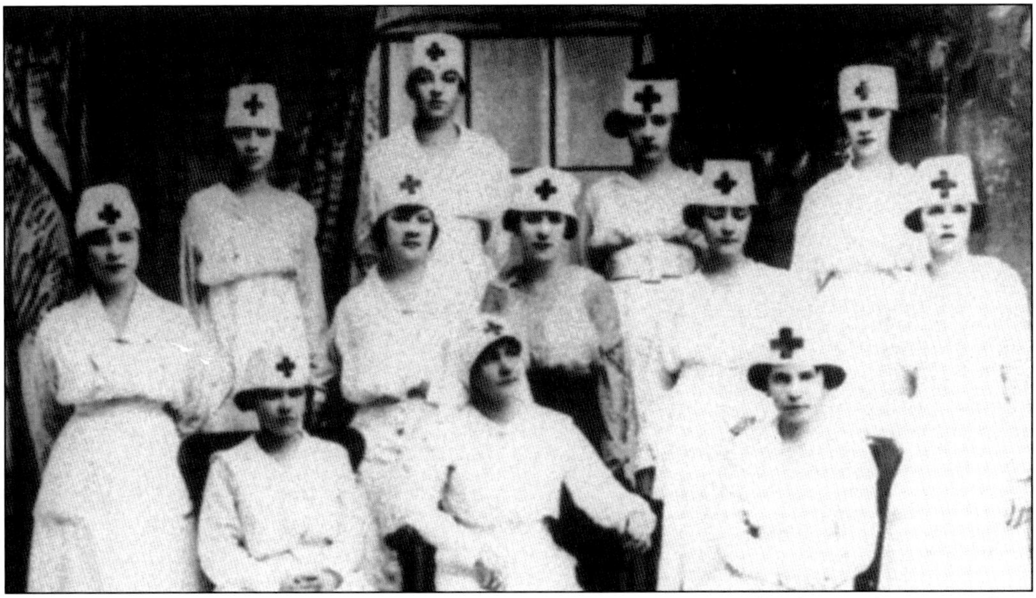

Export Red Cross volunteers, from left to right, are (first row) Mary Bullock, Mrs. James Lindsay, and Mary Ann Moline; (second row) Bertha Foight, Emma Altman, Mae Shearer, Edith Steiner, and Frances Gray; (third row) Jessie Wallace, Elizabeth Jones, Margaret Paul, and Eleanor Stevick. Mary Dixon, Dr. Dixon's wife and a Red Cross volunteer with a merit award (1964), initiated the first bloodmobile and polio vaccine programs. The Dixons cared for the town's youths and were also marriage counselors.

A PAGE FROM THE ROSTER OF EXPORT PATIENTS AND DOCTORS DURING THE 1918 FLU

NAME	DATE ADMITTED	AGE	DATE DISCHARGED	PHYSICIAN
John Wall	10-23-18	29yrs.	Oct. 31st,'18	M.H. Smithgall
Frank Schubs	10-23-18	43	Nov. 3rd, '18	" "
Mary Barbonne	10-23-18	10	Nov. 1st, '18	E. L. Piper
Mary Ivancovich	10-23-18	15	Nov. 1st, '18	J. C. Skelly
Sam Ivancovich	10-23-18	17	Nov. 1st, '18	" "
Eli Ivancovich	10-23-18	8	Nov. 2nd, '18	" "
Alice Skarlitt	10-23-18	6	Nov. 2nd, '18	" "
Mary Skarlitt	10-23-18	13	Nov. 2nd, '18	" "
Annie Skarlitt	10-23-18	9	Nov. 2nd, '18	" "
Miller Skarlitt	10-23-18	10	Nov. 2nd, '18	" "
Mike Skarlitt	10-23-18	17	Nov. 1st, '18	" "
William Grebosky	10-23-18	18	Oct. 31st,'18	" "
Leah Baldowin	10-23-18	7	Nov. 2nd, '18	M. H. Smithgall
Catharine Molen	10-23-18	28	Nov. 2nd, '18	J. C. Skelly
Jullian Scapona	10-23-18	3	Nov. 1st, '18	M. H. Smithgall
Dominik Scapona	10-23-18	7	Nov. 1st, '18	" "
Jennia Scapona	10-23-18	25	Nov. 1st, '18	" "
Mary Scapona	10-23-18	7 mo.	Nov. 1st, '18	" "
Donella DeStypony	10-23-18	28yrs.	Oct. 26th,'18 Died	" "
Annie Chika	10-23-18		Nov. 1st, '18	J. C. Skelly
Frank Shuster	10-23-18	38	Oct. 26th,'18	E. L. Piper
Baby Dolenc	10-23-18	18 mo.	Nov. 1st, '18	J. C. Skelly
Deloro Careta	10-24-18		Nov. 1st, '18	M. H. Smithgall
Mrs. F. Shuster	10-25-18	32yrs.	Oct. 26th,'18	E. L. Piper
Baby Shuster	10-25-18	9 mo.	Oct. 28th,'18	" "
Maggie Shuster	10-25-18	7yrs.	Oct. 31st,'18	" "
Frank Shuster Jr.	10-25-18	4	Oct. 31st,'18	" "
Cinco Germore	10-25-18		Oct. 27th,'18 Died	" "
Jennie Susach	10-25-18	11	Nov. 1st, '18	J. C. Skelly
Annie Susach	10-25-18	9	Nov. 1st, '18	" "
Chas. Susach	10-25-18	6	Nov. 1st, '18	" "
Mrs. J. Kern	10-25-18	31	Oct. 31st,'18	E. L. Piper
Geo. Ivancovich	10-25-18	12	Nov. 1st, '18	J. C. Skelly
John Morgan	10-28-18	30	Oct. 30th,'18 Died	M. H. Smithgall
Valentine Chabuka	10-28-18	36	Nov. 1st, '18	J. C. Skelly
A. Martensik	10-28-18	12	Nov. 1st, '18	" "
Jerome Roslin	10-28-18	45	Nov. 2nd, '18	M. H. Smithgall
Mrs. S. Calocia	10-28-18	26	Nov. 3rd, '18	E. L. Piper
Mrs. Paul Grebosky	10-28-18	21	Oct. 30th,'18 Died	" "
Andrew Verbonich	10-28-18	33	Oct. 30th,'18 Died	" "
Jack Sodnac	10-28-18	24	Nov. 1st, '18 Died	" "
Glen Mill	10-28-18		Nov. 1st, '18 Died	" "
Frank Vetta	10-28-18	54	Nov. 4th, '18	" "
Matilda Passaventa	10-30-18		Oct. 31st,'18 Died	M. H. Smithgall
Baby Passaventa	10-30-18		Oct. 31st,'18 Died	" "
Ellen Ivancovich	10-30-18	11	Nov. 4th, '18	E. L. Piper
Geo Previc	10-30-18	35	Nov. 4th, '18	" "
Matt Melelak	10-30-18	49	Nov. 2nd, '18	" "

This page from a medical roster reveals patients in Export's temporary hospital, set up in the 1912 school. There was little time for funerals. Other physicians in the Export-Murrysville area included a Dr. Haymaker, William Bierer, Charles Smithgall, Howard J. Thomas, John Krick, and John Hart. Jeremiah Murry's grandson was Dr. James S. Murry, specializing in hydrophobia cases. Dr. Benjamin Burrell was Murrysville's first physician and the father of judge Jeremiah Murry Burrell. The next local doctor was Charles J. Kenley.

Slovene Anna "Ann" Rulyak, Export's certified midwife, sits beside Anna Roth (left) on October 4, 1919. Rulyak delivered over 500 babies, including her grandchildren—just about every baby in town. Midwives were not permitted to deliver twins or breech births, even though they often taught doctors. With the help of Rulyak, a mother, after giving birth, presented her newborn to her husband and boarders and packed their lunches that same night. (Courtesy of James Rulyak.)

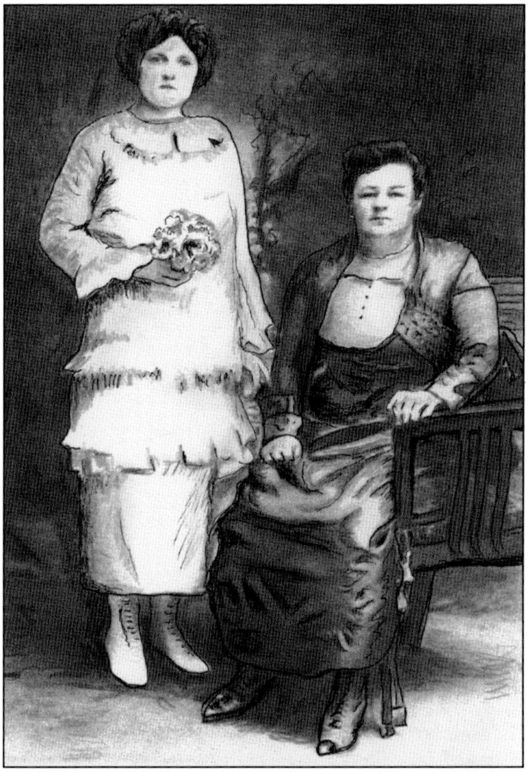

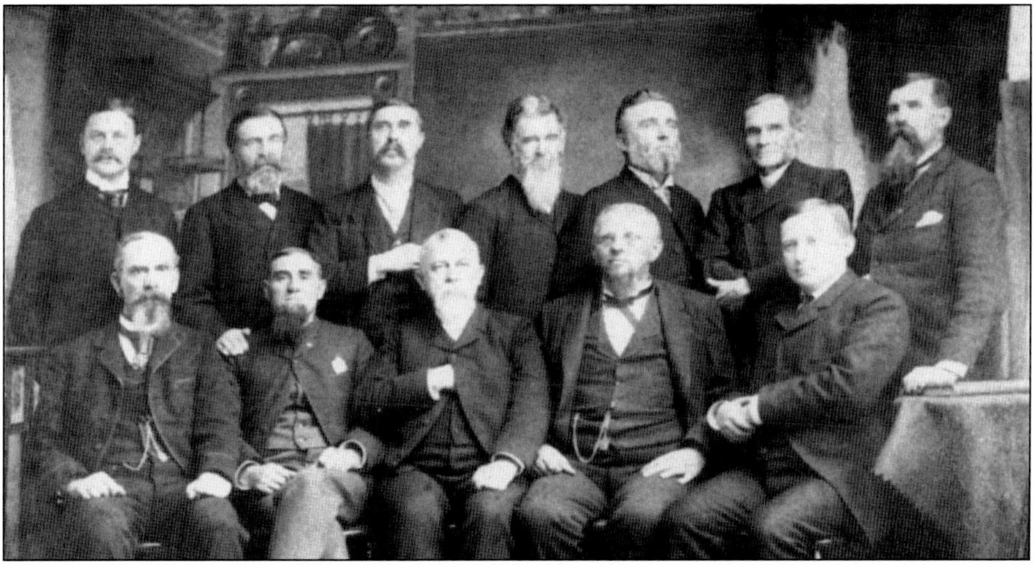

John George Foight (Voight) from Wurtemberg, Germany, saw Napoleon's army march against Russia. Foight's log house and store stood on Northern Turnpike. His son, also John George, joined the Franklin Blues during the Civil War. He was elected to the Pennsylvania legislature in 1888 and helped organize Export's First National Bank. He (first row, second from left) is next to Gov. James Beaver (with hand in vest), who served from 1887 to 1891. Both promoted Pennsylvania roads. The elder John George married Eliza Berlin, and he died in 1872. Son John George married Mary Brinker.

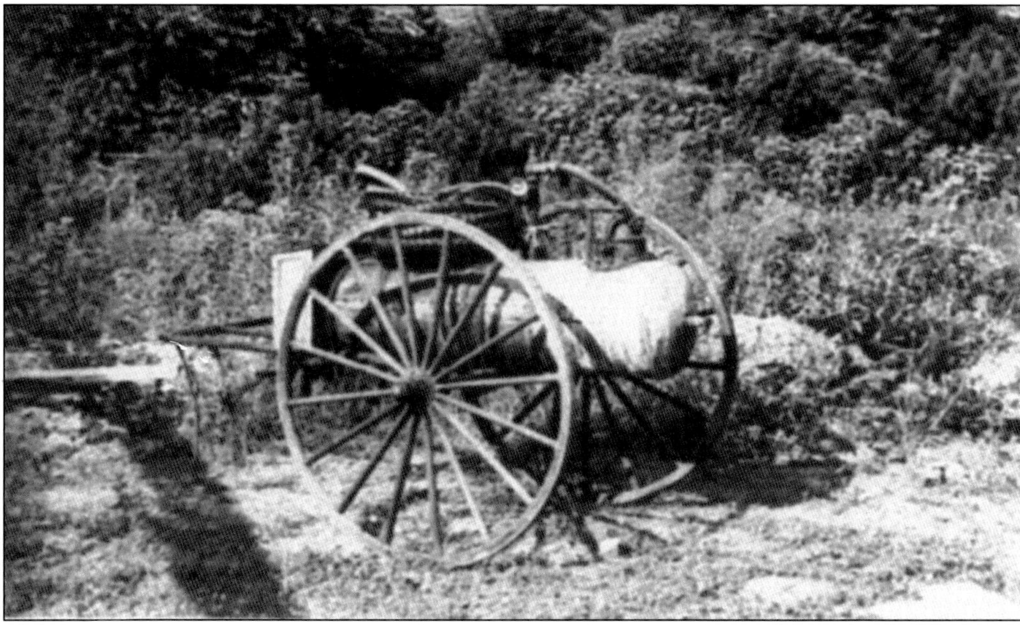

The steam whistle at the Westmoreland coal mine sounded fire alarms until the borough had its own siren. Volunteer firefighters and police represented total dedication to humanity in both communities. Pictured is a simple hose contraption of the period. Export had two machines mounted on a Ford chassis. Previously, fires were extinguished by bucket brigades of men passing water from man to man, which was the first method of organized firefighting.

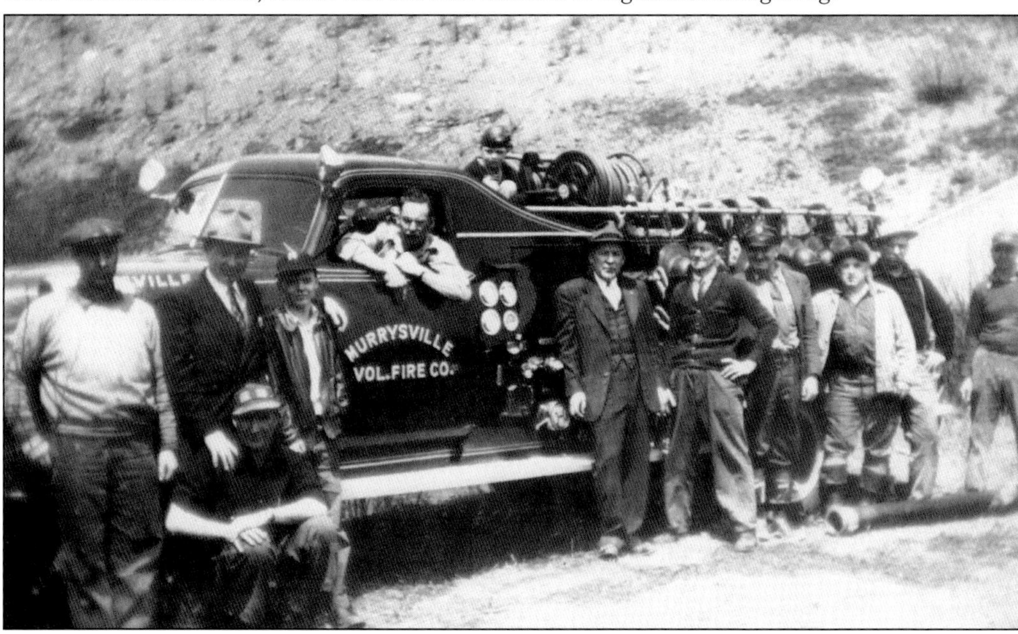

The Murrysville Voluntary Department honors Harry Steiner Patty in 1951. Volunteers built the town's post office and the First United Methodist Church annex. The picture of this 1949 fire truck was taken along Haymaker Run. Known men on the left are, from left to right, fire chief Harry S. Patty, John Haymaker, Vernon Stouton, Charles McGurk, and Carl Patty Sr. Carl Patty Jr. appears in the back of the truck near the hose. (Courtesy of Ralph Carl Patty.)

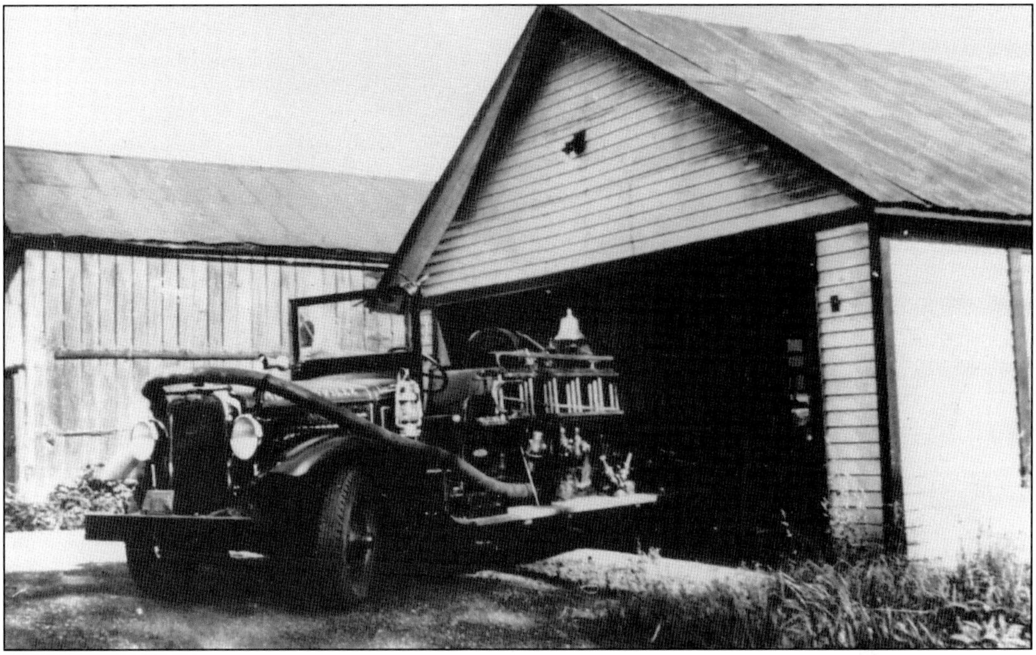

Murrysville's 1930 Dodge Howe Pumper is headed out for an event from a fire-station garage next to Patty's barn. The barn was a landmark long into modern times. The fire department was formerly behind Ferri's supermarket on the Town Square. (Courtesy of Randy S. Marts.)

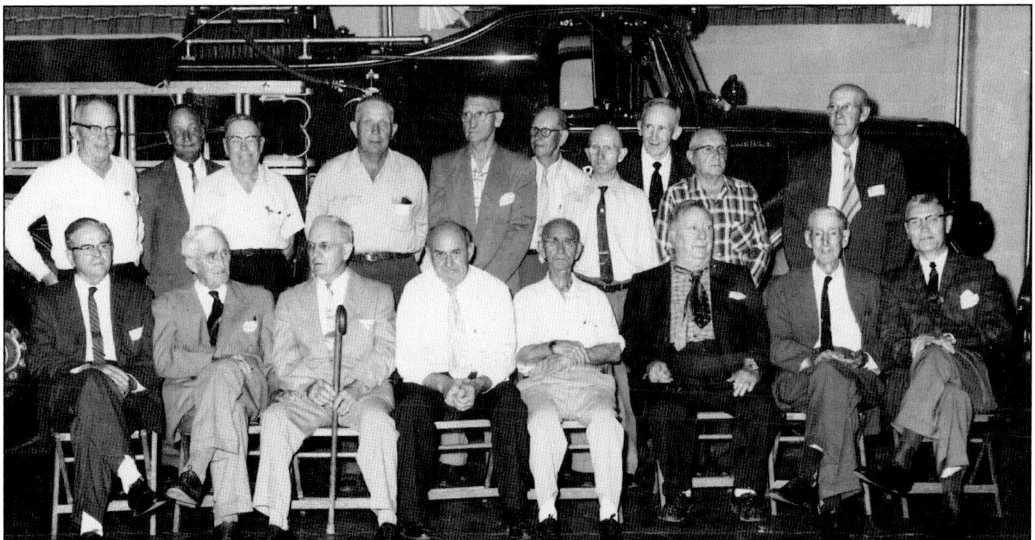

Murrysville's Volunteer Fire Company, pictured on its 35th anniversary, includes, from left to right, (first row): Lloyd King, F. Morse Sloan, Thomas King, John Haymaker, William Ringer, Samuel Stout, Billie Rose, and James Tallant; (second row) Charles Brunecke, Roger Apel, Clyde McCall, Donald Simons, Leon McElfresh, Harry Patty, Clayton Patty, Rubin Elliot, William Rose, and Charles Thompson. Murrysville's first firemen to volunteer were Bell, Bigley, Burt, Creigton, Fellington, Griffith, two Kings, McElfresh, McKee, two Pattys, Rauboc, Riley, Ringer, Ross, Smith, Snyder, Stark, two Stouts, Swauger, Thompson, and Williams. (Courtesy of Randy S. Marts.)

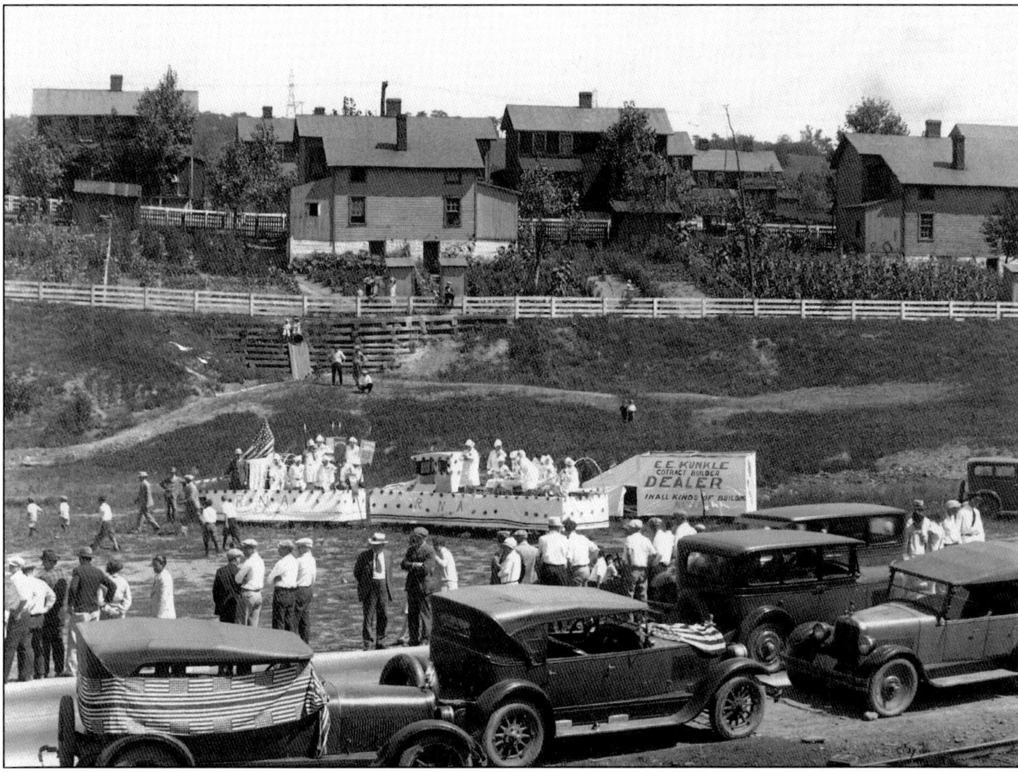

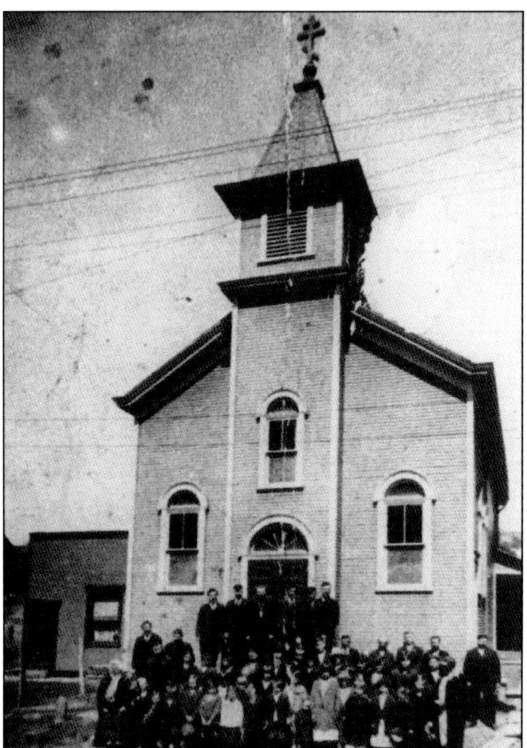

Miss Export, Laura Mae Schell, who collected $699 for the firemen, is featured on a float in a parade that the firemen sponsored in 1927. J.D. Hart, Export's tax collector for many years, won a Crosley refrigerator for the grand raffle prize that day. The first call for Murrysville firemen was made at the Patty Brother's store. Prior to that, bucket brigades quenched fires with church-bell alarms. (Courtesy of Raymond Meehan.)

Fortunately, Export Fire Department volunteers put out the fire at this Russian Orthodox church and saved its historic architecture.

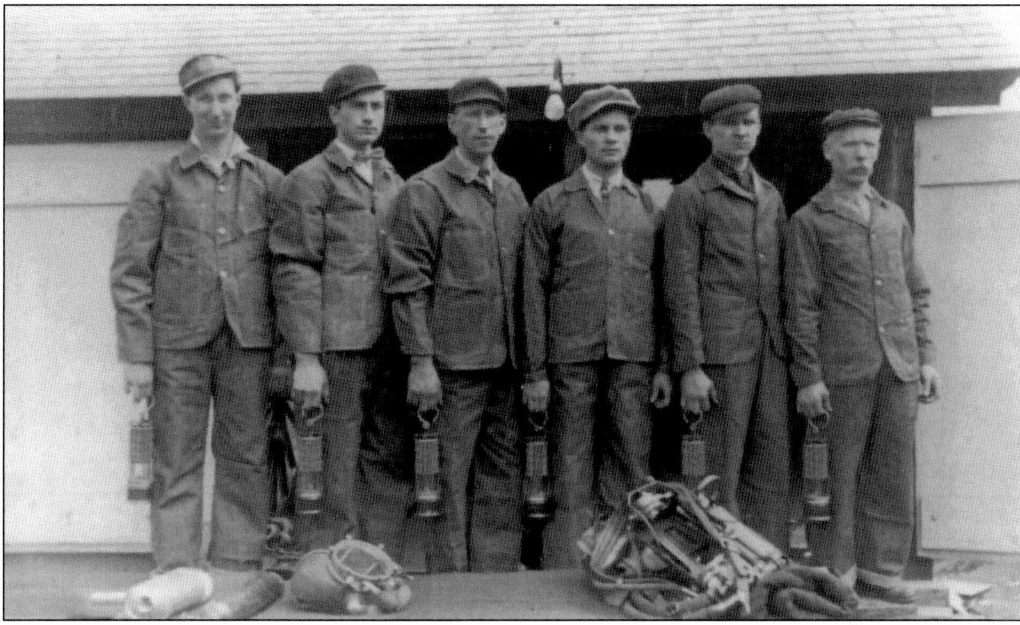

Members of the Westmoreland Coal Company rescue crew display their equipment and a canvas stretcher. The men are holding mine lanterns essential for work in collieries. Mine accidents were frequent in industrial towns, and cave-ins often caused deaths. When a miner died, his body was placed in a sack, or at best, in a wicker basket, and delivered to his widow or co-renter. (Courtesy of Raymond Meehan.)

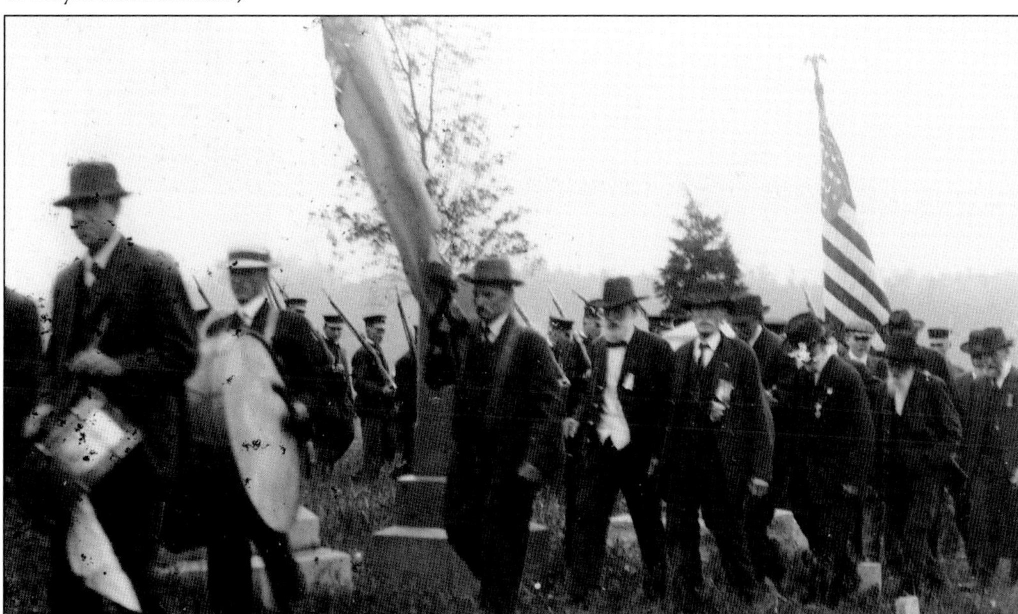

During the Civil War, 400 women disguised as men are said to have experienced active combat, as women have in most wars. Here are Civil War veterans in First Presbyterian Church Cemetery on North Hills Road in Murrysville. Samuel Patty is last man on the right. This 1915 picture of Grand Army of the Republic member (and Jeremiah Murry's house [pictured later]) are from Frank Stimmel's antique glass-plate negatives. (Courtesy of Stephen Simpson.)

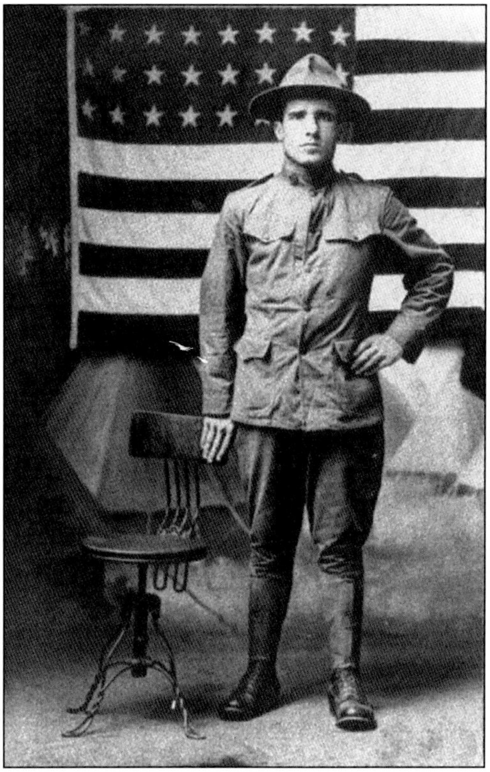

Anthony Barber from Export is pictured in his World War I uniform, posing patriotically in front of the American flag. From Export, 71 men served in that war. Those who lost their lives were Emanuel Geiger, Levi Glunt, John Irwin, Harold Jones, Harry Woods, and Miller Wuslich. More than 30 served in the Korean War, and more than 50 enlisted in the Vietnam War.

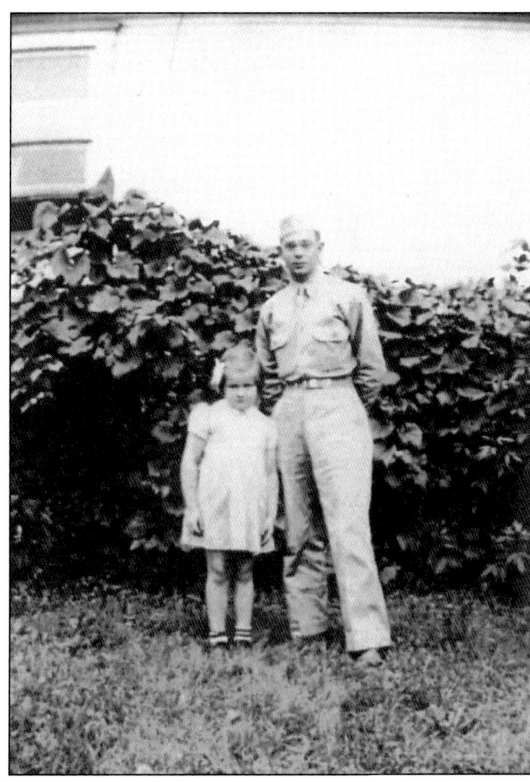

Harry Lloyd Patty (pictured with his niece Marian Heaven), became Murrysville's first World War II casualty, killed in a plane crash in Australia while heading for New Guinea on his first bombing mission. Harry Patty, Lloyd's father, operated a telegraph office on Mill Street where he received the tragic news in November 1942. In 1965, Frank Kohosek Jr., a pilot in 101st Airborne Division (civilian), was missing at sea. Kohosek's father and grandfather died in Export mines. (Courtesy of Carl Patty.)

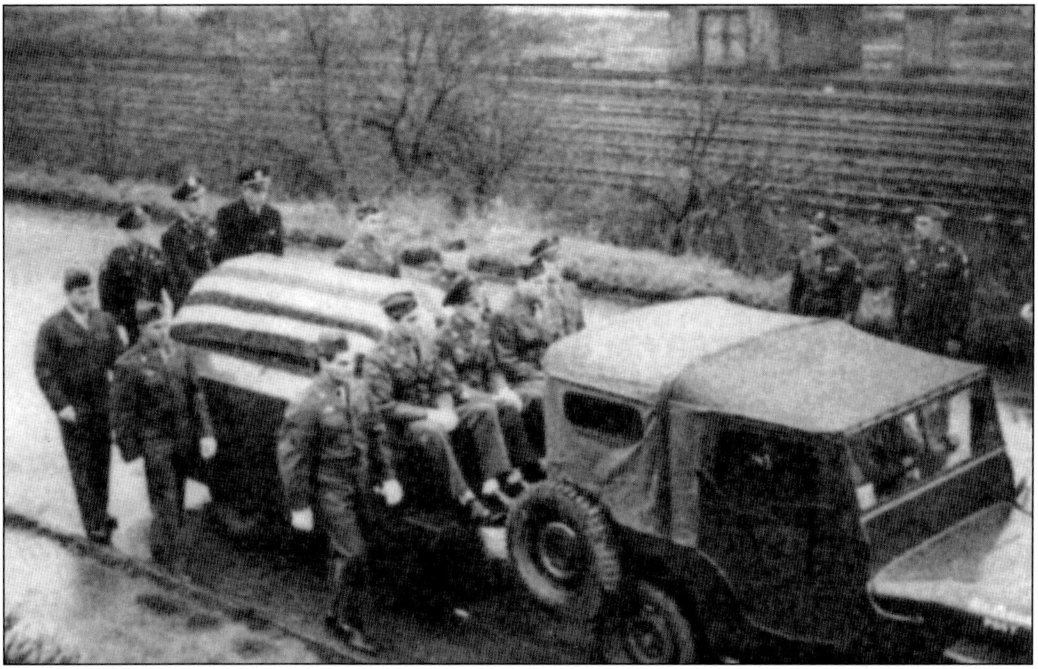

This is Frank Cain's World War II–era funeral in Export. Of the 578 local people who served in that war, 23 lost their lives. Besides Cain, they included Frank Kapusta, John Cain, Bernard Cohen, William Collins, Chalmers DeCecco, Nick Gazibara, William Geiger, Floyd Glunt, Robert Hamilton, Louis Kapera, Michael Karan, Leo Kovacic Jr., Frank Medved, Albert Oslosky, Earl Painter, Phillip P. Primozic, William Shifler, Pete Slavic, George Stepetich, George Susich, George Yakovick, and Raymond Zucco.

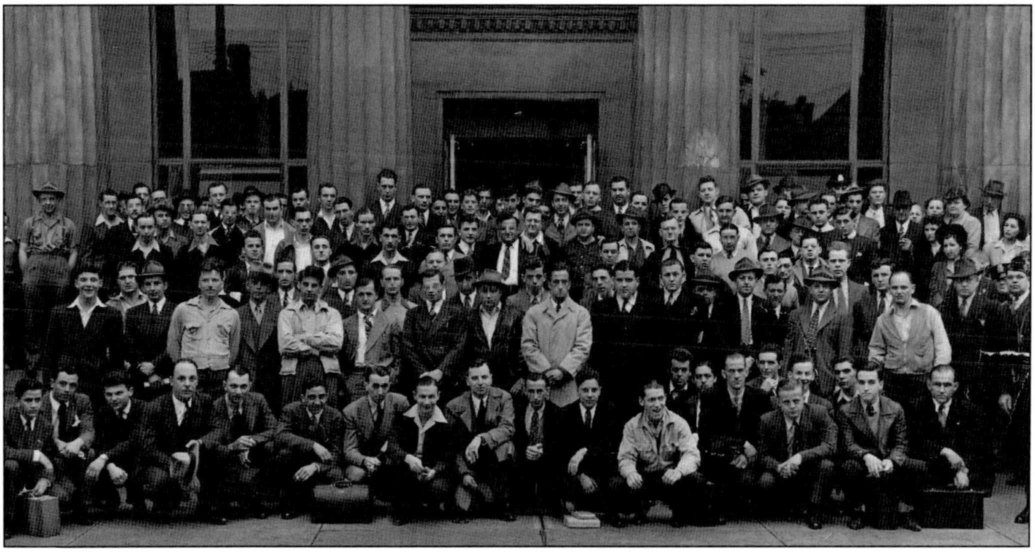

These well-dressed men, many with shirts and ties, are Army recruits posing for photographer Hartzell with their carrying cases. The men in this 1942 photograph are from Export, White Valley, Irwin (the Westmoreland Coal Company headquarters), and neighboring communities and ready to serve during World War II. There were many men from the small village of White Valley in old Franklin Township. Some brave soldiers never came back. (Courtesy of Raymond Meehan.)

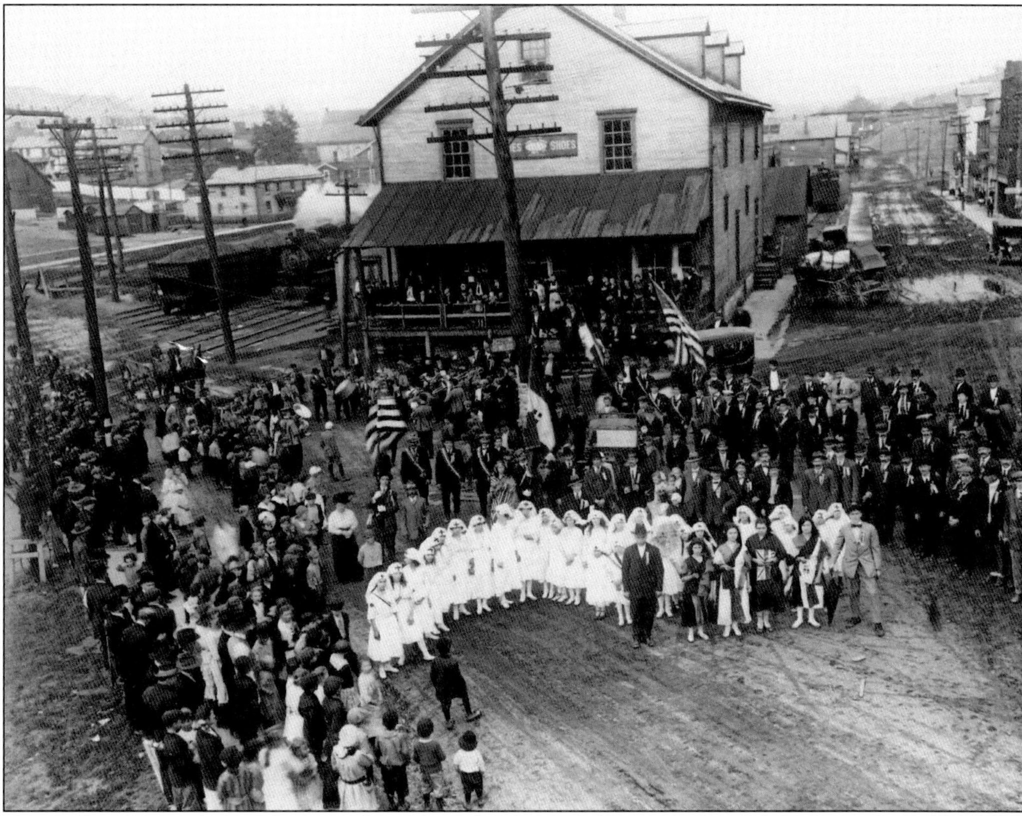

This photograph of Export Town Square (with 15-mile-speed-limit and shoe signs visible) captures a 1918 Columbus Day ceremony honoring soldiers serving in Europe during World War I. Red Cross volunteers, who made bandages to be sent overseas, are in front of a woman wrapped in patriotic bunting. Several ladies at right represent allied nations. A locomotive beside Westmoreland Coal Company Store puffs smoke from its coal-fired boiler. (Courtesy of Raymond Meehan.)

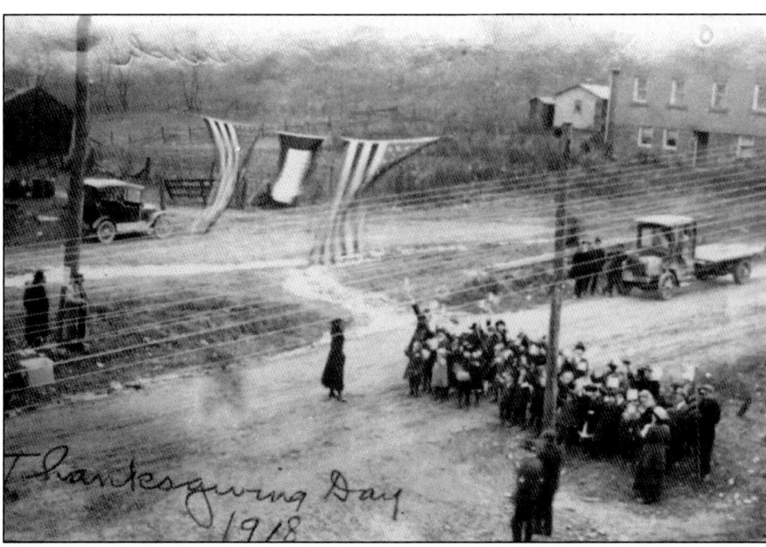

This Thanksgiving ceremony in 1918 takes place in the Murrysville Town Square where a war memorial was later erected. The First Methodist Church is on the right in the background. A choir and their director are performing. The end of World War I was a time to be thankful. (Courtesy of Stephen Simpson and Ray Meehan.)

Seven

Good Sports, Community Spirit

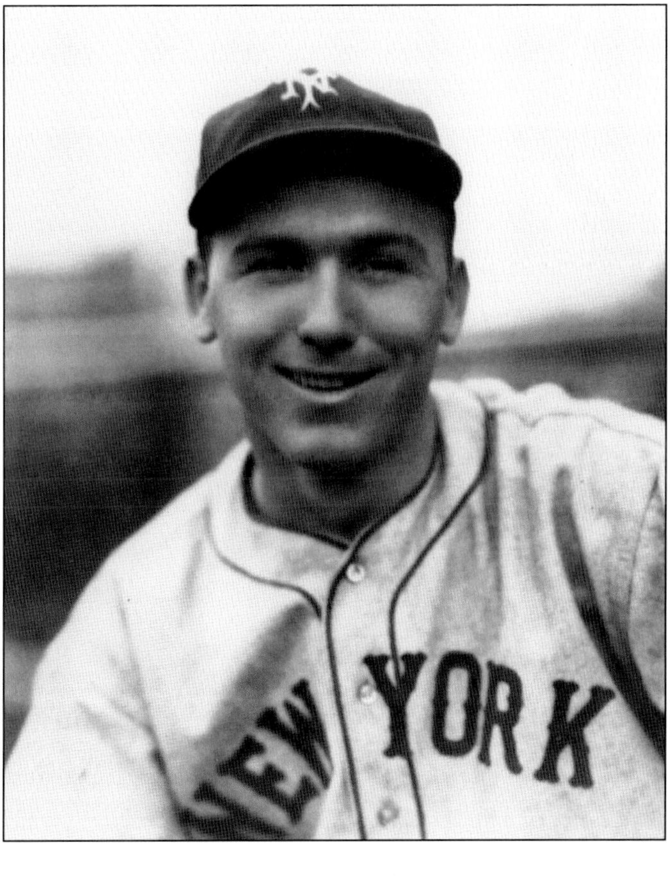

James A. Ripple (1909–1959), was Export's first major league baseball player, an outfielder who began his career in 1929 with the Mid-Atlantic League. He played with the Montreal Royals in the International League, advanced to the New York Giants in 1936, was traded to Brooklyn, and then to the Cincinnati Reds and Philadelphia Athletics in 1943. At 2,000 at bats, he struck out only 89 times. (Courtesy of James Ripple, his son.)

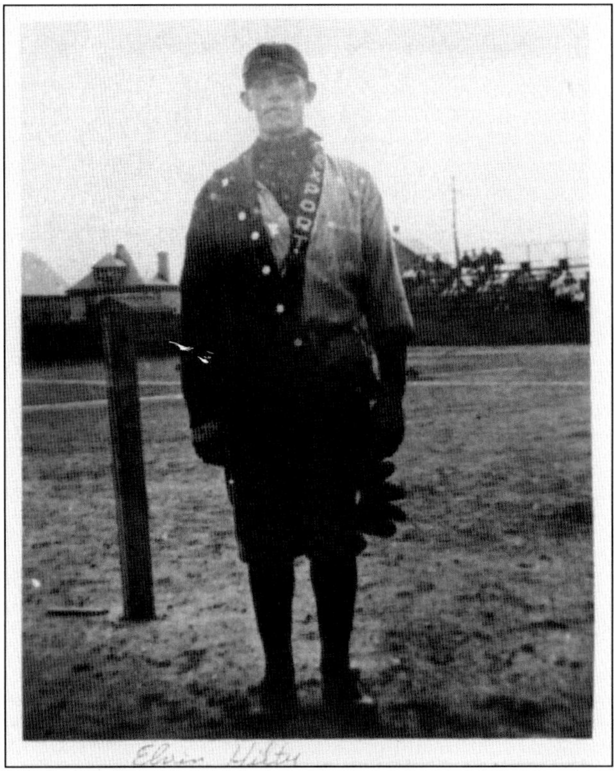

John McGaw, New York Giants manager, offered Export's Elvin P. Hilty (pictured), known as "Count Hilty," a contract he refused: "I can make more money working as a plumber for the railroad and pitching semipro ball than I can in the big leagues." Pitching ball and chewing slippery elm, he was as "good a spitter as anybody," but baseball outlawed spitballs in 1920. Cum Posey, Homestead Grays' manager, said Hilty was "one of best pitchers ever."

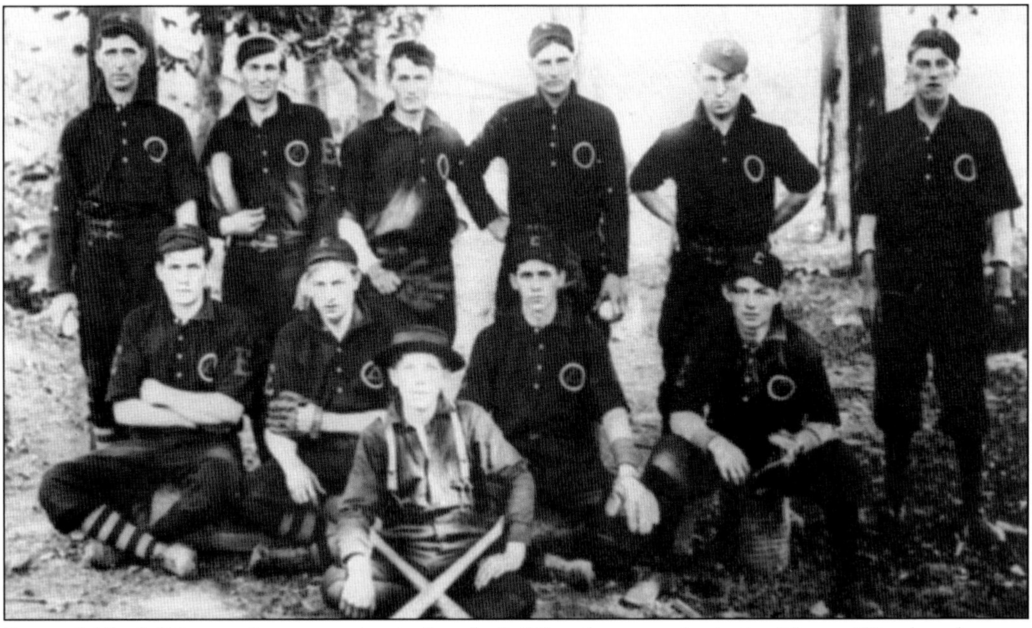

Export's Black Diamonds were active in baseball. They knew and admired James Ripple, who was inducted into the Pennsylvania Sports Hall of Fame at Harrisburg (1983) and the International League's Hall of Fame. Ripple, from neighboring Delmont, married Helen Berlin from Export where they lived. In winter, Ripple loaded his car with a shovel and ashes to help people stuck in snow. (Courtesy of Raymond Meehan.)

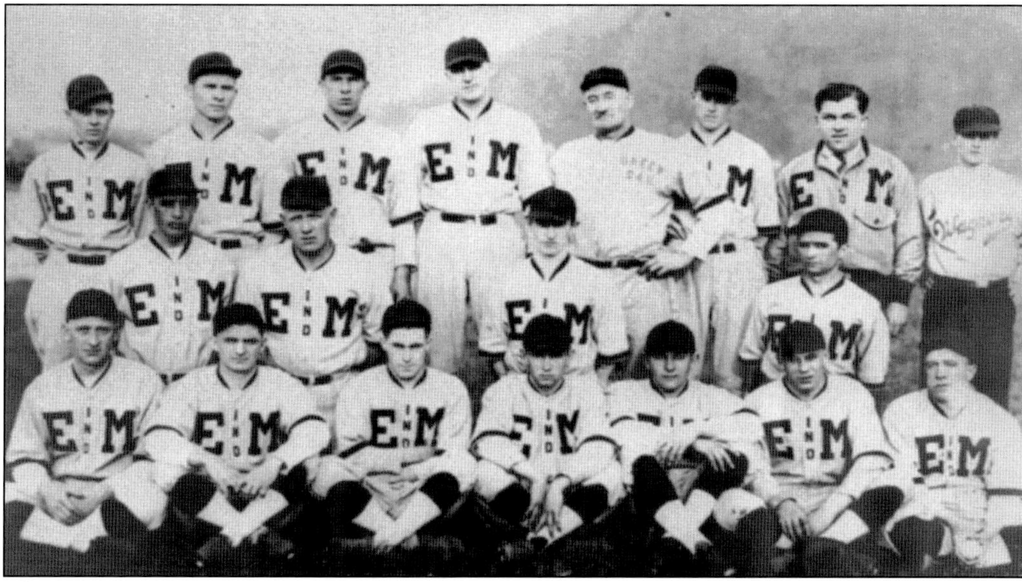

This Export-Murrysville Independents baseball c. 1950 team photo includes, from left to right, (first row) Leon McElfresh (M), Clayton "Sonny" Millberg (E), Claire Houston (M), Edward or Carl Whipkey (M), Peter Slongo (E), Selwyn Jones (E), and manager Robert Shirey (E); (second row) Harry Horell (M), Donald Simon (M), Ralph Thompson (M), and Nick Visnick (E); (third row) Milton Stuck (M), Peter or Ray Shannon (M), Nick Kukich (E), Roy or William Speer (E), Honus Wagner (Pittsburgh), James Thompson (M), business manager Lawrence Sloan (E), and an unidentified sport store employee.

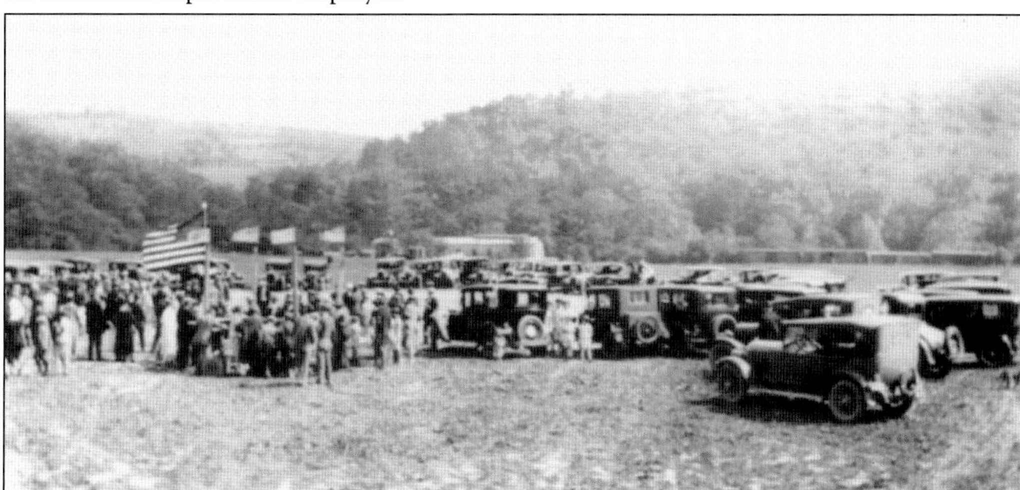

J.P. "Honus" Wagner, the "Flying Dutchman," is known as the greatest shortstop in baseball history and was elected to National Baseball Hall of Fame as one of its first five inductees, which included Ty Cobb and Babe Ruth. He sold Murrysville-Export team uniforms from his Pittsburgh store. This 1925 image shows when Wagner brought Albert Kennedy "Rosey" Rosewell, the head Pittsburgh Pirates radio announcer, to a game at this ballpark. During home runs, Rosey was known to say, "Close the window, Aunt Minnie, here it comes!" Wagner had his picture removed from tobacco-sponsored baseball cards, so cards with his image are very valuable. (Courtesy of Carl Patty.)

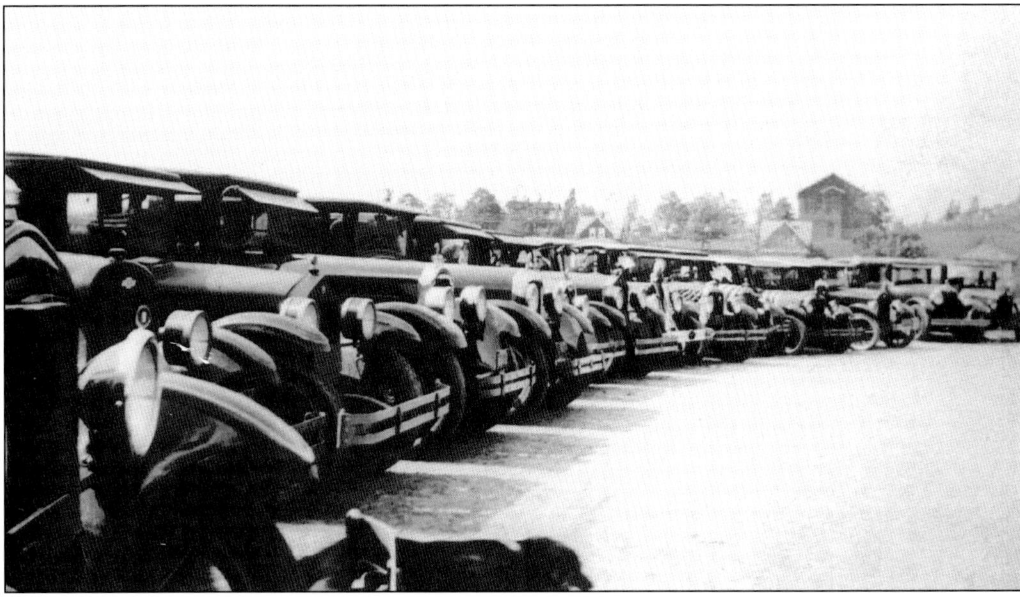

Export's Robert Moose played Murrysville's Little League team and went on to become a major league baseball player. Moose was the only member of his Little League team to make it to the majors, years after playing on this sandlot, seen here much earlier surrounded by vintage cars parked for a 1925 celebration of the opening of Old William Penn Highway. The First Presbyterian Church is on the hillside in the center. Moose's entire pro career was with the Pittsburgh Pirates from 1967 to 1976. He died in an automobile accident in 1976. (Courtesy of Carl Patty.)

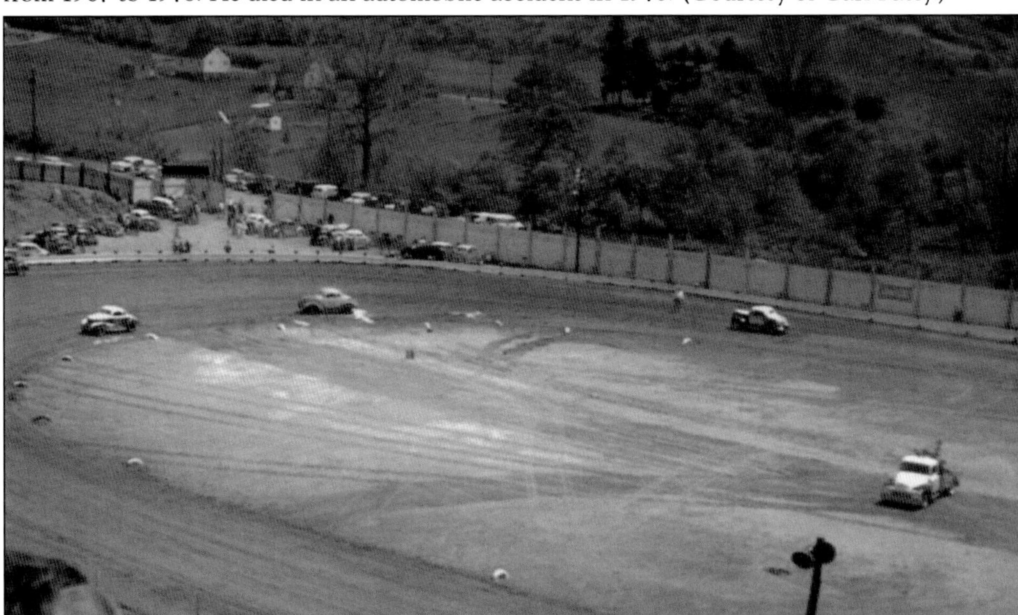

Another popular field sport in old Franklin Township, now Murrysville Municipality, was car racing. Here is Mon-Duc Racetrack, the site of the community's ball field in 1925. This course was known by the abbreviated names of its active sponsors, Monzo and Duquette. The dirt track was located below the new Old William Penn Highway, also called the Northern Pike, on the West Pike Street hillside running from Export's western border. (Courtesy of Raymond Meehan.)

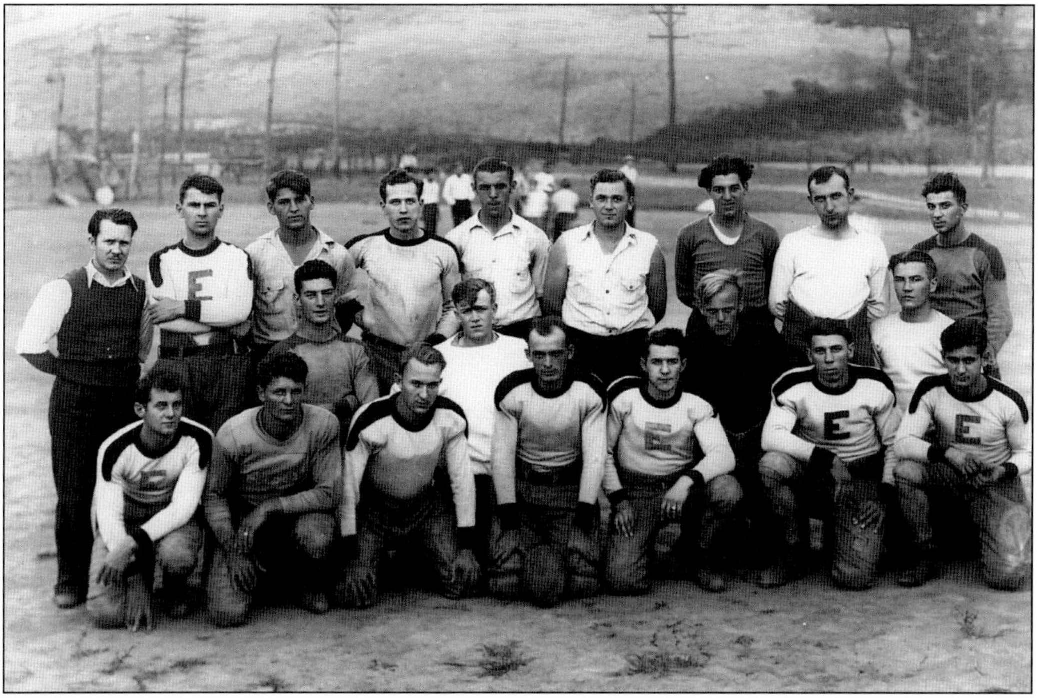

Export's football squad (with 27 wins and 4 losses from 1931 to 1934), includes, from left to right, (first row) Stephen Ruliak, Ector Depizzol, Miller Korach, Miller Manovich, Sereno Depizzol, Miller Wuslich, and Nick Manovich; (second row) William McHugh, Duncan Shearer, Peter Basara, and William Gutman; (third row) Theodore Krushinski, Andrew Laurence, Charles Cupe, Henry Sowaski, Samuel Kerach, Harry Bickerstaff, Wetty Battalgia, Keko Regoni, and Charles Chupa. (Courtesy of Raymond Mehan.)

John Sartoris photographed the Export girls' basketball team for the 1929–1930 season. At Murrysville in 1976, the Franklin Regional High School girls' basketball team won the Western Pennsylvania Interscholastic Athletic Association (WPIAL) championship, and the following year, it won the Pennsylvania Interscholastic Athletic Association (PIAA) championship. In 2005, Franklin Regional took home the state PIAA football title. (Courtesy of Raymond Meehan.)

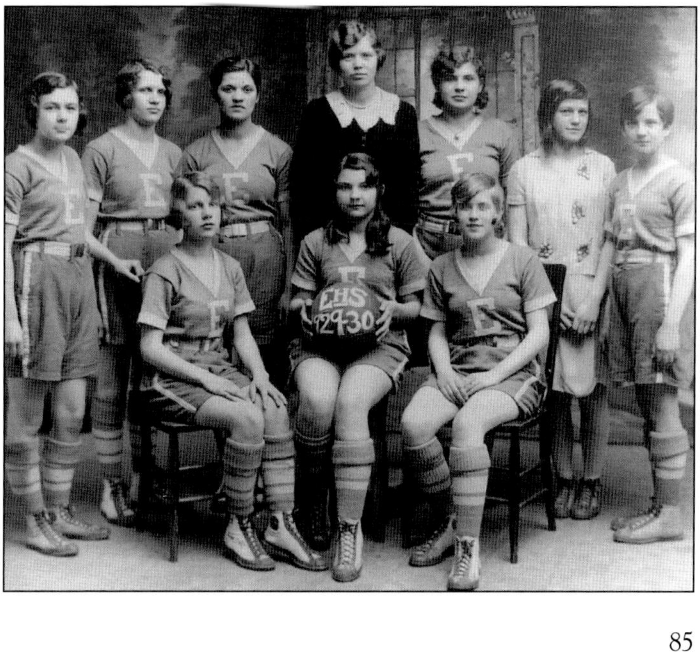

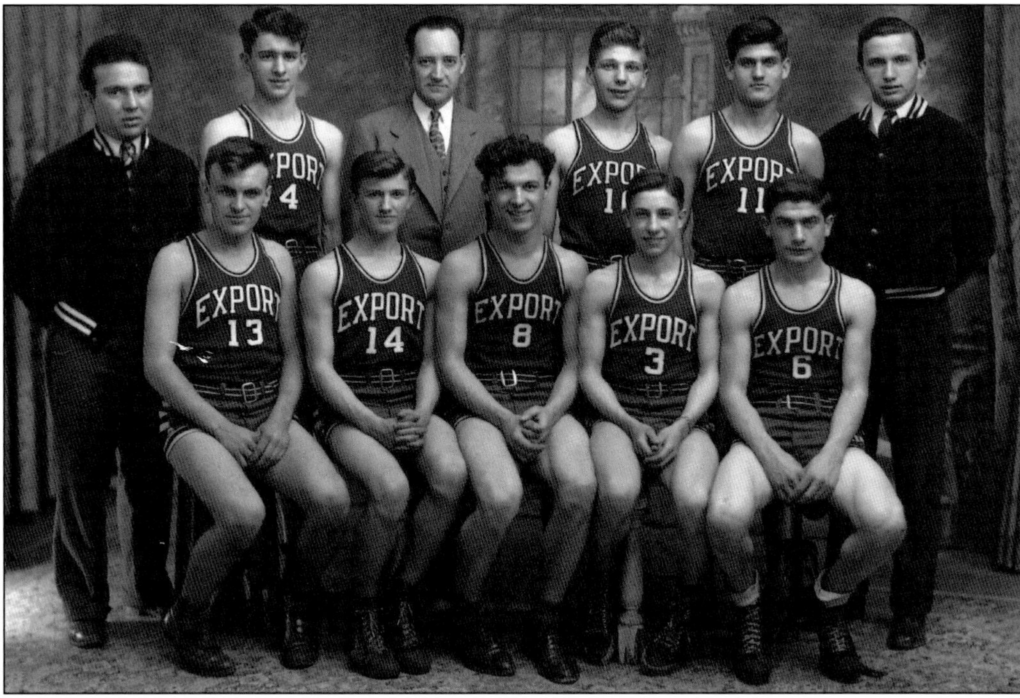

Members of the Export boys' high school basketball team include (first row) Guildo Trento (13), B. Manovich (14), George Stepitich (8), Leroy Kemerer (3), and Daniel Cherill (6); (second row) John Mione (4), unidentified man in tie, Pete Visnick (10), and Walter Delong (11); coaches Bruce McHail (left) and James Ternchine flank the players. Panther basketball players won the first WPIAL section title in 1945. Team member Lawrence Lapcevic received an all-state small school honorable mention. Murrysville-Export resident Frank Klaus, his father a coal miner, was the world middleweight boxing champion in 1913. Murrysville basketball coach John Onder (1959–1960) took his team to the WPIAL semifinals. (Courtesy of Raymond Meehan.)

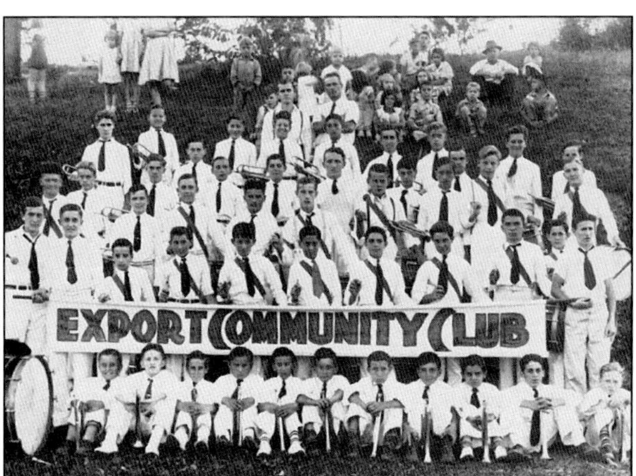

In addition to Export Community Club, there were other musical groups and individuals, such as John Lindsay, a Westmoreland Coal employee, who, as shortstop, cut a hole in his glove to catch better. He sang with Moses Good, Charles Shannon Humes, and George Fink. Harmonizers were Jake Deible, Walter Hart, Ruben Foight, George Geiger, Roy Speer, and Arthur Shaw. Aber Shaw sang with Billy Sunday's choir. Cliff Baughman, a musician and composer, was aboard the USS *Wakefield* transport when it caught fire in 1942.

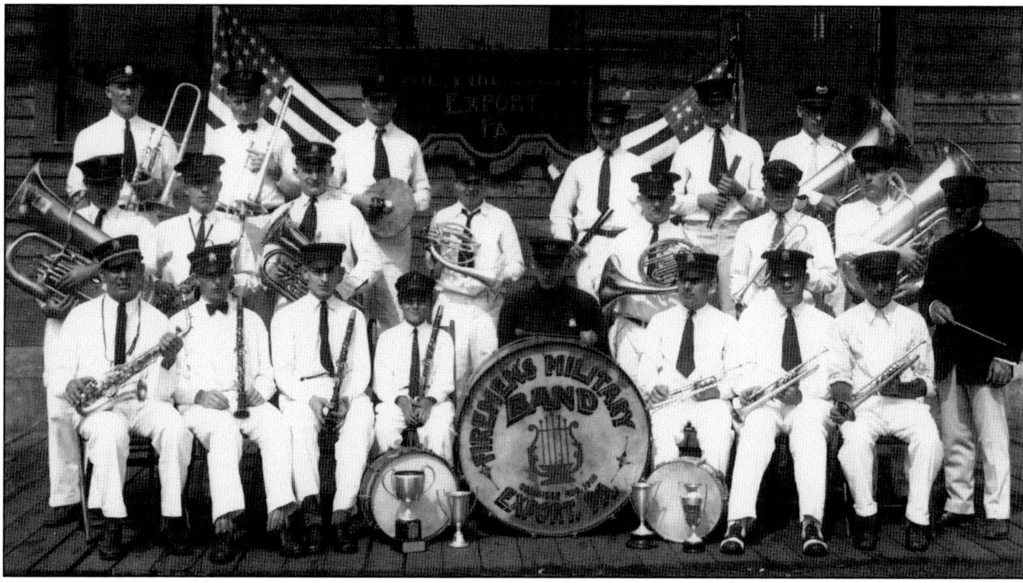

The Export Firemen's Military Band was organized in August 1928; some members also played baseball. The deparment's other band included women, such as majorettes Roberta Thompson, Mary Ann Plechey, and Naomi Reich (pictured below). (Courtesy of Raymond Meehan.)

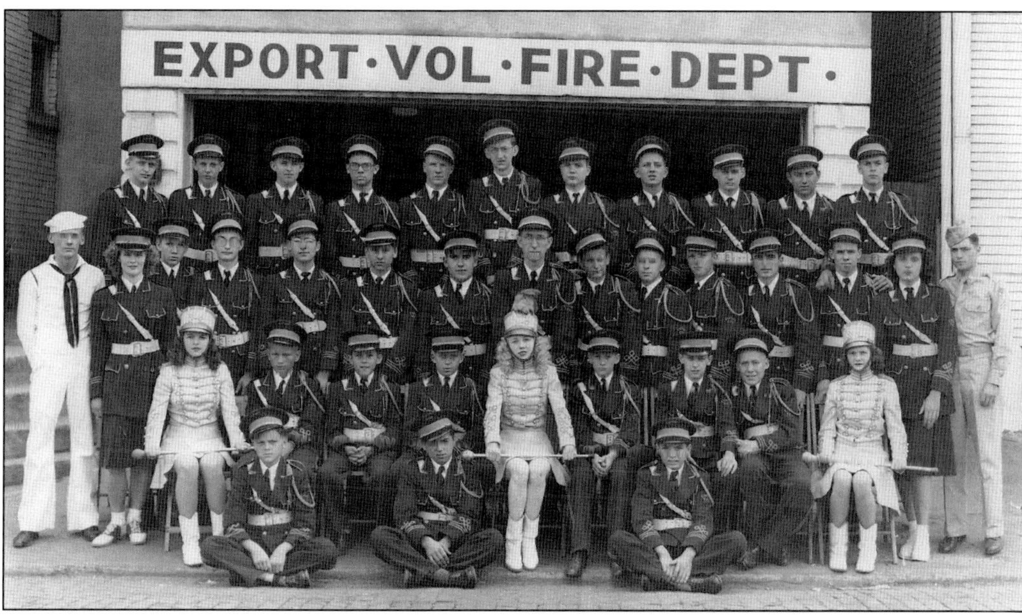

From left to right are (first row) Peter Fisher, Joseph Pafretti, and James Cappa; (second row) Ronald Beltz, Nick Orlic, Edward Warzinski, Robert Cargnel, Hector Luscri, and Edward Lachmanek; (third row) Charles Gray, Mildred Stanovich, Frank Senchur, William Marsiglio, Daniel Djubek, Leroy Oddis, Louis Mediate, Harold McHail, Frank Fidei, Ronald Sauers, William Lemmon, George Cherellia, Bruce Tsironis, Natalie Pocalyka, and James Geiger; (fourth row) Edward Hand, Louis Corgnel, Charles Nesbit, Edward Previc, Charles Borland, Edward Zychal, George Coffen, Joseph Skandara, Donald Gazibara, Charles Djubeck, and William McClain. (Courtesy of Raymond Meehan.)

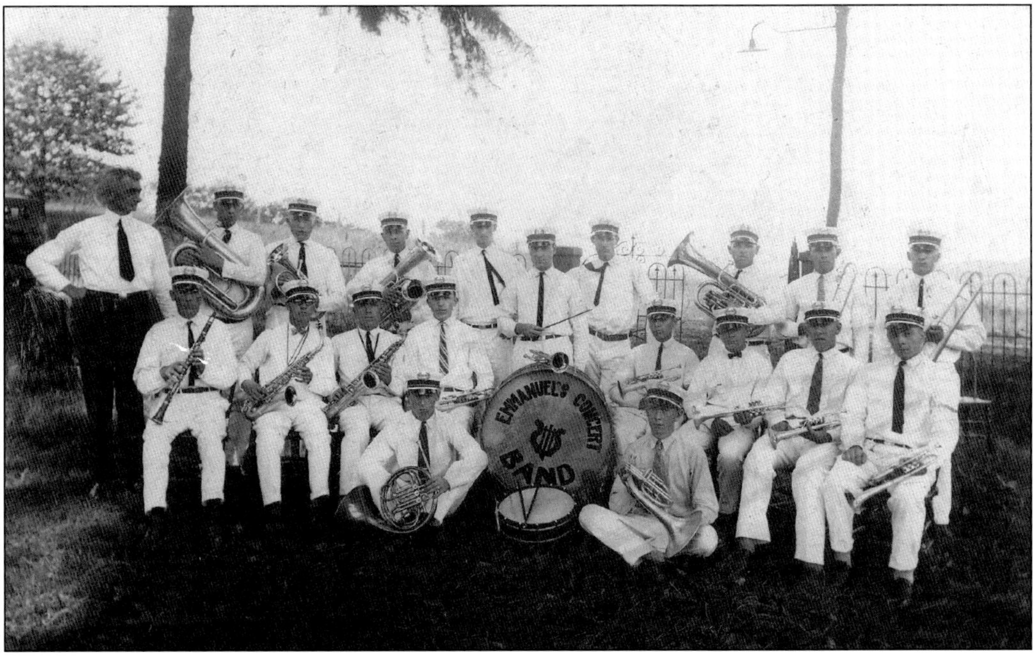

Hills Emmanuel Church Concert Band from Murrysville includes director Louis Remaley, William J. Duff, James Remaley, and Edgar Martz, who lived in judge Thomas Mellon's house on Hills Church and Cline Hollow Roads. Export also had its Star Brass Band of 1909. Athletics and bands were popular and exceptional in Export. (Courtesy of Raymond Meehan.)

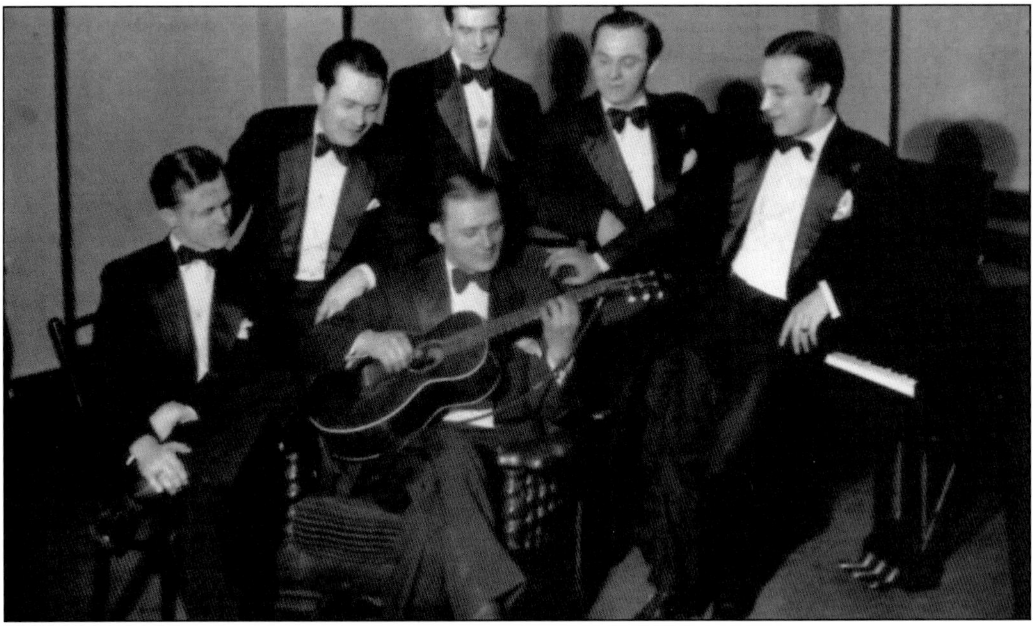

Seven Export Krushinski brothers played for vaudeville, later joining Lee Crossley's Orchestra on WWSW radio. These musicians are, from left to right, Frank, Edward, William, Theodore, Henry, Bert, and Sal. Around 1938, Anthony Rosance played with the band, as did Peter Wuslich. The brothers were called "the burgess, the coal dealer, and men around town." Edward is missing in this photograph because he was in Honolulu at the time. (Courtesy of Nan Krushinski.)

Perry Como, a barber from Canonsburg, auditioned for Crossley's orchestra. He was told that his voice was too soft and that he would never make it in the music world. The Krushinskis played for Freda Pope's Showboat in New York. Here, Frank Krushinski leads a practice session. He worked as a loader and a dealer on the tipple for Westmoreland Coal. (Courtesy of Nan Krushinski.)

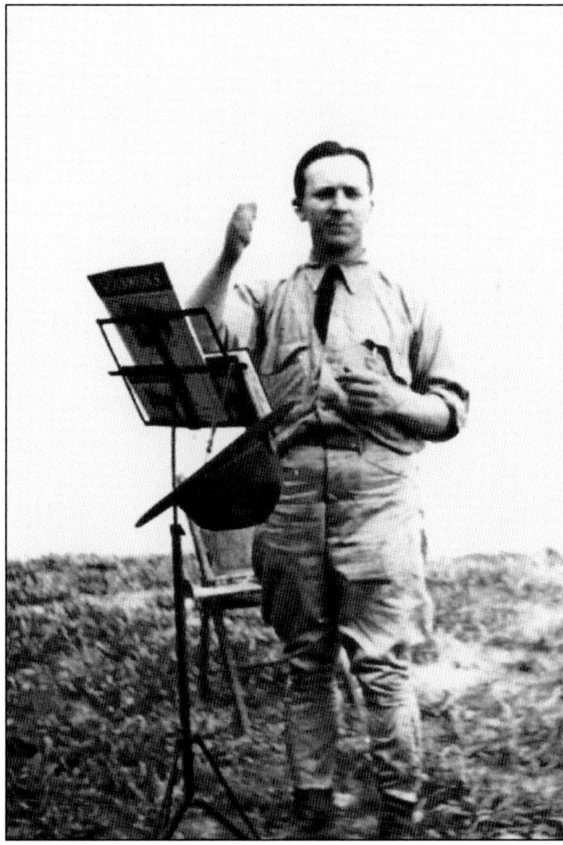

Export's Frank and Leokadia Krushinski are pictured with family members at their home, which is still standing. They promoted their children's musical interests. On this lawn, where music still seems to echo in the air, their sons practiced gymnastic feats. Other stuntmen in town were James Ripple, doing somersaults on the baseball field, and miners Ron Hamilton and J. Harold "Chick" Ake, who climbed flagpoles. (Courtesy of Nan Krushinski.)

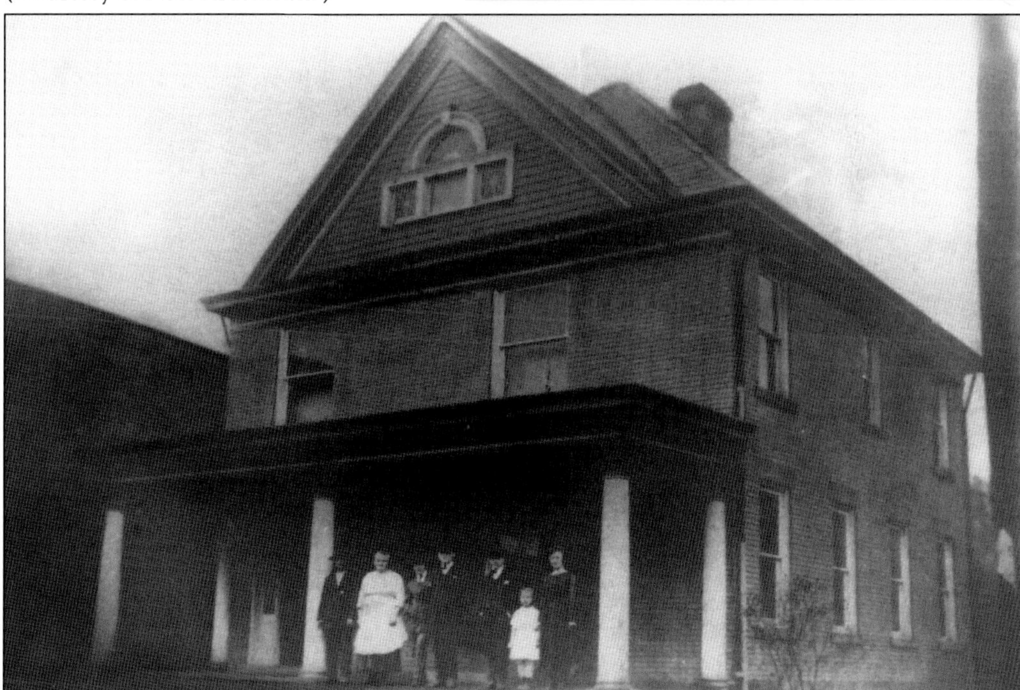

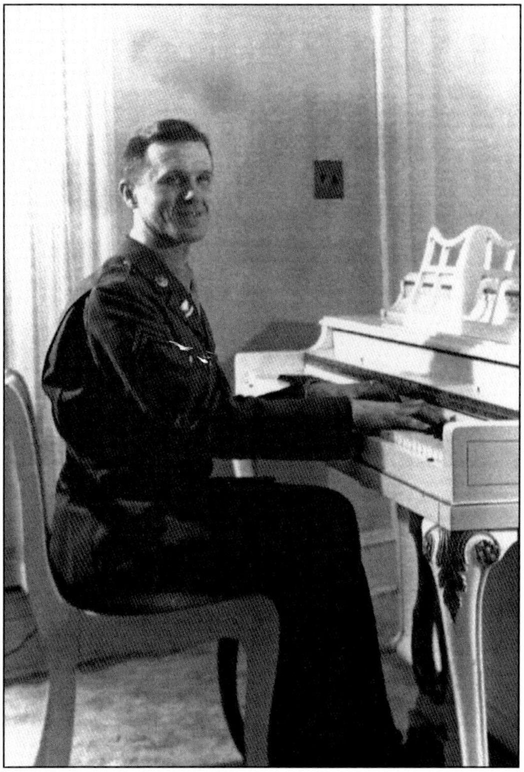

Pianist Edward Krushinski served in World War II and was concertmaster of the US Army Band in Honolulu. The Krushinkis' band was the first to broadcast over KDKA in Pittsburgh, the first commercial station in the nation. They joined Wesley "Freckles" Barry's Hollywood Harmony Hounds and helped produce one of America's first sound movies. Another local musician and a student of Joseph Mediate (next page), Alfred Sturchio had a band and taught music at Red Eagle Tavern. (Courtesy of Nan Krushinski.)

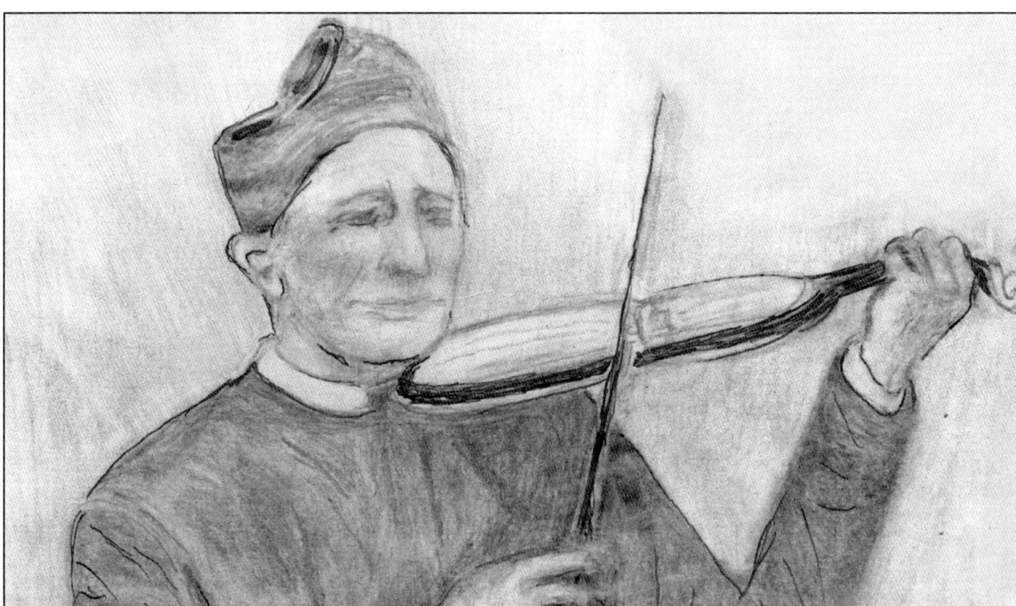

Polish artist-musician the Reverend Peter J. Rendziniak (seen in this drawing by the author) played his violin during his priesthood at St. Mary' Church from 1937 to 1957. People from both communities were familiar with him, as Murrysville residents attended this Export church until their own church was later built. He took his personal artwork with him when he moved to New York City. Another talented Export man was Joseph Story, known as the "mail-carrier fiddler."

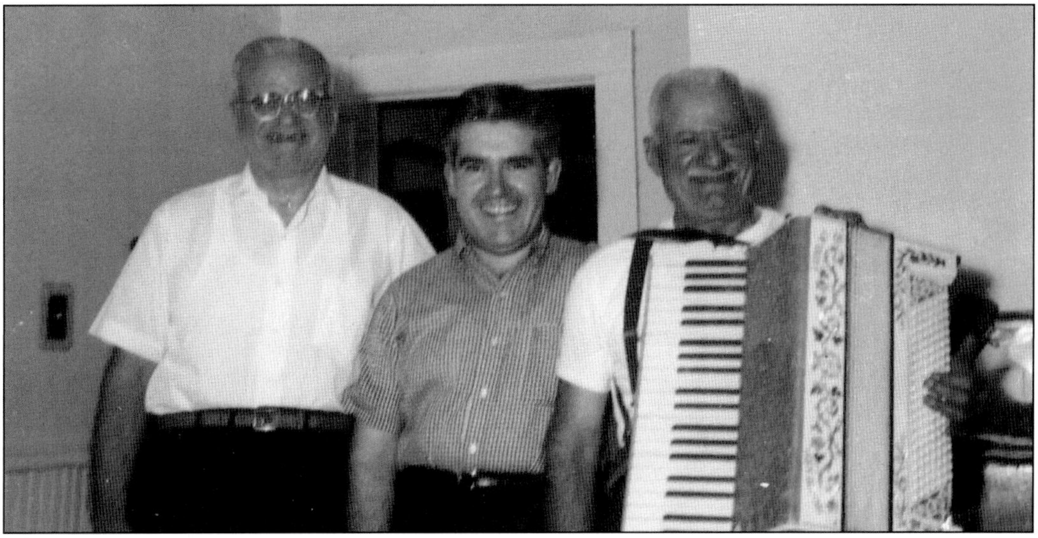

Joseph Mediate (right), a railroad employee and the acknowledged accordion king in Export, gave music lessons that went on as long as he wanted them to last. One of his students was Anthony Rosance, later the owner of a music conservatory in Texas, who wanted to have Mediate's accordion on display there. Louis Mediate (left) is happy his father kept the accordion that gave him so much pleasure. The other man is Louis's son, whose name is unknown. (Courtesy of Louis Mediate.)

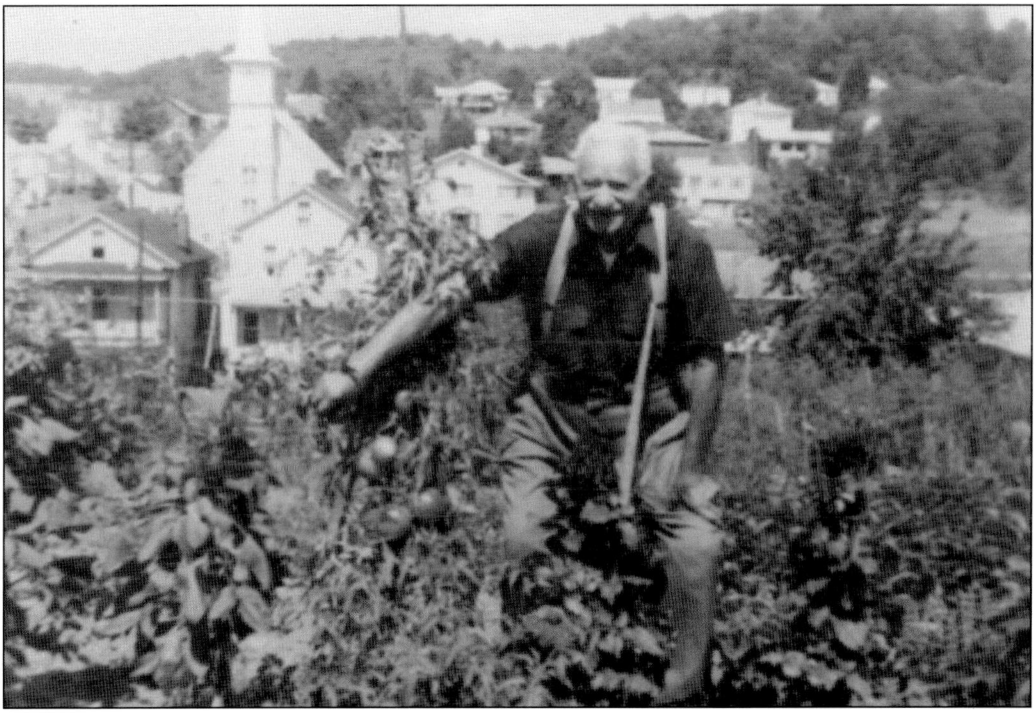

Joseph Mediate, who lived on Manor Street in Export, raised vegetables for his family and others and flowers for his wife in his garden overlooking the town. Numerous people cultivated gardens and sold vegetables from their homes in this community. Mediate was the uncle of Anthony Mediate (father of Rocco Mediate, golf professional). Anthony and his brother Joseph Mediate were Louis's cousins (next generation) and both local hairdressers. (Courtesy of Louis Mediate.)

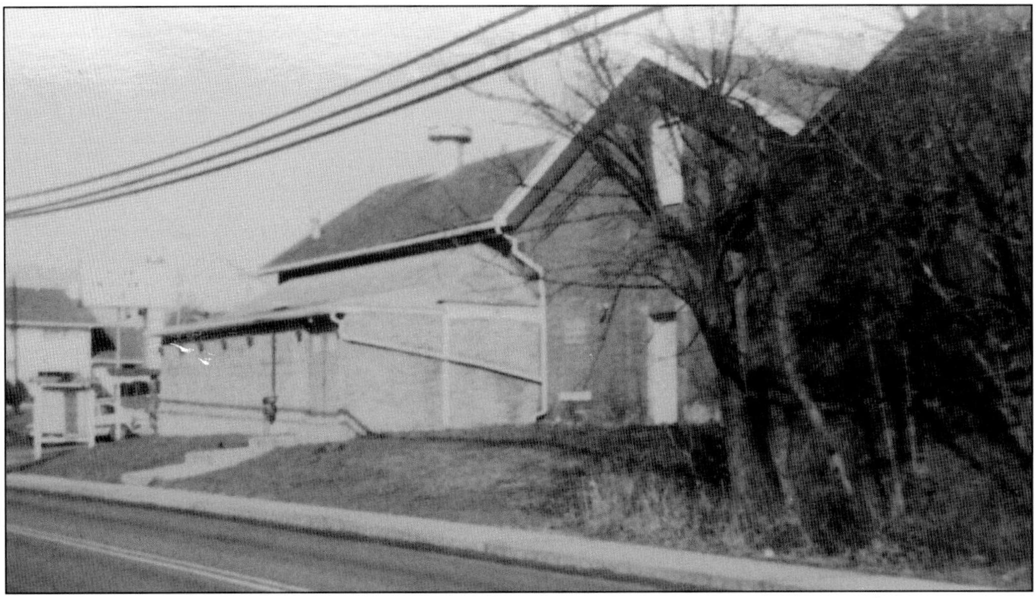

Often, ethnic clubs began in private homes, such as Louis and Mary Scarton's Italian American Club (IAC), in the former Westmoreland Coal Co. building, seen here on Madison Avenue in 1934. With its black shutters, the Scartons' home is still standing on the hill overlooking the later IAC Club. Today, the IAC flourishes at 5930 Kennedy Avenue (a section of Old US 22). It opened in 1957 in a former Westmoreland Coal building. Former mayor Sherry Lynne Stover is the granddaughter of the original club owners and now manages the club.

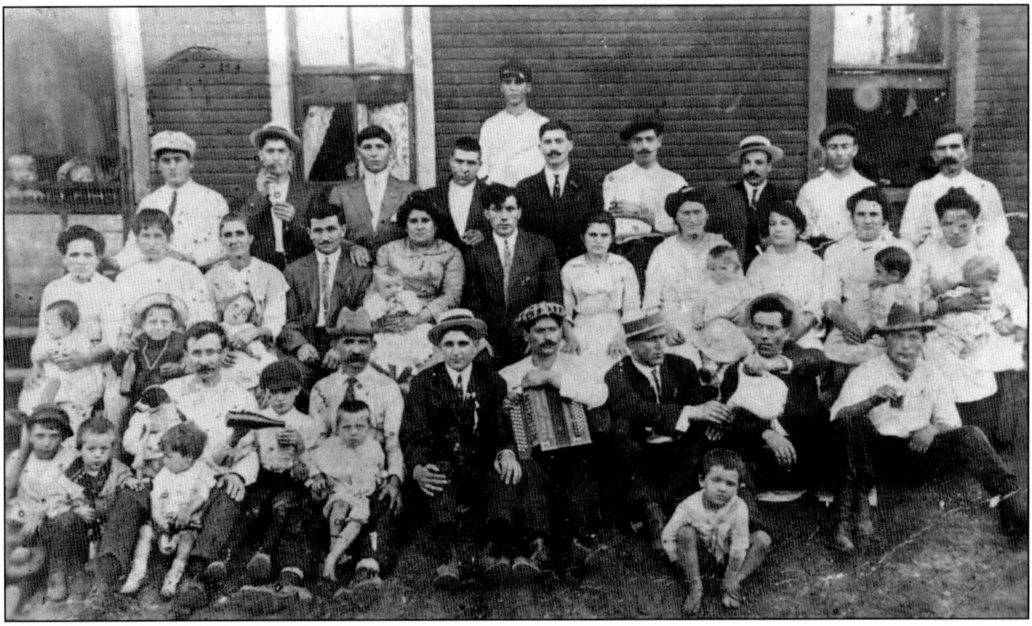

At this Mediate family reunion in Export, Joseph sits in the front row with his accordion. He played for area festivals and weddings. Two children peek above the porch railing. One boy (far left) has a bat over his shoulder and a ball and glove at his side. In the third row, a man smoking a cigar holds up cards, and in the first row, adults pour themselves drinks as children also appear to enjoy this festive gathering. (Courtesy of Louis Mediate.)

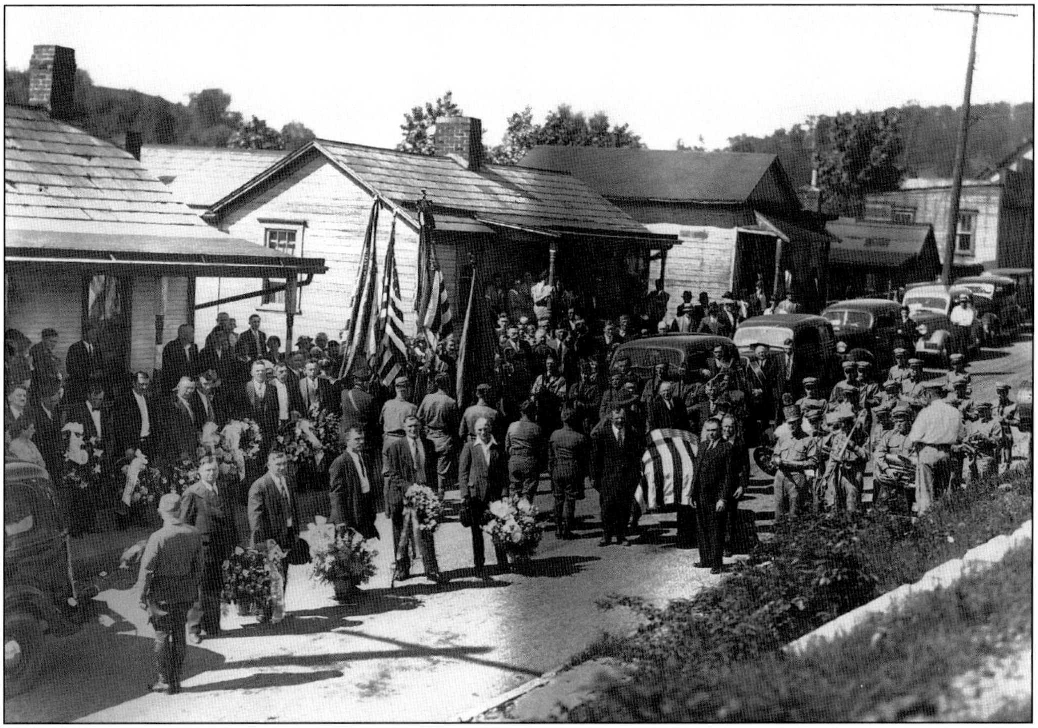

This 1937 funeral memorial service on Italy Road in Export honors Joseph (?) Mance. A band, whose director went by the nickname Wheatie, plays on the right, and an American flag is draped on the coffin. The deceased was a member of the Italian American Club. The Mance family operated a dance hall and restaurant on that street where many of these houses still stand. (Courtesy of Raymond Meehan.)

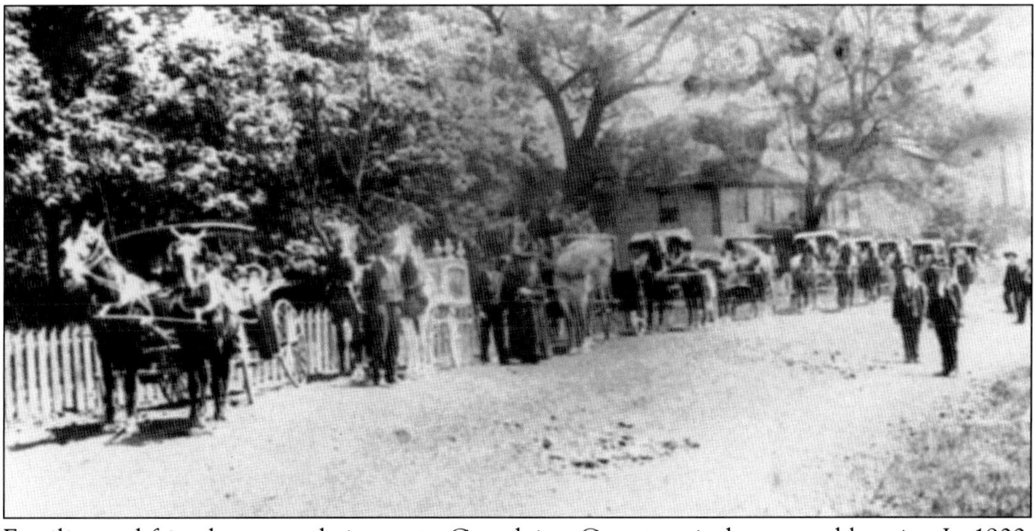

Families and friends are on their way to Grandview Cemetery in horses and buggies. In 1900, Albert Alexander Earnest, a wagon maker, was Export's earliest mortician. The Harts were funeral directors in Murrysville. Years ago, wakes were held in private homes. Special table drawers held ice to keep the body cold for viewings, after which a tablecloth was spread for a meal. Guests often brought fresh, fragrant flowers from neighboring gardens with them.

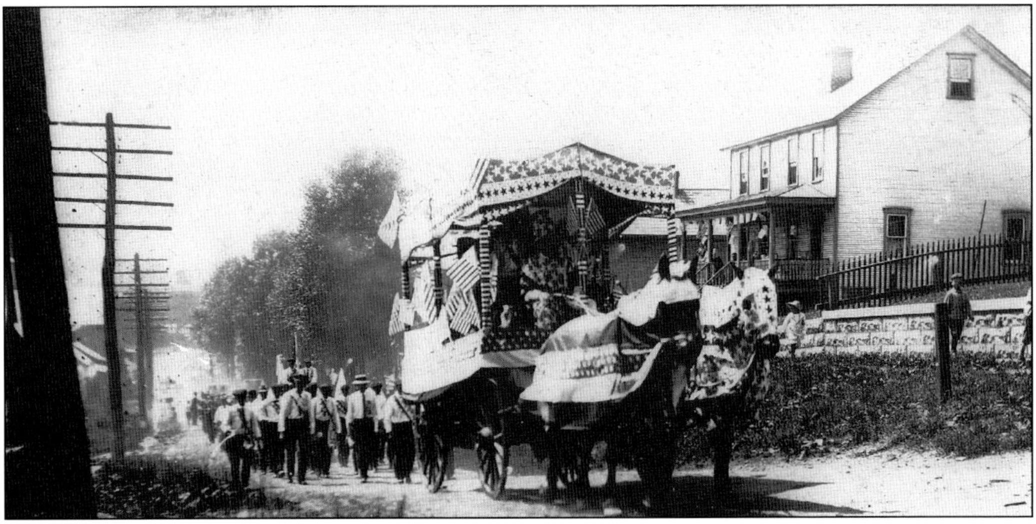

Export's spirits ran high with ethnic band clubs. This festive float in a parade passes a house on Kennedy Avenue, a section of Old William Penn Highway, on its way to Star Park. In both Murrysville and Export, music was especially important. After social events in one of the towns, those who participated often followed railroad tracks homeward and sang songs while walking under a moonlit sky. (Courtesy of Raymond Meehan.)

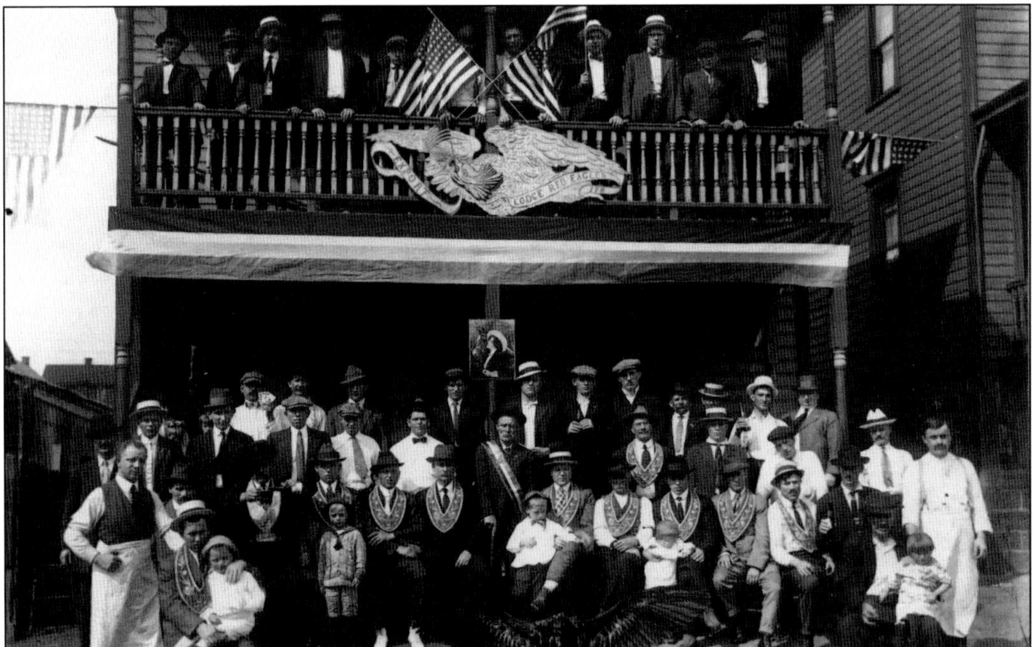

In 1915, the Red Eagle Tavern plays host to the Slovene National Benefit Society. Ethnic organizations provided insurance, and farmers depended upon the Grange. Before lodges, miners joined secretive Knights of Labor meetings in woods. In the image, Squire Berlin (center, wearing sash) carries a cane. During renovation, removal of floorboards revealed evidence of it Prohibition-speakeasy days. "Pick handle" (moonshine with tobacco juice added for color) was often concealed in mines, out of the eyes of revenue men. During Prohibition, one Export woman sat on keg of illegal liquor, concealed under her skirt.

Export's Polish Club served as a store. As Westmoreland Coal was more lenient than most labor-controlled towns, miners could sell and raise produce. The company held contests for gardens and awarded prizes. Until 1910, if any miner made purchases from independent shops, the price was docked from his paycheck. Such a situation inspired Merle Travis's song "Sixteen Tons," made famous by Tennessee Ernie Ford and from which comes the line, "I owe my soul to the company store." (Courtesy of Raymond Meehan.)

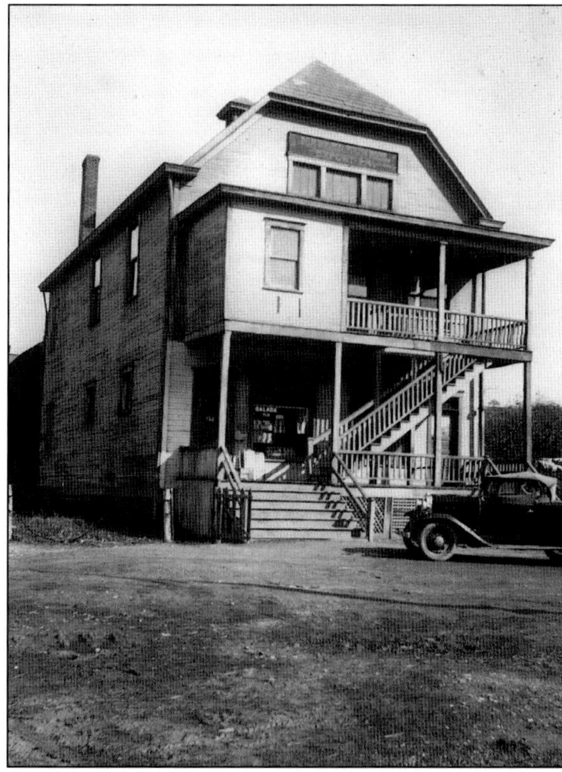

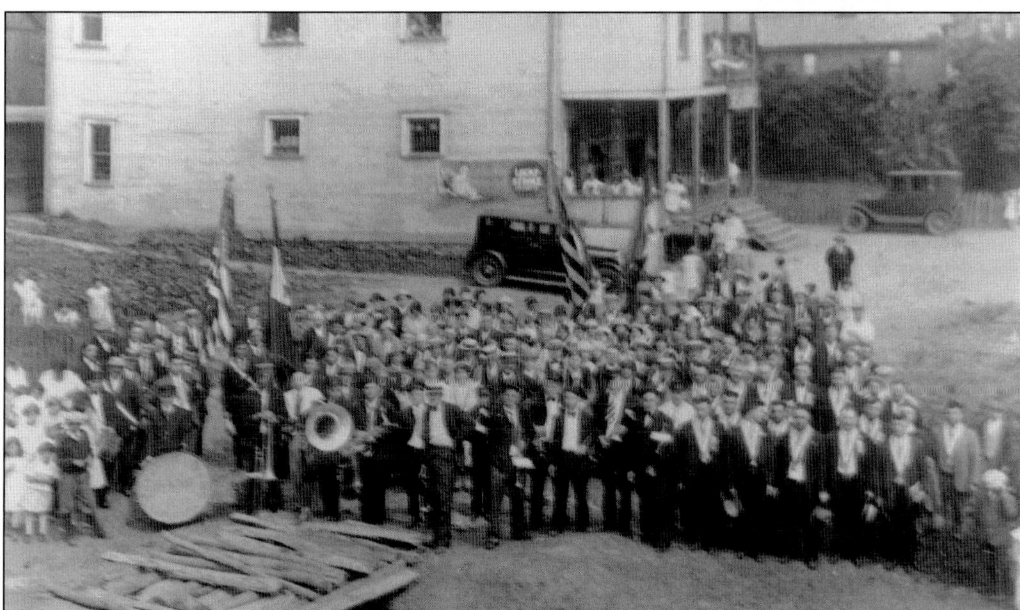

At this ethnic clubhouse, band musicians and Polish members gather with their musical instruments for a celebration. Lithuanian Club members met in William Zaboaky's home on Roosevelt Street behind Berkowitz's Store before 1929. The Russian Club held meetings in a private home. The Serbian Sisters Circle met in Mance Hall (first named Rizzardi) on Italy Road. The American Fraternal Union (AFU No. 57) was established in 1902. (Courtesy of Raymond Meehan.)

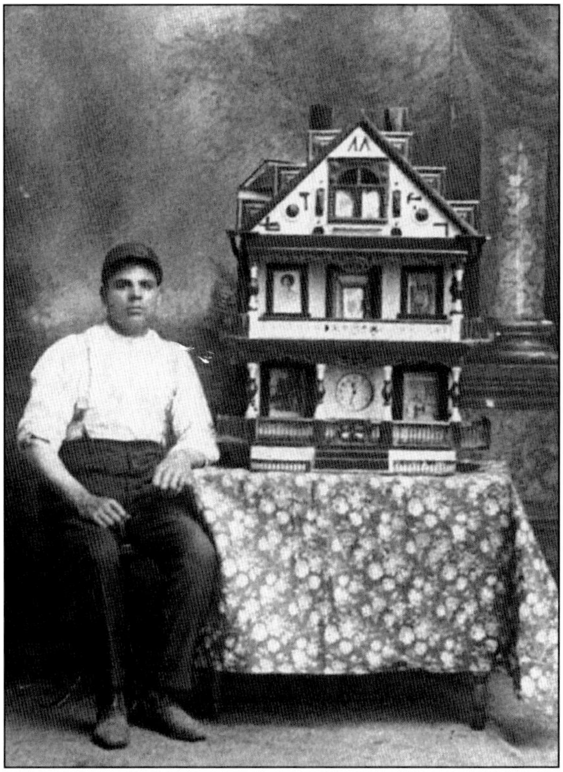

The spirit of creativity is evident in this Export miner's woodcraft clock. Another artist, Edward Manetta of St. Mary's, came from Italy around 1920, and went on to teach at St. John's University in Jamaica, New York. In 1985, he was asked to contribute his immigrant boat painting of Manhattan Island for a New York art show. When interviewed, he said, "We are just grateful that here we can do the kind of work we want."

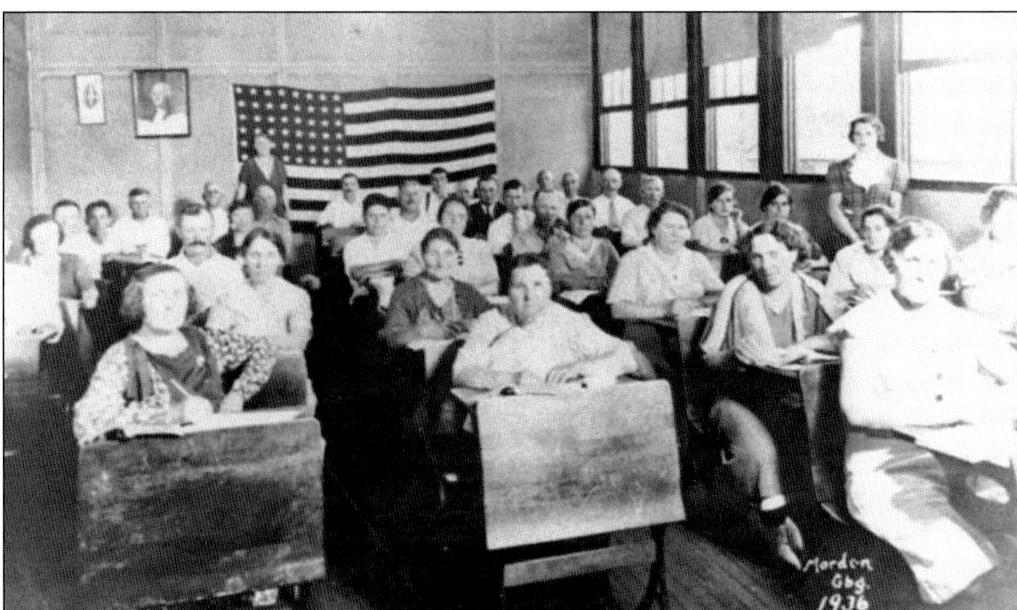

Patriotic-minded immigrants from both communities took citizenship courses, such as the one pictured in this photograph. Either at Ellis Island in New York City or in the gas- and coalfields, their names were often simplified by paternalistic measures. Similar actions suppressed the lives of Native American people living in the area. Their children were often forced to go to repressive military schools, one of which was in Carlisle.

John "Mutt" Wuslich of Export, pictured in his Serbian hat, felt the same sentiment as Manetta—that of being free in America. Children and adults alike enjoyed his stories of former days in town and the country of his birth. Wuslich was interested in the people and life around him. With a strong inclination for archaeology, he used to collect minerals, interesting rocks, fossils, and projectile points left behind by the original peoples of America.

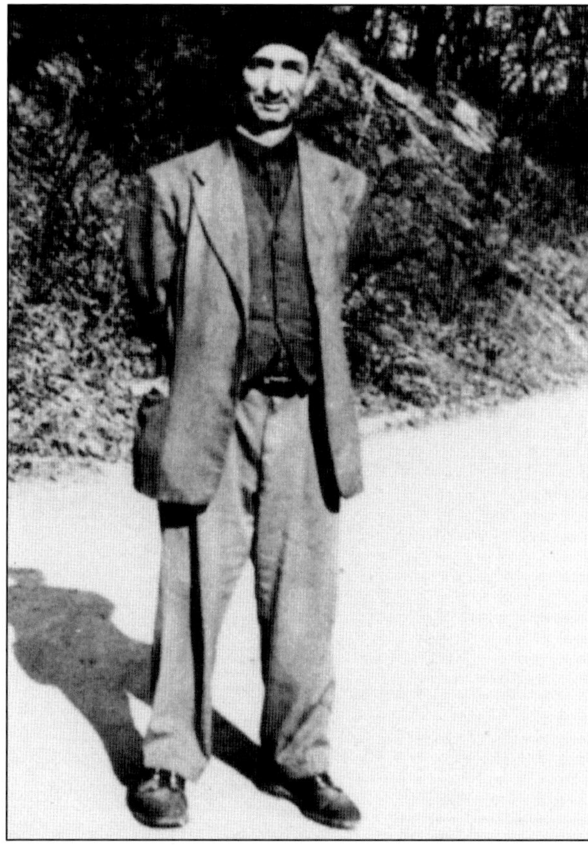

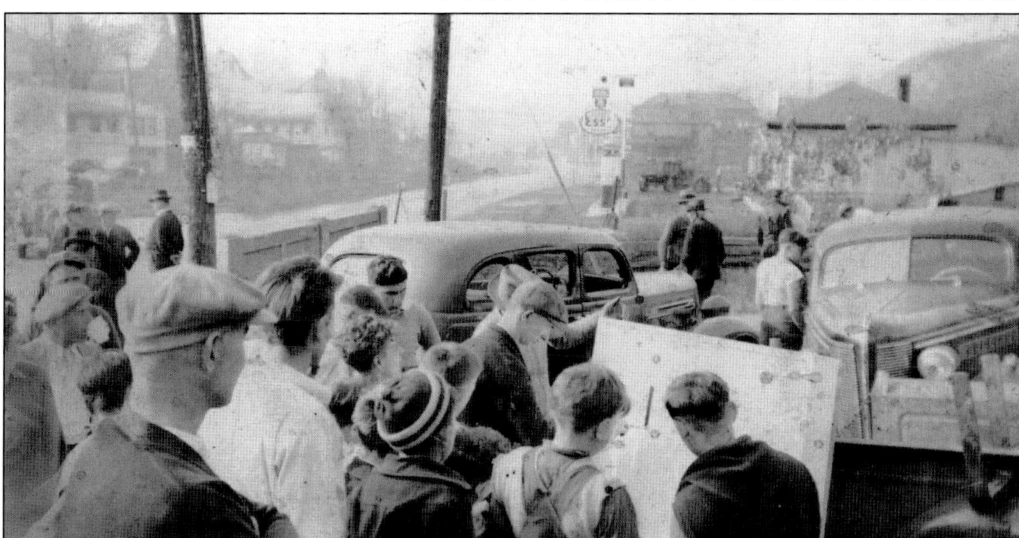

Wuslich drew pictures at Greer's Corner, Export's company store where Export men bragged that more coal was dug there than in the mines. He displayed his paintings inside and outside his art studio, a little frame shack at which he was often the center of attention. Wuslich's epitaph on his 1967 tombstone at Grandview Cemetery reads, "Whomever you are, I salute you with thanks for stopping by."

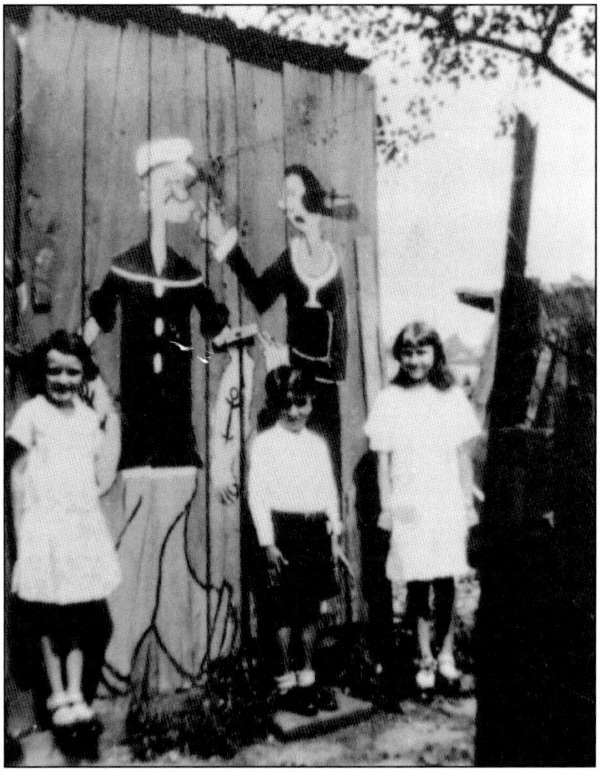

Young fans pose with John Wuslich's rendition of Popeye and Olive Oyl, a popular mural on his Town Square art shop. He was inquisitive about everything and kept a detailed daily diary. Well-read, Wuslich shared his knowledge and philosophy of life with others. He and Paul Good kept a town journal of weather and special community affairs at Good's Gasoline Station at 5800 Roosevelt Avenue in Export.

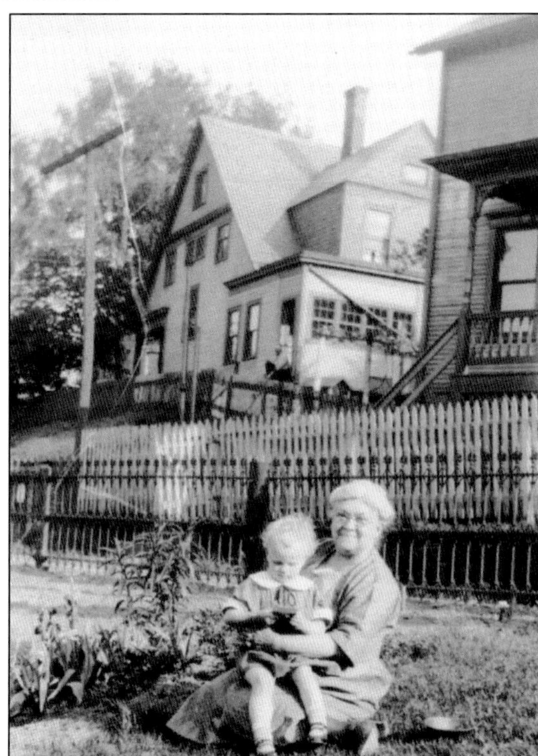

Pictured here is a little girl by the name of Olive who especially liked Wuslich's painting of Popeye and Olive Oyl. Her grandmother Mayhew is holding her on the front lawn. People young and old appreciated Wuslich's artwork and fascinating folk stories. He and Karl Koch, who also recorded his memoirs, were good friends and often discussed Export's pioneer history as well as its coal mining industry.

Eight

People, Their Homes, and Places

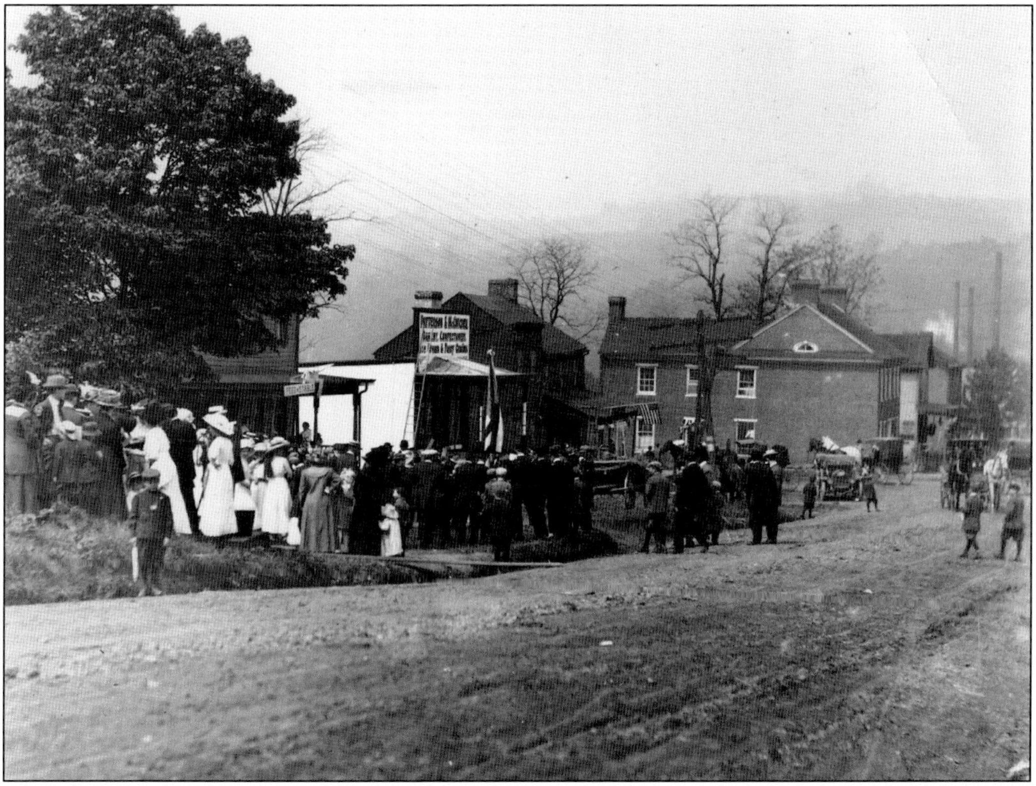

Jeremiah Murry, Murrysville's Irish-born founder and once a peddler, lived in this so-called mansion, on Town Square near Patty Brothers' stores. In 1781, Murry emigrated to America, traveling through Cumberland Valley where he met his wife, Ann Montgomery. Murry used his earnings to buy land from the government. A Mr. Cole also bought land, as did William Meanor from an Indian via what was called a tomahawk survey; Meanor paid for the land (later owned by John Rubright) with tobacco and a rifle. Old Peoples Gas Company smokestacks are on the right. (Courtesy of Stephen Simpson.)

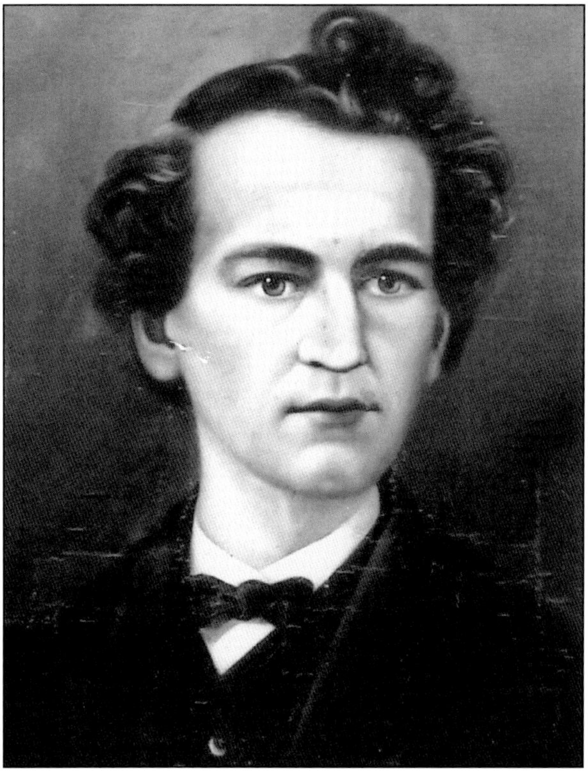

This 1784 portrait of Capt. Jeremiah Murry, Murrysville's founder, was preserved by ancestor James Murry Stewart. Jeremiah served in the state militia, as did his son, Gen. James Murray. The Murrys owned the original Town Square where their mansion stood. Along with other brick Murry houses, it was demolished in May 1987, a decision often regretted. Jeremiah said, "I can walk five miles in any direction and be on my estate." (Courtesy of Murrysville Historical and Preservation Society.)

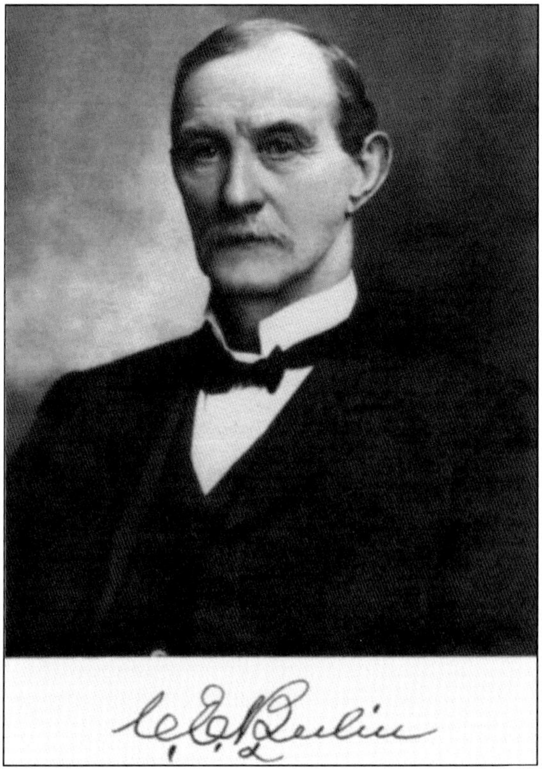

Squire Cornelius Elias Berlin, founder of Export, supplied Westmoreland Coal with land and built the first three houses; one was renovated for the coal company. His father, Col. Elias Berlin, came west during the Whisky Rebellion and later served in the state militia. Around 1795, Cornelius Berlin's ancestor Jacob lived between Finks and Lauffers. John and Elizabeth Lauffer's son Joseph married Esther Berlin, the granddaughter of Colonel Elias and Sarah Ament. Berlin's general store telephone number was "ring 3."

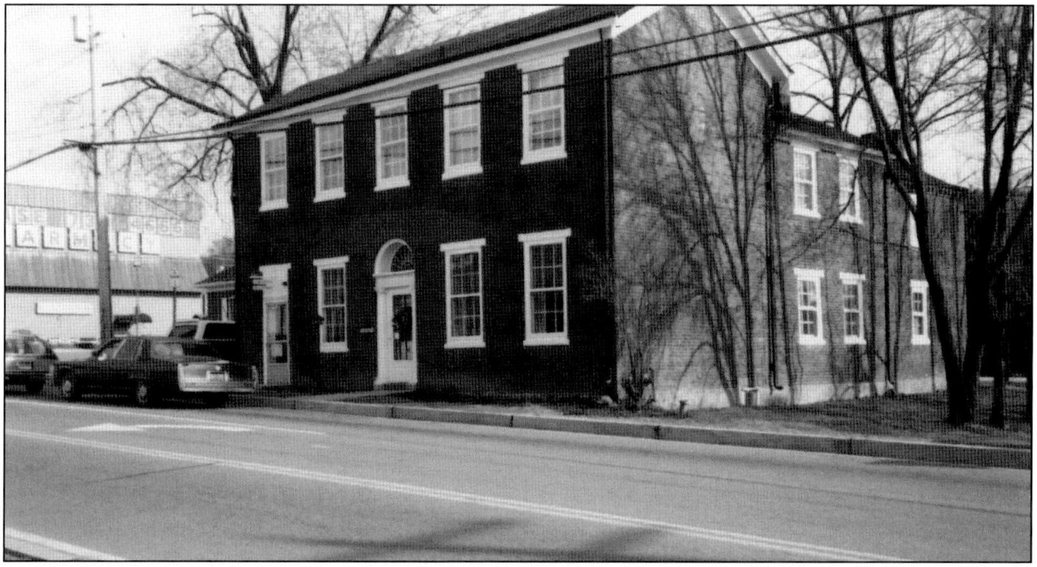

Jeremiah Murry was the first owner of this brick house (later owned by Bossart). Murry's daughter, Sarah, married Dr. Benjamin Burrell, father of judge Jeremiah Murry Burrell (who has two townships named for him). He was the first county judge elected by the people. Murry had one slave, who was willed to his daughter Betsy. Besides Bossart, Rev. O.L.M. Sargrove, the McElroys, and Michael and Ann Murry Haymaker owned this house over the years.

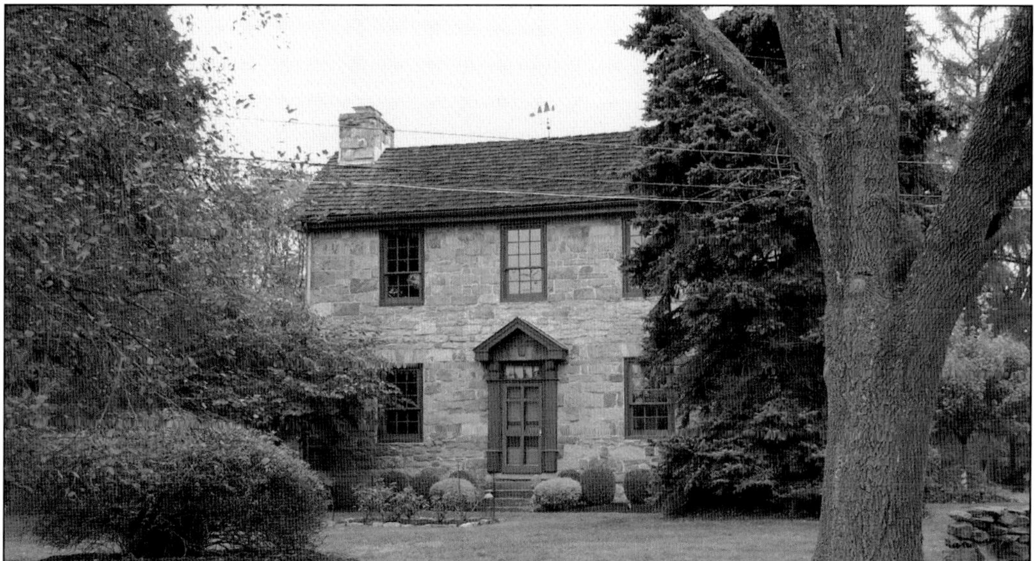

The Michael Rugh house near Bulltown and Sardis Roads was restored by the Miller family. In 1778, Indians captured the family, burned their log house (now the site of Meadowink Golf Course), and took the Rughs to Canada as prisoners. An infant son died along way. They were released three years later and returned home. After being adopted by the Indians for some time, their daughter Mary married Jacob Haymaker in 1794. In 1783, Rugh built a new log cabin. He was a member of the first Pennsylvania House of Representatives and built this stone "Philadelphia House" after his term. He died in 1820 and wife, Phoebe, predeceased him in 1809. Their son John still lived in the residence in 1876. (Courtesy of Laurel Smith.)

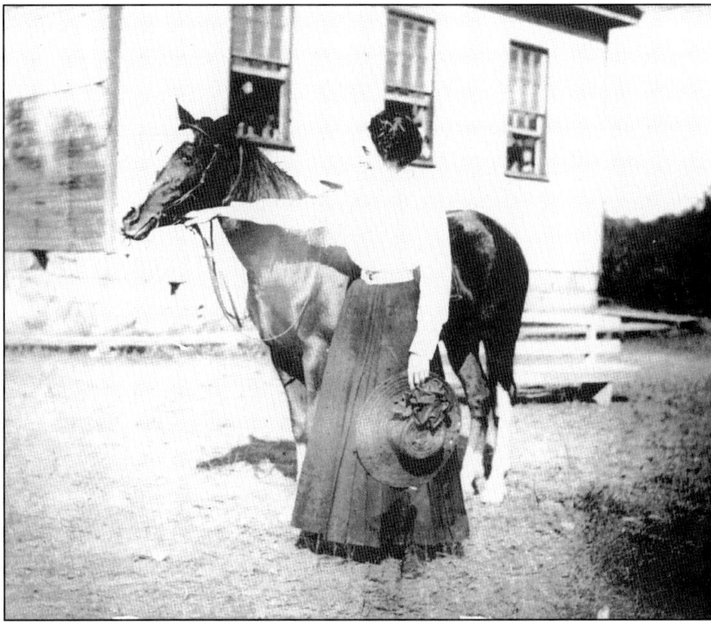

Bessie I. Staymates (honored in 1955 for teaching 50 years) stands beside her horse and Clark School, one of 14 where she taught. Receiving $30 a month, she swept the floor, cleaned windows, and kept one-room buildings warm. As a principal, she introduced hot meals at school, organized civic clubs, and was president of the Export Women's Club. "Be a mother plus—integrity, understanding, sympathy, and inspiration" was her motto. (Courtesy of Carl Patty.)

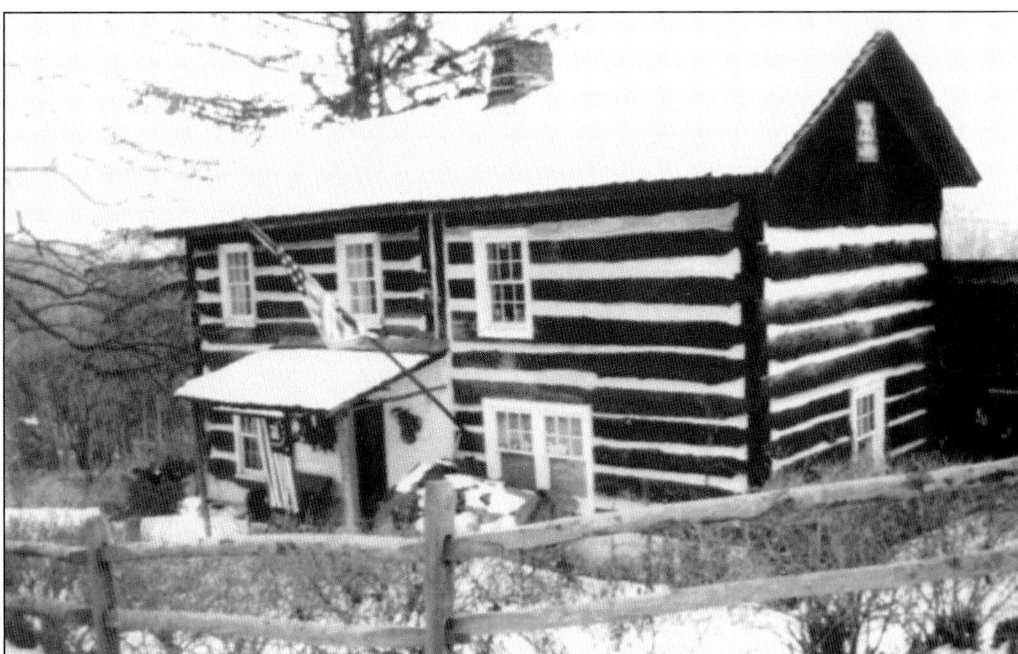

Bessie Staymates's house (1910 photograph) is on Round Top Road at Murrysville Park at the Old Forbes Road. She was a descendant of Philip von Steinmetz, a Prussian hussar lieutenant who also fought under General Washington. Her home, built around 1785–1790, and barn are now a museum. When she graduated from eighth grade, Bessie supported her mother and 11 siblings after her father's death. (Courtesy of Carl Patty.)

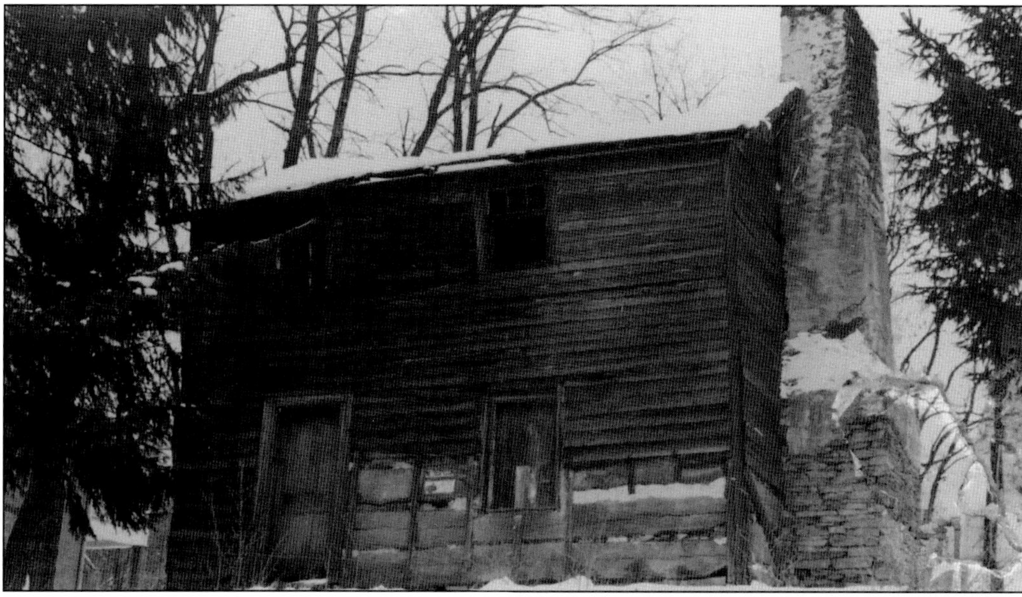

This rustic 1700s log house on Hill's Church Road in Murrysville belonged to John Duff Jr. and his wife, Mary Ann (Patterson). Duff's Belfast Scottish-Irish father was John Duff (McIlduff), and his mother was Ann (Wallace). They were pioneers at old Manordale and neighbors of Jacob Longannecker, John Milo Torrance, Jacob Barleign (Berlin), George Keister, and Jacob Cline. The Duffs intermarried with the Hall, (Bethune) Christy, Hill, Kemerer, Richey, Silvis, and Tallant families.

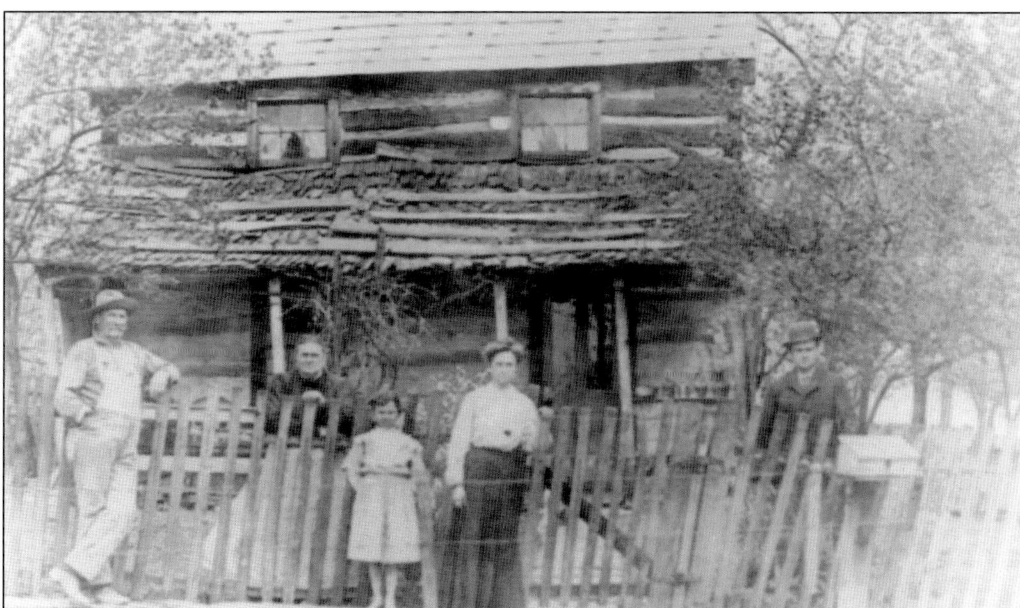

This early log house with a slat fence was located on Crowfoot Road in Murrysville at the present site of the Crowfoot Rod and Gun Club. It was owned by the Glunts. They are, from left to right, Lewis Johnson, Sarah H. Ament (neighbor), Eliza Belle Glunt Duff, and Lewis. Charles Hall's ancestor was William James Hall, born in Ireland in 1795. He was a weaver and a farmer who married Susanna Glunt. (Courtesy of Charles Hall.)

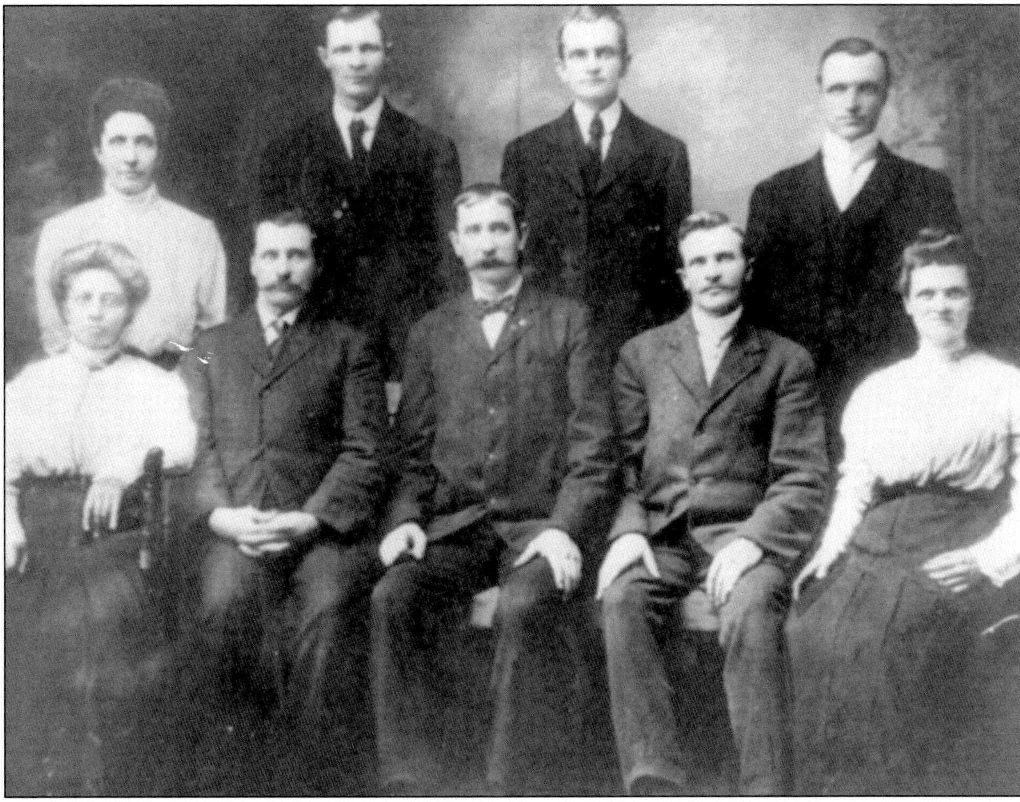

The William John Hall family, shown in 1900, includes, from left to right, siblings (first row) Susan (Masters), William James, Robert Caldwell, George Orbin, and Annie Irene (Branthoover); (second row) Margaret Jane (Porter), John Pugh, Guy Peter, and Charles Murray. Eldest Mary Elizabeth died at age six. William James lived with his brother Dr. Orbin in the homestead for some time. John Pugh, also a doctor, was on the Laird Institute board. Guy Peter was a pharmacist. (Courtesy of Charles Hall.)

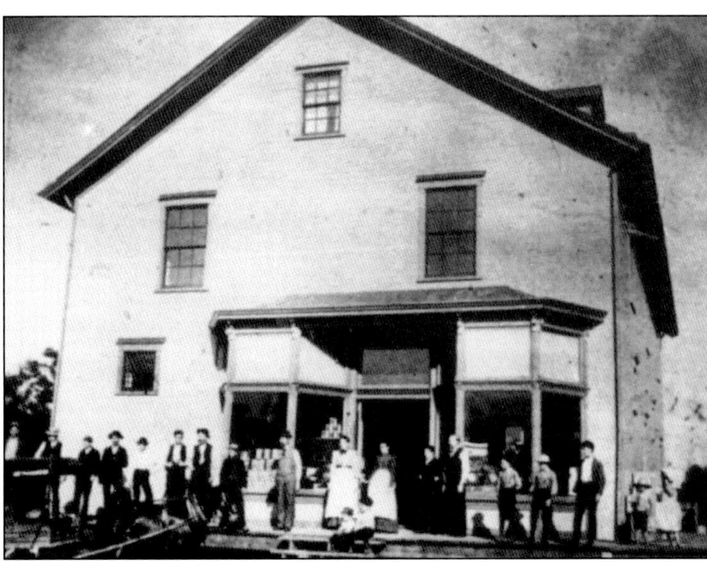

Murrysville residents shopped at Westmoreland Coal Company's store on the town corner on Westmoreland (now Washington) Avenue. They often talked about the latest activities in the coal and gas well businesses inside and outside on a porch familiar to both communities.

In this vintage photograph taken around 1933, the Hall brothers, from left to right, are (first row) Dr. John Hugh and William James; (second row) Charles Murray, Dr. George Orbin, and Guy Peter. The Halls have been prominent community leaders for decades. Many of them lived on Town Square where the original Mill Street was later named Vincent B. Hall Street. For years, they have been members of First Methodist Church across from Ferri's supermarket. (Courtesy of Charles Hall.)

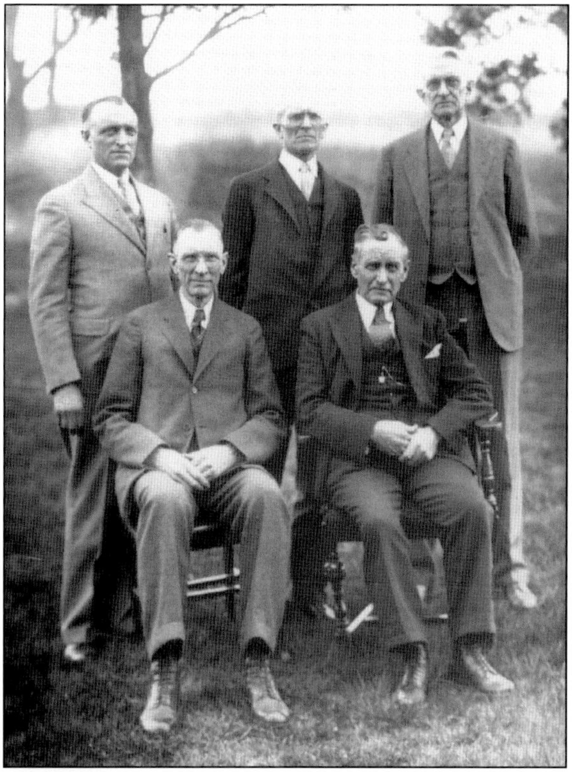

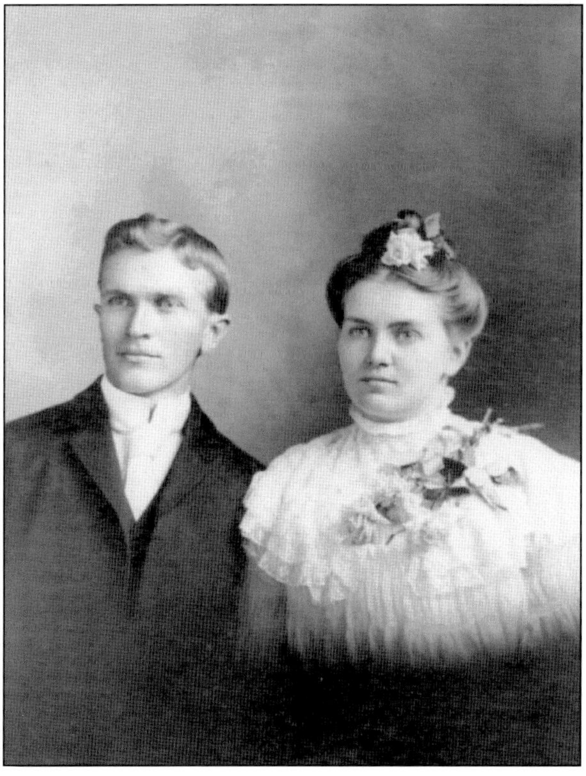

Pictured are George Orbin Hall and Roma Best Hall at their wedding in 1905. The Halls lived their entire married life at their homestead in the community. It was here that people in Murrysville came not only for medical help but also to discuss the latest news and events. (Courtesy of Charles Hall.)

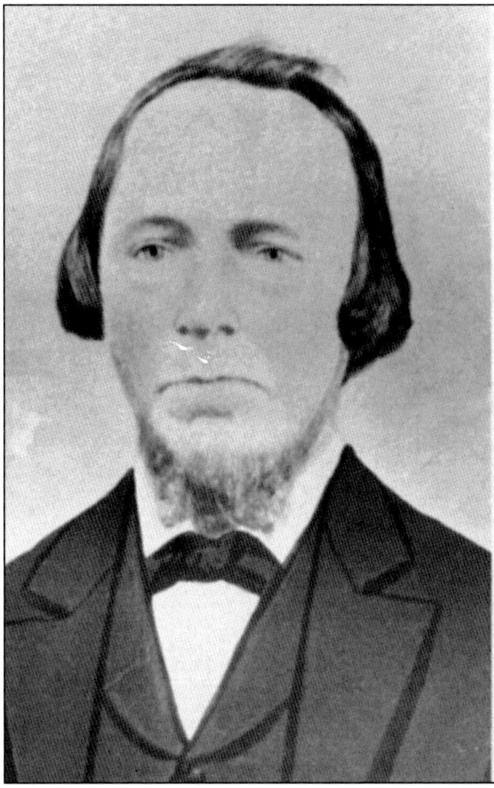

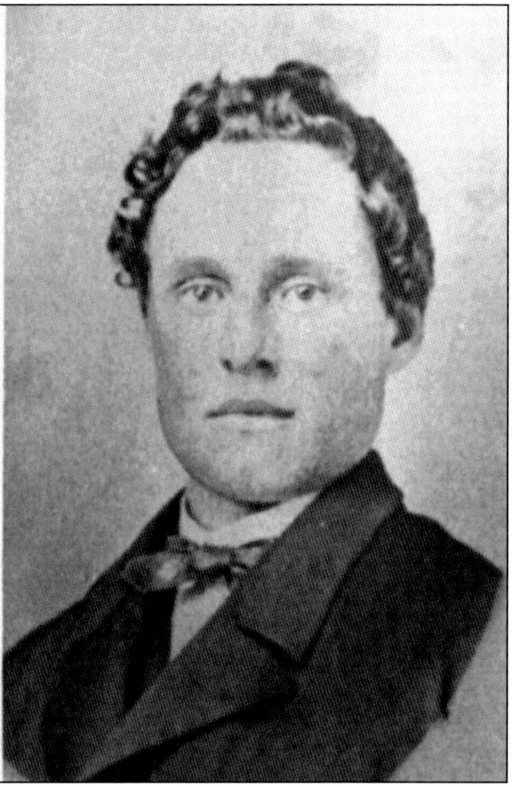

Alonzo Ryckman (left) fought during the Civil War in the 2nd Pennsylvania Calvary until he was captured and imprisoned in Andersonville, Georgia. He was transferred to Florence, South Carolina, where he died as a prisoner of war. Ryckman's son Levi was also incarcerated in both prisons. Levi, once the postmaster in Manordale, had a horse farm and opened a shoe shop in Murrysville in his log house after he returned home.

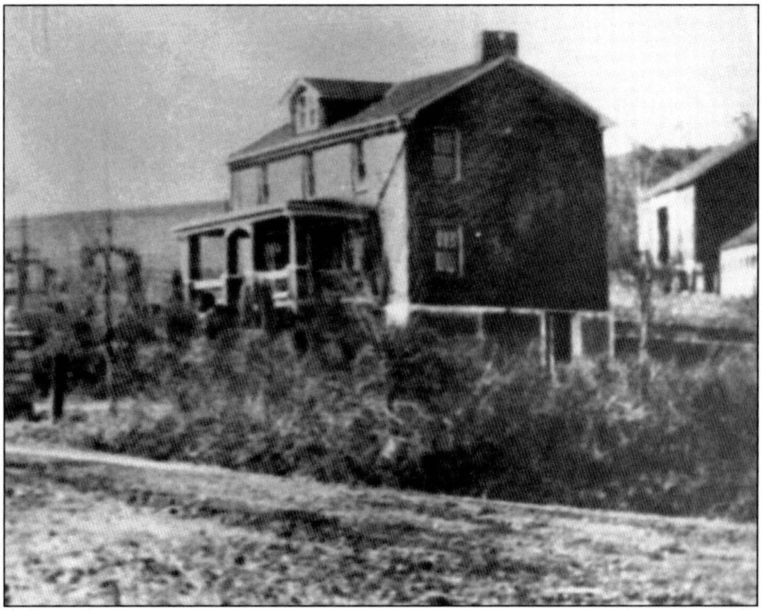

This log home (owned by Ryckman) was covered with red brick. In recent years, the house was painted with a buff color. It still stands on Old US 22 near west Export. For years, his shoe shop was located in an unpainted frame building in front of his house next to a muddy dirt road. Levi also operated a pharmacy and general store. He sold it to John H. Foight in 1905.

Export's beautiful Mary Borga in her wedding dress and ethnic veil is remembered in a porcelain portrait on a tombstone in Grandview Cemetery. Tranquillo Ciotto of Jeannette transferred photographs of the deceased onto porcelain (which is also a good source of records for people interested in their genealogy). Gravestone photographs come from an early European memorial custom. Many of these priceless images have been vandalized and shot with BB guns.

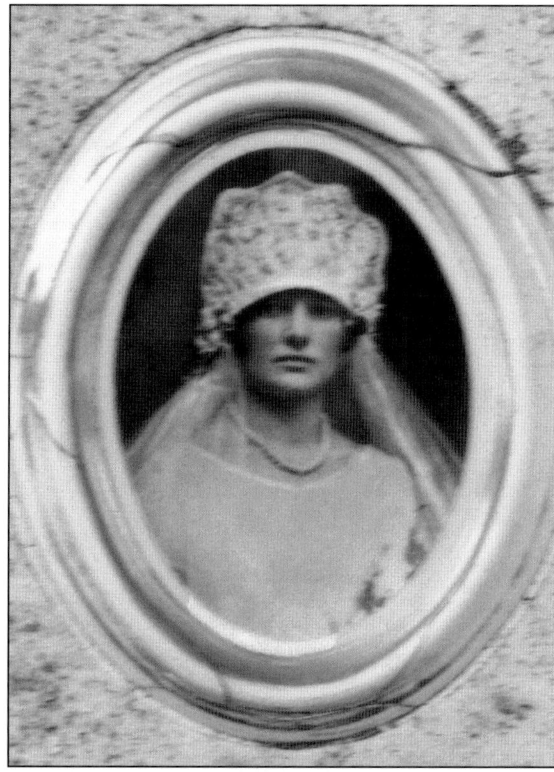

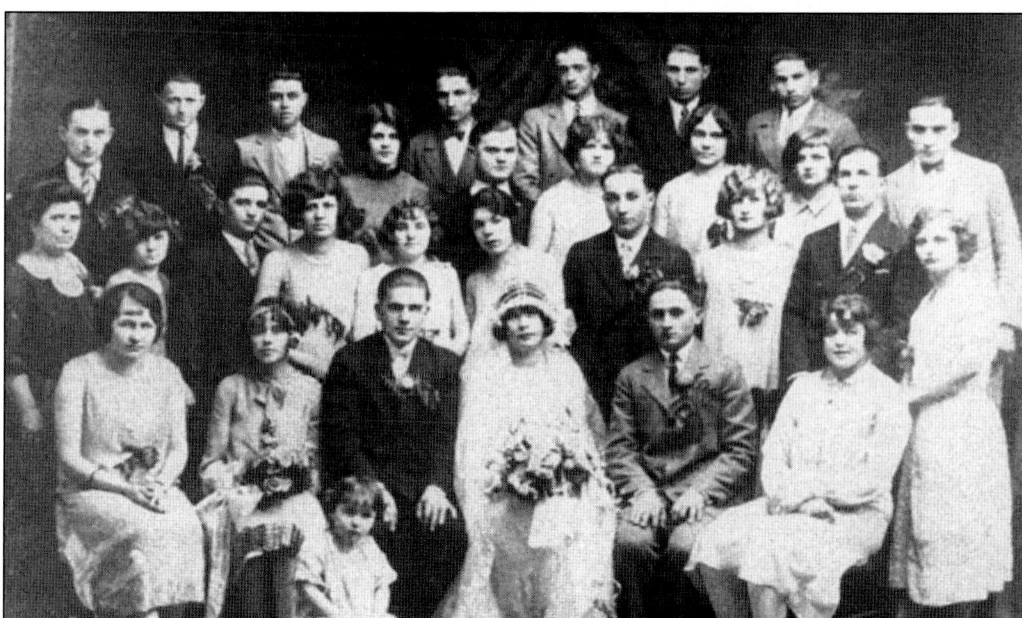

In his well-known poem "Ode on a Grecian Urn," John Keats writes, "Thou still unravish'd bride of quietness, / Thou foster-child of Silence and slow Time / . . . / She cannot fade, though thou has not thy bliss, / For ever wilt thou love, and she be fair!" Another beautiful bride is pictured in this early Export wedding portrait, with family and friends gathered around her.

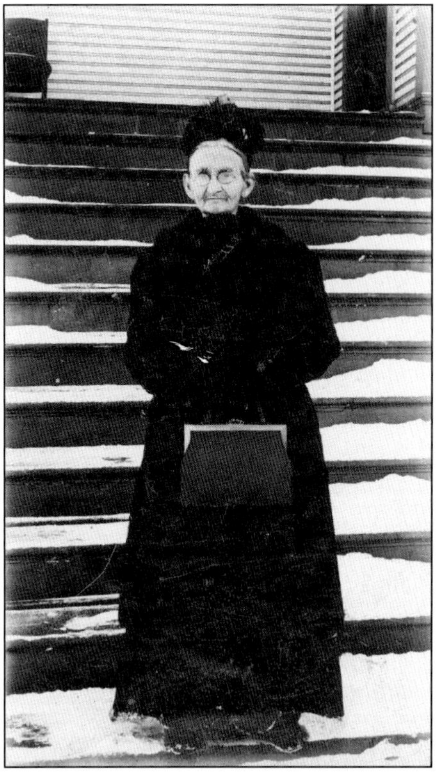

Pictured is Karl Koch's Grandma Karp clutching her favorite purse. In her times and still to this day, valleys were called hollows, while creeks were named runs. From the time that Karl was six years old, he heard stories from his grandmother and picked up folklore from Scott's barbershop in the basement of Export's bank-borough building (once a bank and now home to borough offices). His published memoirs include exciting excerpts from his journals.

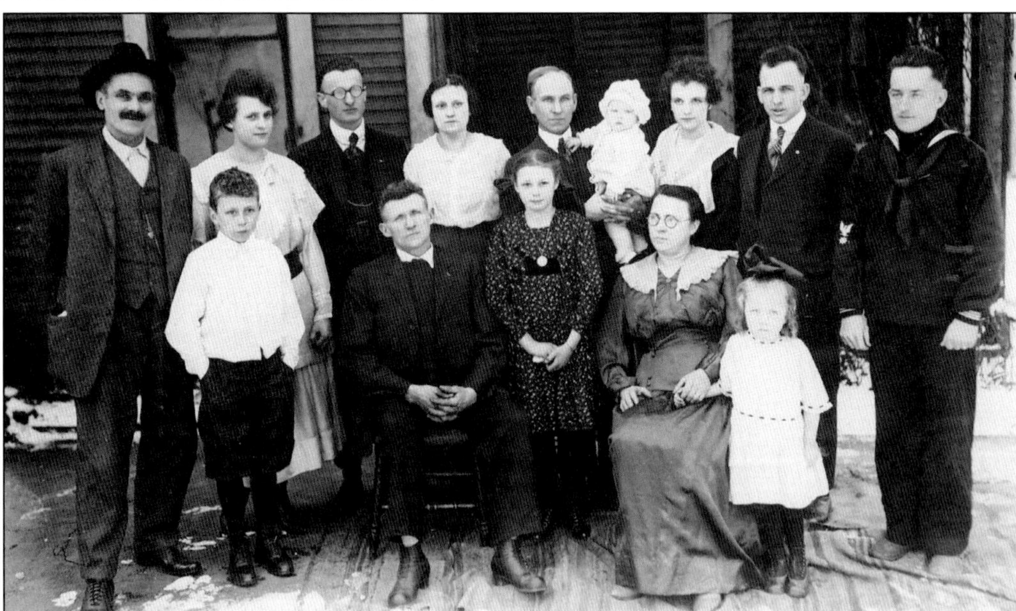

In 1915, Karl Koch is at the far left in the first row beside his father, Charles (Karl) Koch, at their home in Export. To the right are his sister Mildred, mother Wilhelmina (Minnie), and Margaret Nelda Good. In the second row are, from left to right, Chris Wigle, sister Lorna Koch, James Craig (Lorna's friend), his sister Hulda and her husband, Herbert Kiggens holding daughter Lorna, sister Lillian, Roy Kunkle (Lillian's husband), and Arthur McCoy (Lillian's friend).

Judge Thomas Mellon, Mellon Bank founder, emigrated from Ireland with his family in 1818 and lived in Captain Cook's stone house in Crabtree.

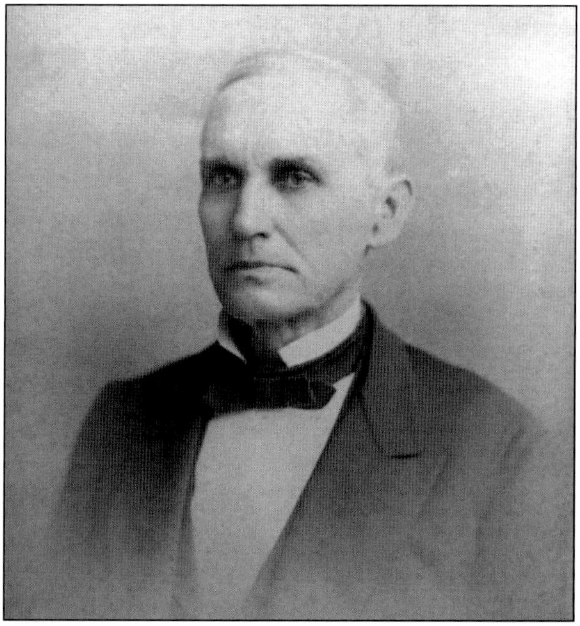

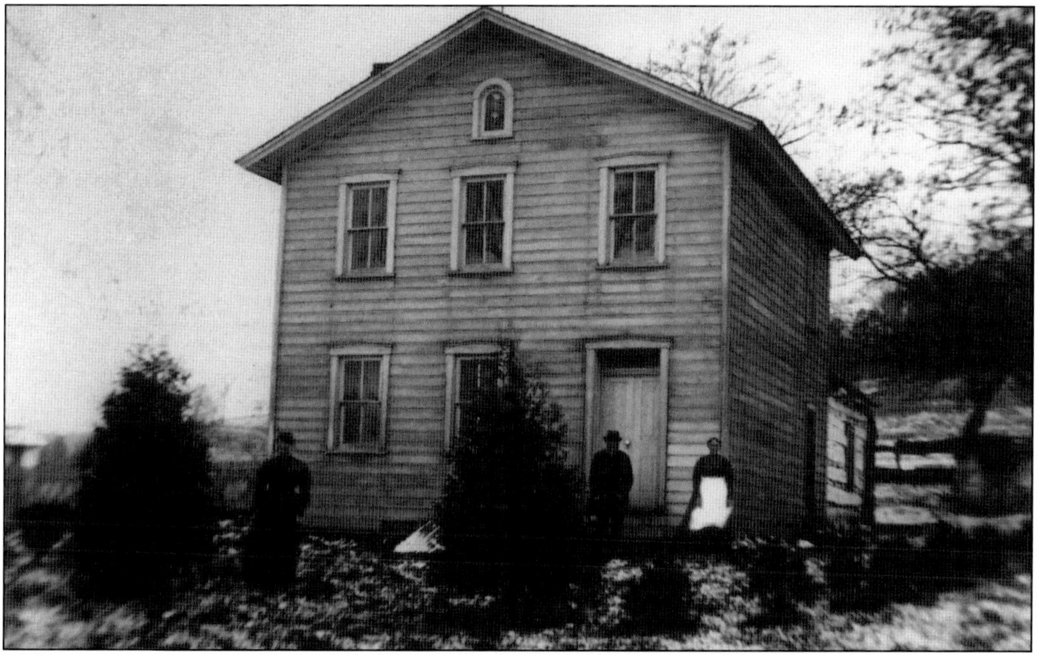

Mellon and his father built this house at Hill's Church and Cline Hollow Roads. Here, Cline-Pipher family members stand in front of the home. Mellon called the area Poverty Point. The Westmoreland County Historical Society erected a large stone with a historic plaque here. Scaifes, related to the Mellons, also lived in Murrysville on Sardis Road. A story goes that wishing to purchase farmland for his son, father Andrew Mellon left Tom at home to cut lumber. The future capitalist ran to the courthouse to stop the transaction. Years later, when Mellon returned to his homestead in a shiny, black horse-drawn carriage, he called his secretary his amanuensis, to the amusement of Plummer Duff and his neighbors. When the Mellons' Fifth Avenue mansion in Pittsburgh was razed, the materials were used to build Mount St. Peter Church in New Kensington.

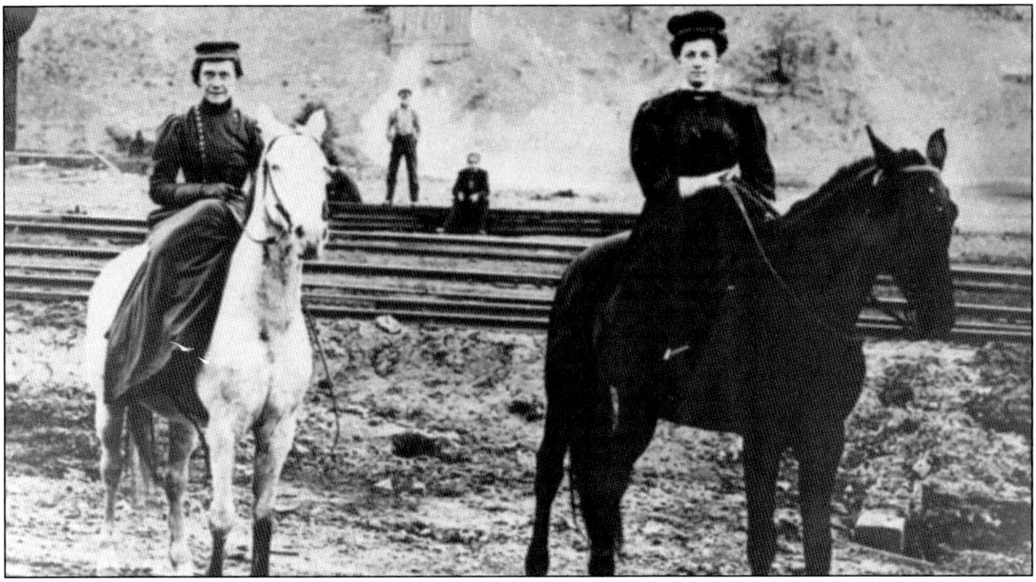

Many Turtle Creek Valley women were entrepreneurs. Anna Walton (left), a friend of Janet Stout Snyder, rode her Arabian horse named Pride between towns. In 1893, she was fined for riding her horse too fast. After her mother died when she was 16, Plummer Duff built Anna's house and dress designer shop on East Pike Street. She supported her father and herself. Anna's shop sign was donated to a private museum in Buffalo, New York.

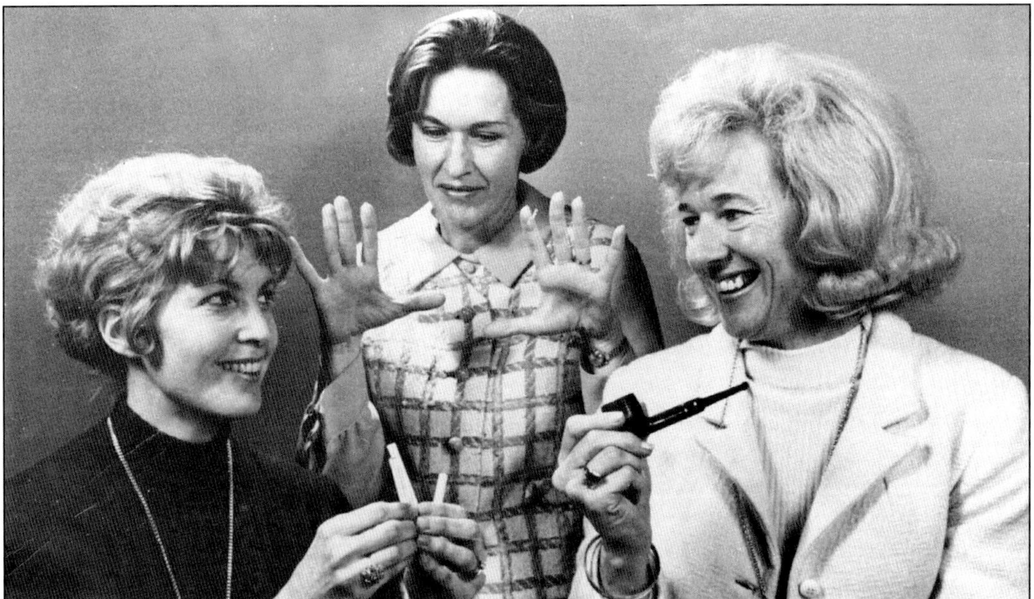

Murrysville is known for its entrepreneurs. From left to right, Helen Smith, Eileen Clark, and Charmaine Stickel (devoted to preserving Murrysville's tree sign) invented a cigarette holder (without an open channel) to help non-smokers and those breaking the habit. A feature article was published in the historic but now defunct *Pittsburgh Press* decades before public smoking was prohibited. Eileen sang in the Sweet Adelines International. Yvonne Rathgeb, also from the community, sang in Pittsburgh's Light Opera.

Nine

BUSINESSES AND HISTORIC BUILDINGS

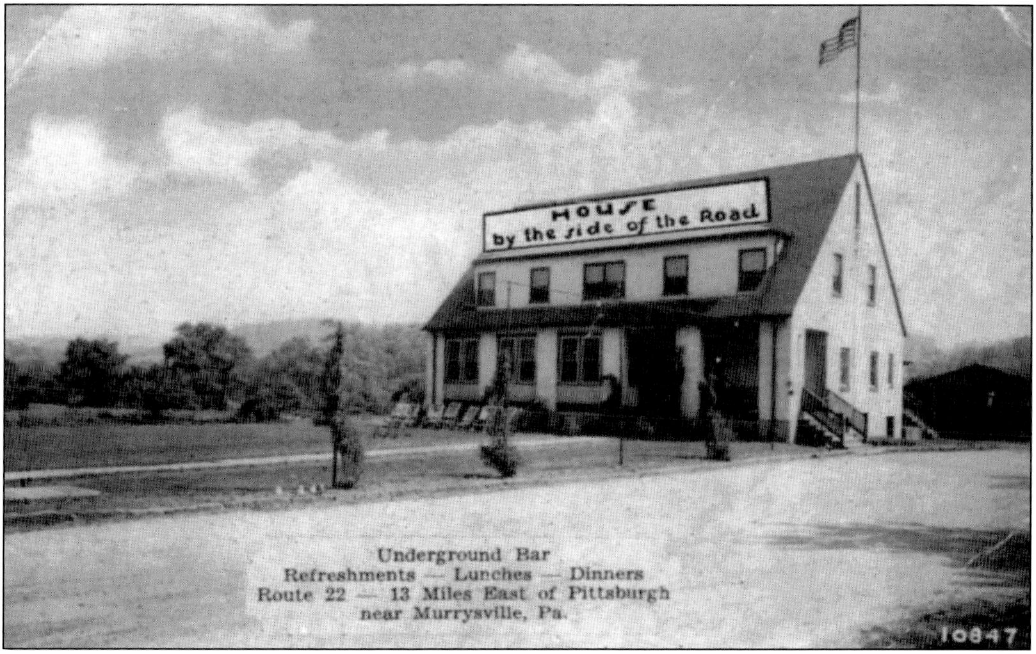

Johnny Miller's House by the Side of the Road on School Road in Newlonsburg was inspired by a poem of that name. *Readers Digest* magazine published an article on this inn that burned in 1949. Inside were owners George Miller (age 82) and his wife, Josephine, their son Joseph, and Wallace Meyer, an employee who tried to save them. All perished. The Murrysville Fire Department acquired better equipment following the fire. (Courtesy of Raymond Meehan.)

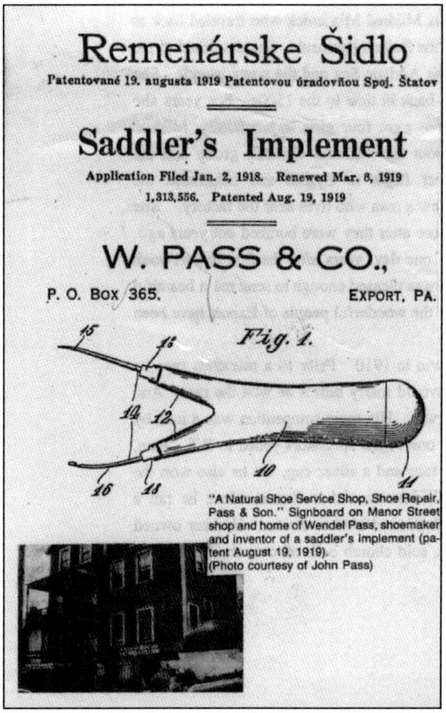

"A Natural Shoe Service Shop, Shoe Repair, Pass & Son." Signboard on Manor Street shop and home of Wendel Pass, shoemaker and inventor of a saddler's implement (patent August 19, 1919). (Photo courtesy of John Pass)

Wendel Pass was the inventor of a saddler's implement he sold to in his shoe shop. He had worked at Westmoreland Coal Company where he contacted "miner's asthma" (black lung). Before Export had sanitary sewers, Pass drained dish- and wash water through terra-cotta pipes he laid in front of his home. He wrote to Pennsylvania Department of Health encouraging them to bring public sewage disposal to Export. Pass died in 1935.

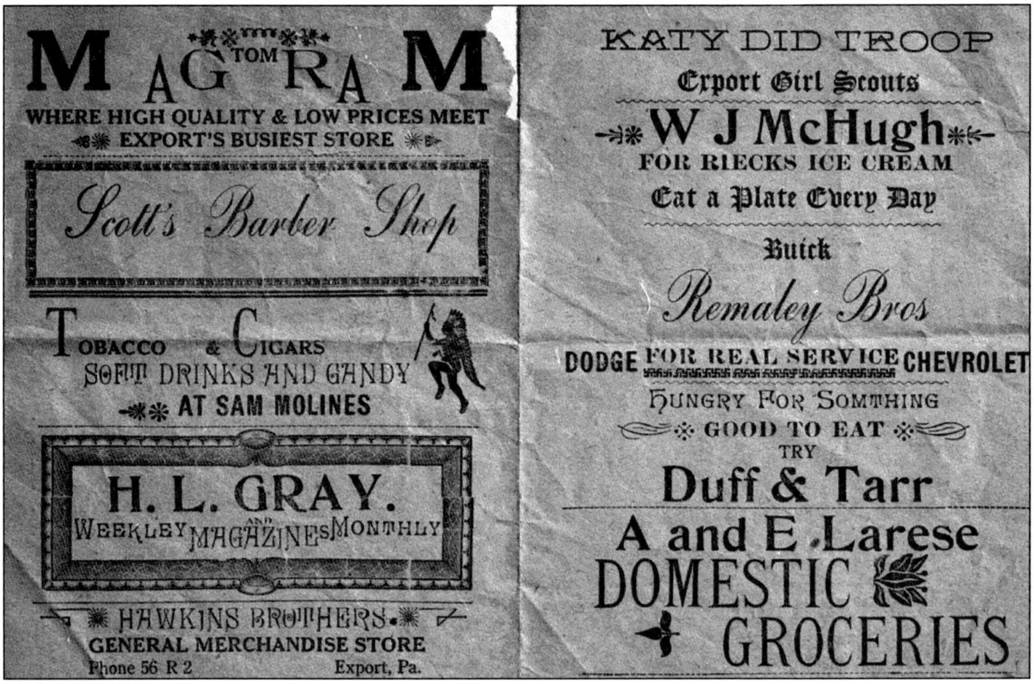

Here is a mixed sampling of vintage business cards (copied together) from Murrysville and Export. These nostalgic advertisements all represent surnames of families stemming from pioneer days in the Turtle Creek Valley. One humorous image shows a rooster chasing a chicken, with a forlorn old hen left on a road behind him. The card reads, "We are after new business." (Courtesy of Raymond Meehan.)

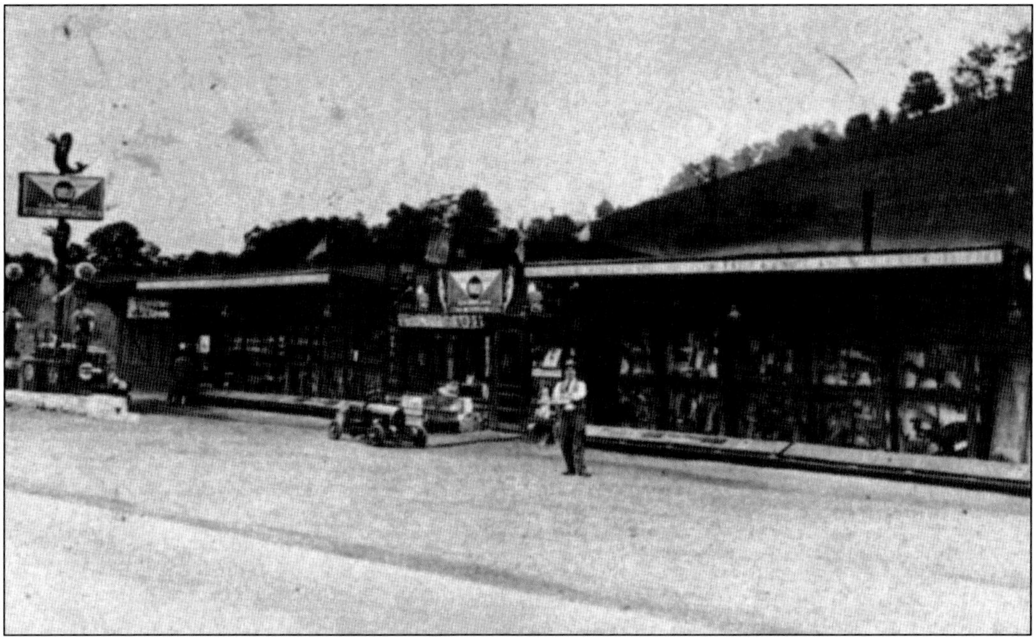

Standing in front of this Murrysville gasoline station and unique store is Charles Altman, the owner (see page 120). (Courtesy of Edward Banks.)

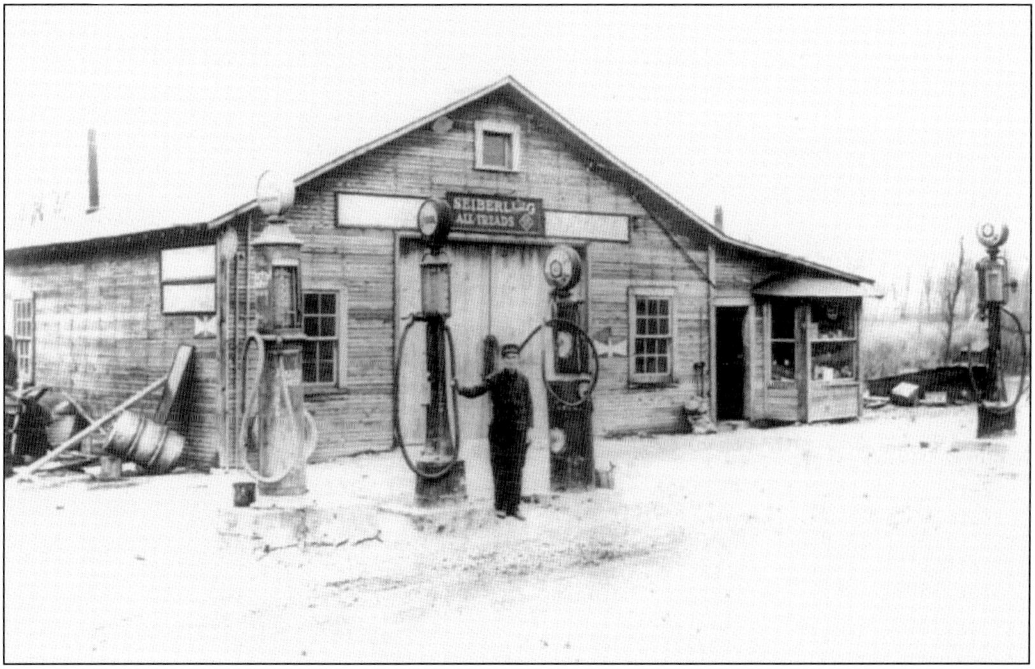

William Valentine Rings, a descendant of 1925 German immigrant Valentine Rings, operated this garage adorned with vintage advertising signs, shown in the 1930s. Newlonsburg's John A. Rings was appointed postmaster at Boyle (now Newlonsburg) through the influence of congressman Charles E. Boyle in 1886. A descendant of slaves from Virginia, Hugh Winston (1900–1978), who worked for Rings until 1971, was called Amos because he enjoyed the *Amos and Andy* radio program. The man in the photograph is unidentified. (Courtesy of Carl Patty.)

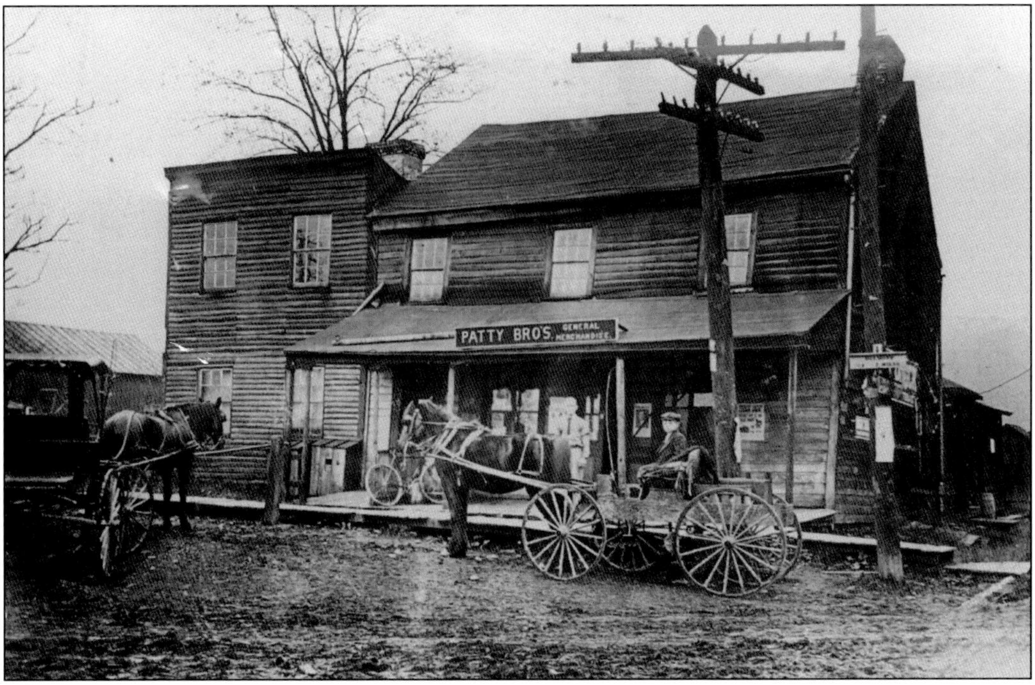

Patty Brothers General Store, a log building with siding on Murrysville's Town Square, was probably Jeremiah Murry's original store. In Export, Joseph Collins Greer, Thomas Baughman, and Walter Jordan, were successive managers of the Westmoreland Coal Company store. There, Murrysville's Bessie Staymates bought shoes for her family using 11 sticks of varied lengths with children's names attached to them. Nick Coco had a small shoe store in the building. (Courtesy of Stephen Simpson.)

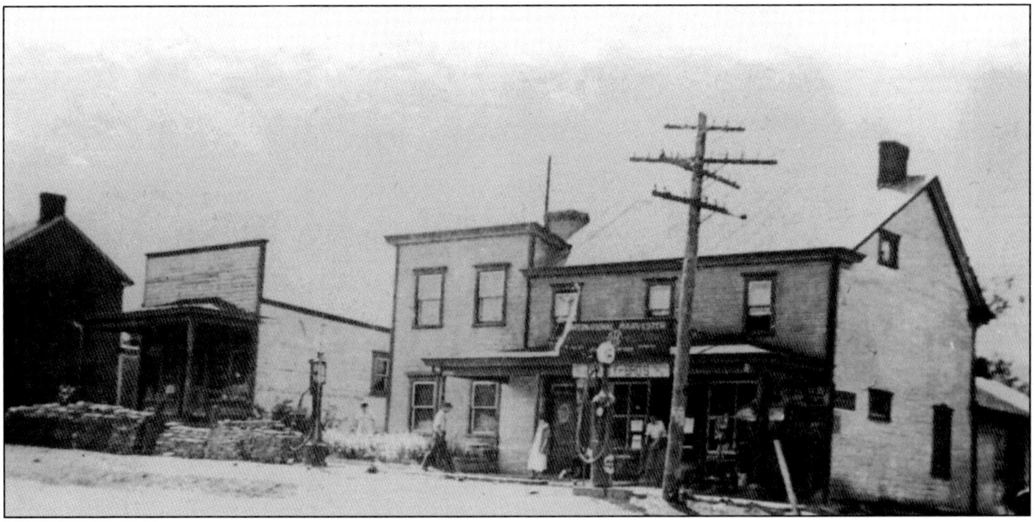

Pictured in 1910, Patty's buildings included a little shop with multiple uses (third from right)—ice cream parlor, confectionery, bakery, and library. Nearby is Heckman's house (not shown). In 1954, Ely-Anson Snyder's store (not visible) was the home of Ferri's supermarket (still in business.) In 1905, H.S. Patty made one battery-operated telephone for his buildings. His gas station was the center of local commerce, but it burned in 1963. (Courtesy of Carl Patty.)

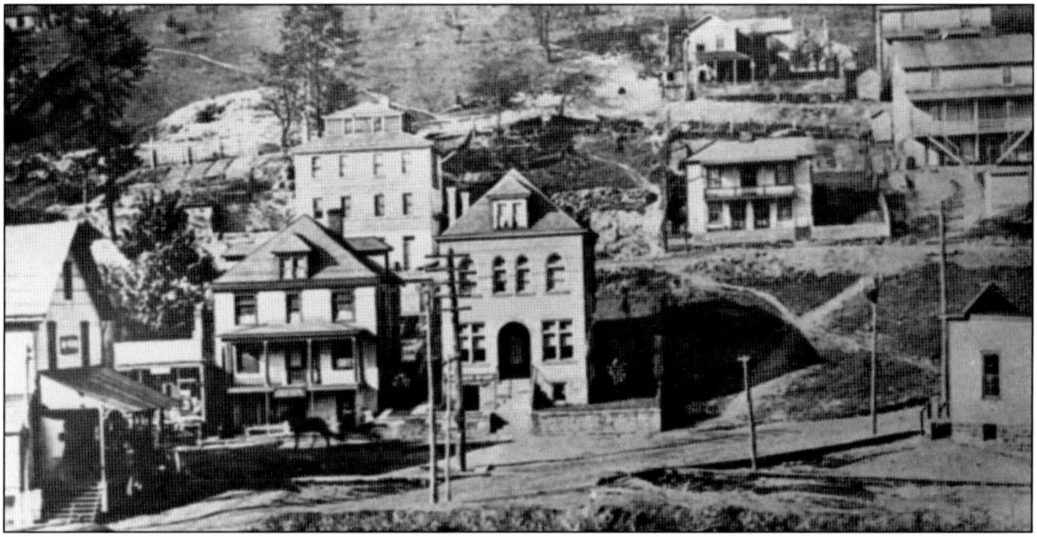

The corner building on Washington Avenue (far left) is the train-track side of the Westmoreland Coal Company Store next to Gus Millberg's boardinghouse. To its right is Export's brick First National Bank, considered the "finest bank in Pennsylvania" and built in 1904 by E.E. Kunkle Lumber Company for $2,800. The first town council met there on January 11, 1912. The present brick volunteer fire department is next door on Lincoln Avenue. Behind Millberg's is the Pauletich house.

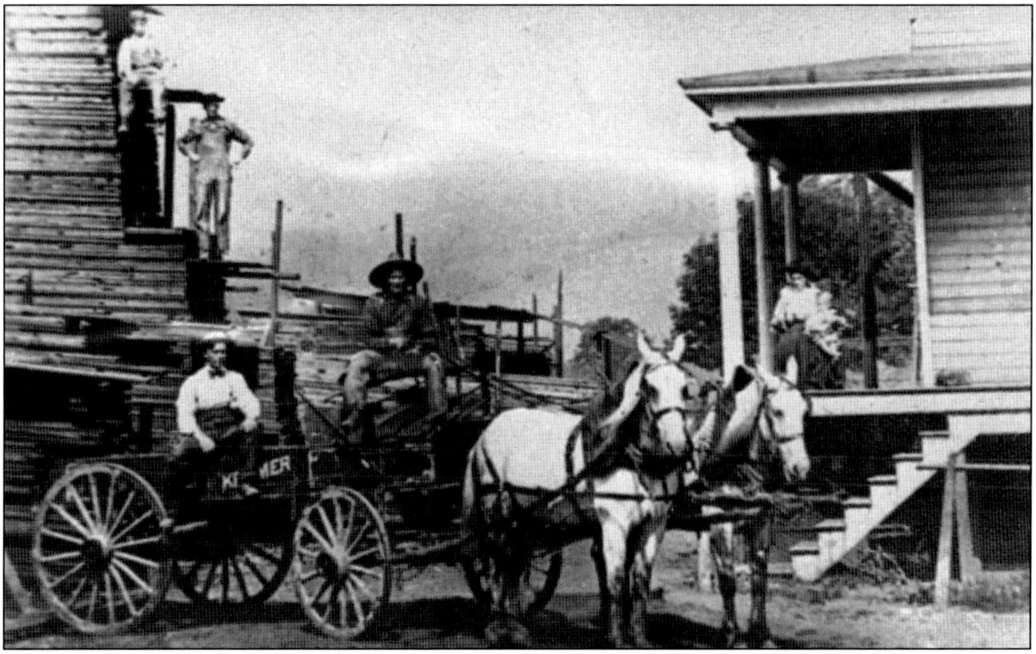

In 1892, when the Pennsylvania Railroad tracks were extended to Export, Grable's lumber company moved its business from Murrysville to Export, which had become a boomtown that needed many wooden building, tipples, and trestles. Originally Lucian and Osmyn Grable's company, it changed its name in 1936 to Export Lumber, where Joseph Wonce was an early employee. In 1891, the Grable family constructed the Westmoreland Coal Company Store, presently Master Automobile Supplies.

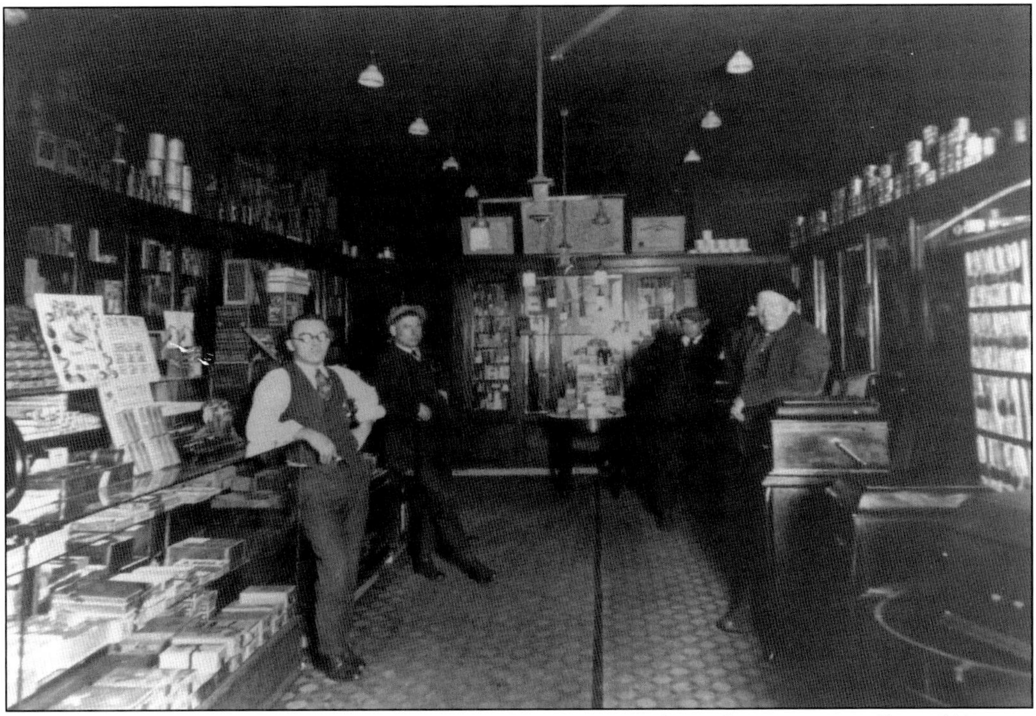

Wigle (sometimes spelled Weigle)'s Pharmacy in Export served people in Murrysville and Export, where there not that many drugstores for competition.

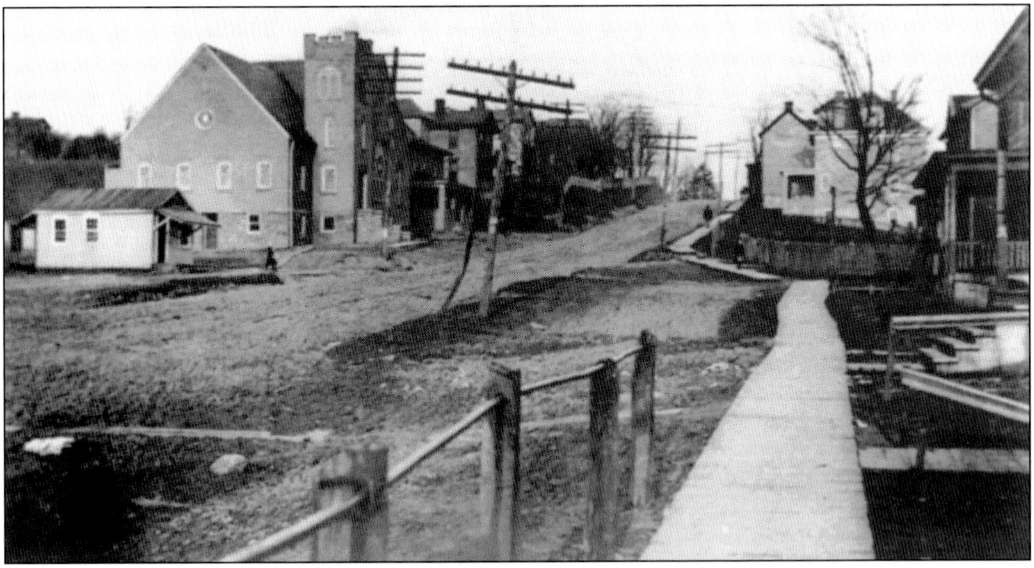

Murrysville's first post office (left foreground) opened in 1818. Pictured in 1914, it was moved across Town Square to avoid mud for the postmistress. An 1800s post office on Logans Ferry Road in Sardis was in the general store. Duncan McAlister was a Civil War veteran and postmaster 35 years. James Watt, a horse-riding postman, traveled from Stewart Station to Murrysville. Jeremiah's granddaughter, Susan Irwin, operated a post office in 1867 in her house. Also at Town Square is Bob's Inn (the former 1830 Methodist church), close to Dean's Barber Shop (a former dance hall). This boardwalk extends to Dick's Diner, owned by the Snyder family. (Courtesy of Carl Patty.)

A Mr. Abbot (left), an Export photographer, stands beside Philip, a tinsmith, in front of Cashdollar's Nickelodeon. Later owner of the enterprise Louis Calisti charged only 10¢ for admission. When children were not able to pay, he let them in free if they brought a lump of coal to donate to help finance the heating bill. Children and adults resourcefully combed railroad tracks for fallen coal.

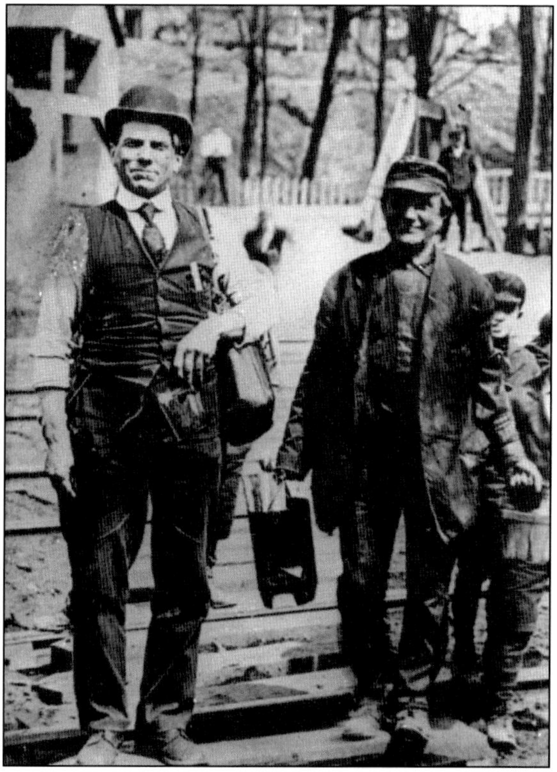

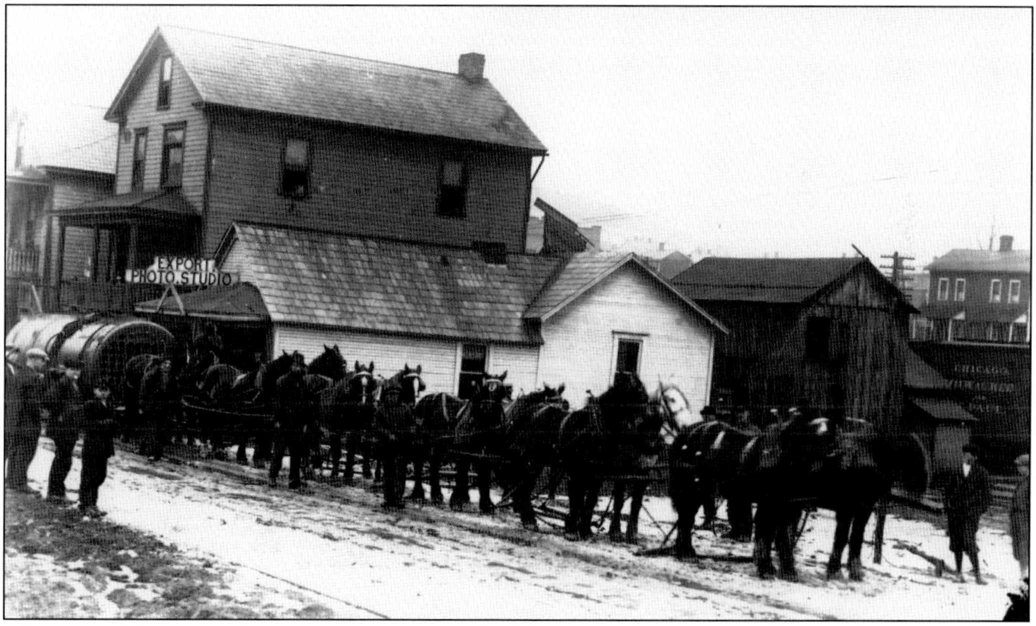

John Sartoris, "Mr. Picture Man," had his studio in a former coal paymaster house (pictured) across from Moose Hall for 50 years. A rollback rooftop provided natural light. His equipment and hand-painted drops were sold for a proposed museum in Beaver. Mr. Kline, an early photographer in Export, operated his darkroom in a boxcar behind the YMCA. Here, a team of horses transports a boiler from the Last Chance colliery.

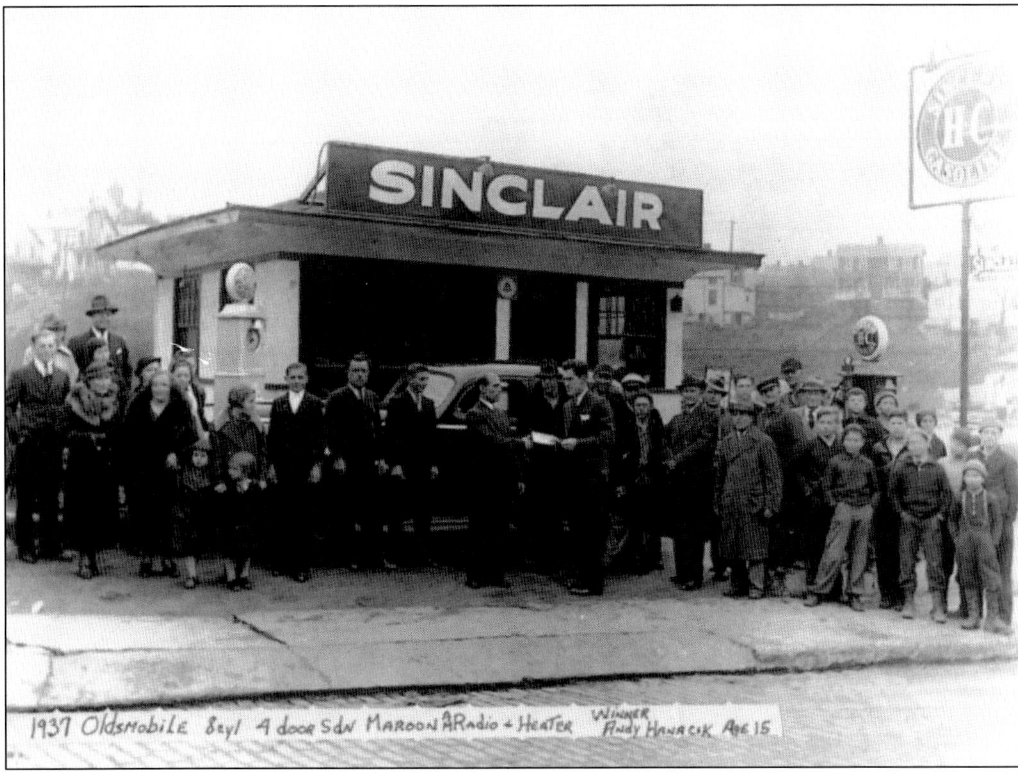

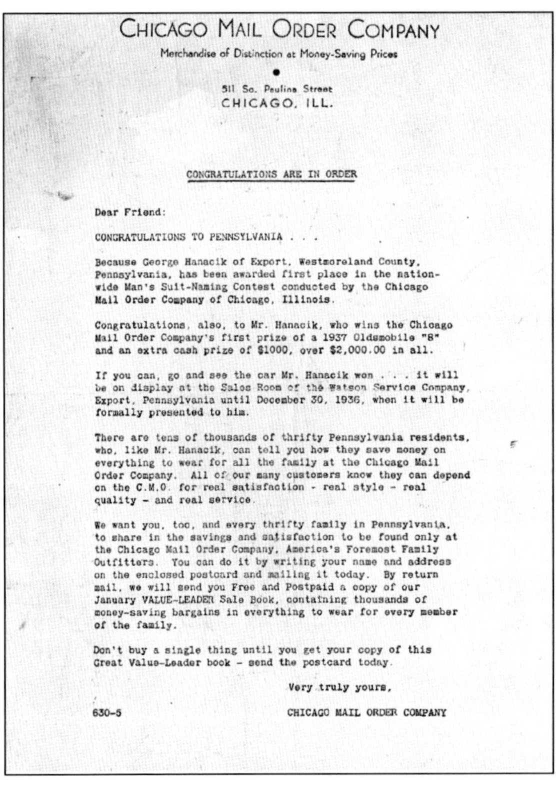
CHICAGO MAIL ORDER COMPANY
Merchandise of Distinction at Money-Saving Prices

511 So. Paulina Street
CHICAGO, ILL.

CONGRATULATIONS ARE IN ORDER

Dear Friend:

CONGRATULATIONS TO PENNSYLVANIA . . .

Because George Hanacik of Export, Westmoreland County, Pennsylvania, has been awarded first place in the nation-wide Man's Suit-Naming Contest conducted by the Chicago Mail Order Company of Chicago, Illinois.

Congratulations, also, to Mr. Hanacik, who wins the Chicago Mail Order Company's first prize of a 1937 Oldsmobile "8" and an extra cash prize of $1000, over $2,000.00 in all.

If you can, go and see the car Mr. Hanacik won . . . it will be on display at the Sales Room of the Watson Service Company, Export, Pennsylvania until December 30, 1936, when it will be formally presented to him.

There are tens of thousands of thrifty Pennsylvania residents, who, like Mr. Hanacik, can tell you how they save money on everything to wear for all the family at the Chicago Mail Order Company. All of our many customers know they can depend on the C.M.O. for real satisfaction - real style - real quality - and real service.

We want you, too, and every thrifty family in Pennsylvania, to share in the savings and satisfaction to be found only at the Chicago Mail Order Company, America's Foremost Family Outfitters. You can do it by writing your name and address on the enclosed postcard and mailing it today. By return mail, we will send you Free and Postpaid a copy of our January VALUE-LEADER Sale Book, containing thousands of money-saving bargains in everything to wear for every member of the family.

Don't buy a single thing until you get your copy of this Great Value-Leader book - send the postcard today.

Very truly yours,

630-5

CHICAGO MAIL ORDER COMPANY

On Export's Town Square, the Hanaciks are awarded a 1937 Oldsmobile from Watson's Garage on the old Merle Cline property as first prize in a man's suit-naming contest in Chicago. The winning name was *Woolrich*. The garage received a World War II government bonus for its service. Robert Watson Sr. and his uncle Harry Diffenderfer sold Jordan and Oakland cars there. (Courtesy of Raymond Meehan and Stephen Simpson.)

A letter was sent to George Hanacik, in regard to his 15-year-old son Andy. Andy was too young to accept the car. In the image above, George accepts the prize, an eight-cylinder, four-door maroon sedan with a radio and heater. George was too young to receive the car, so his father received it for him. Watson's garage, with the Sinclair sign in front expanded to a new building on New US 22 in Murrysville.

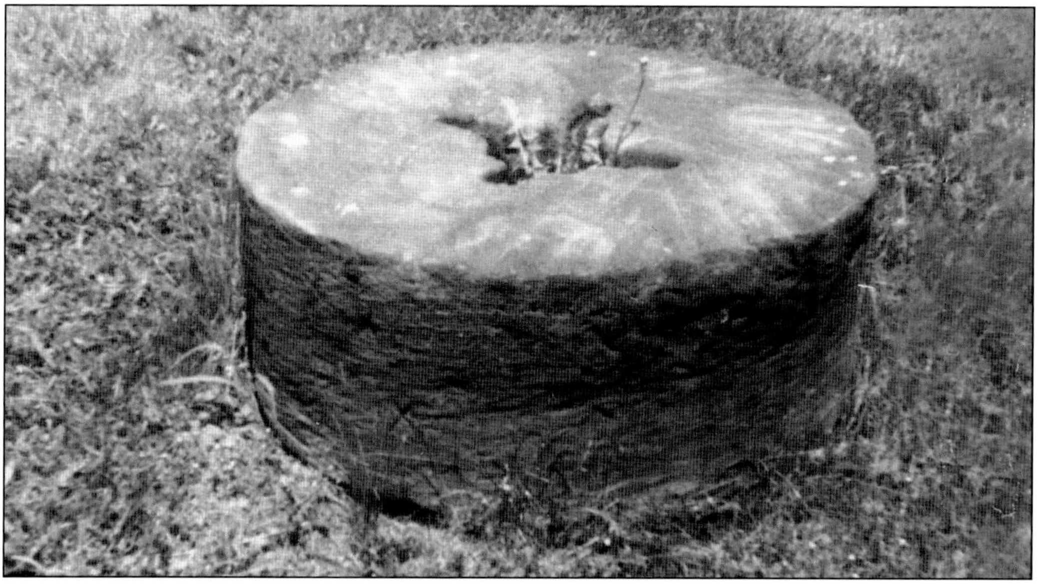

This sorghum millstone in Murrysville is the type scientist and inventor Francis Laird Stewart used to develop millet sorghum from maize. This founder of Laird Institute said the Stewart Process of manufacturing sugar from corn stalks would make the nation "untold millions in wealth." It was demonstrated at an 1885 St. Louis exhibition, bringing him an international gold medal. Prof. Dmitri Mendeleev of Russia, creator of the periodic table of elements, published Stewart's findings in a book.

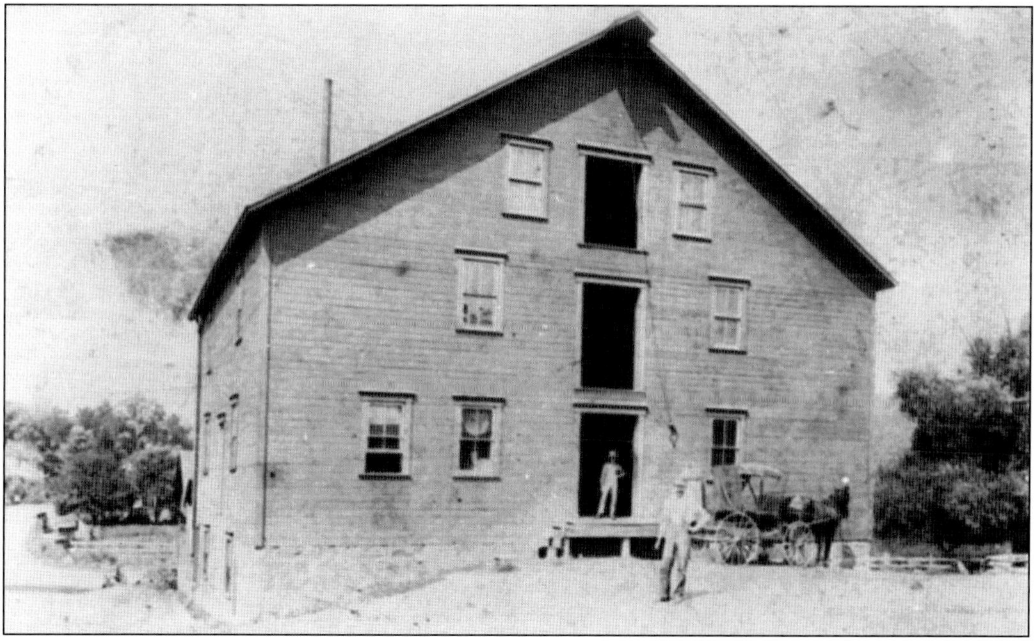

This was a Remaley mill and Murrysville's largest grain center. It burned in 1949. Mills of this kind often caught fire due to structure and contents. Mills constituted Franklin Township's first industry. Jeremiah Murry and William McWilliams, among others, were prominent first millers. There were many Remaley mills in the Turtle Creek Valley. This early family was prominent, starting out in Germany and immigrating to this area.

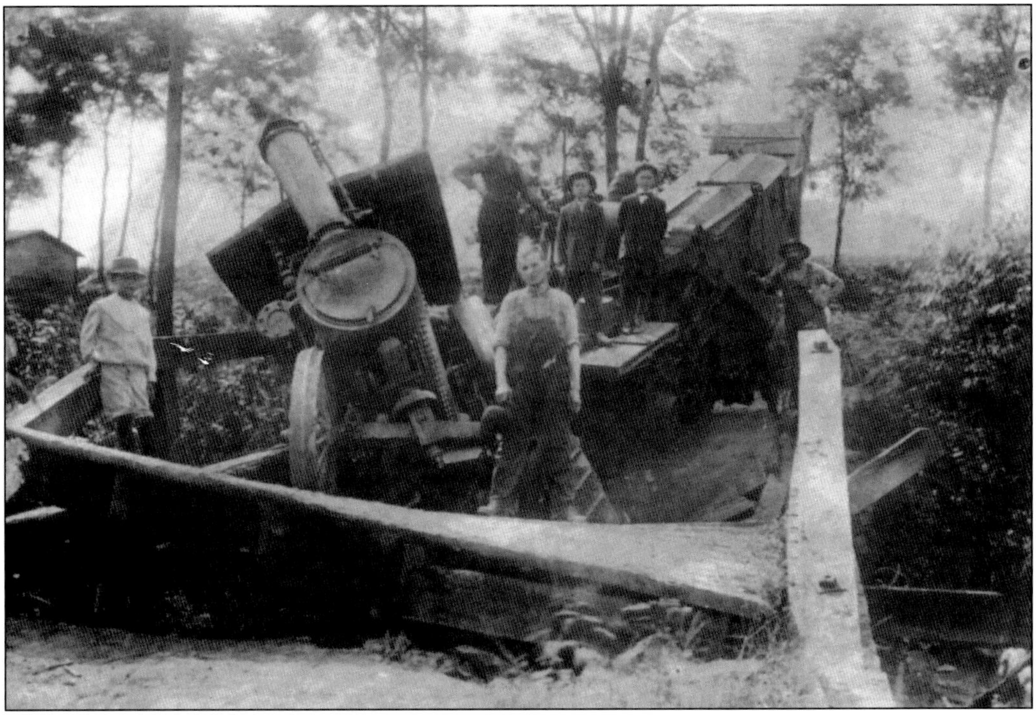

Frank Remaley is at the rear of this image of a bridge broken from the weight of a farm thrasher and a tractor taken over the creek north of one of Remaley's mills. An enthusiastic spectator could not resist the photo opportunity. Michael Remaley, a blacksmith, married Margaret Berlin. One of their granddaughters married James Duff. Louis Geiger's son William married Sadie Remaley. (Courtesy of Raymond Meehan.)

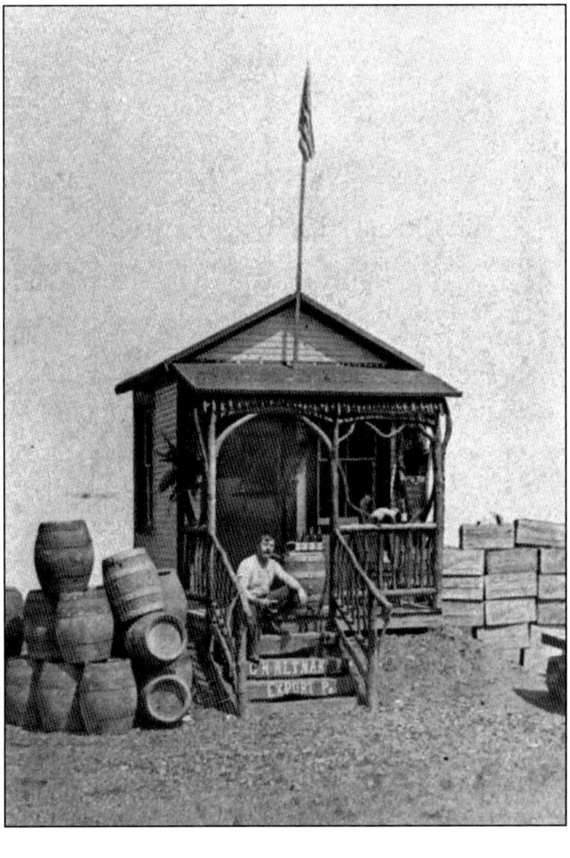

Seen here on the steps of his cider mill in Export, Charles Altman, who built Star Park for Westmoreland Coal Company, also was a beer distributor, dropping off kegs or barrels at homes in both communities. Altman's concession stand/amusement park, now long gone, only had one building on it. It used to belong to a Mr. Pristou before the Banks family purchased; the Bankses still own the property.

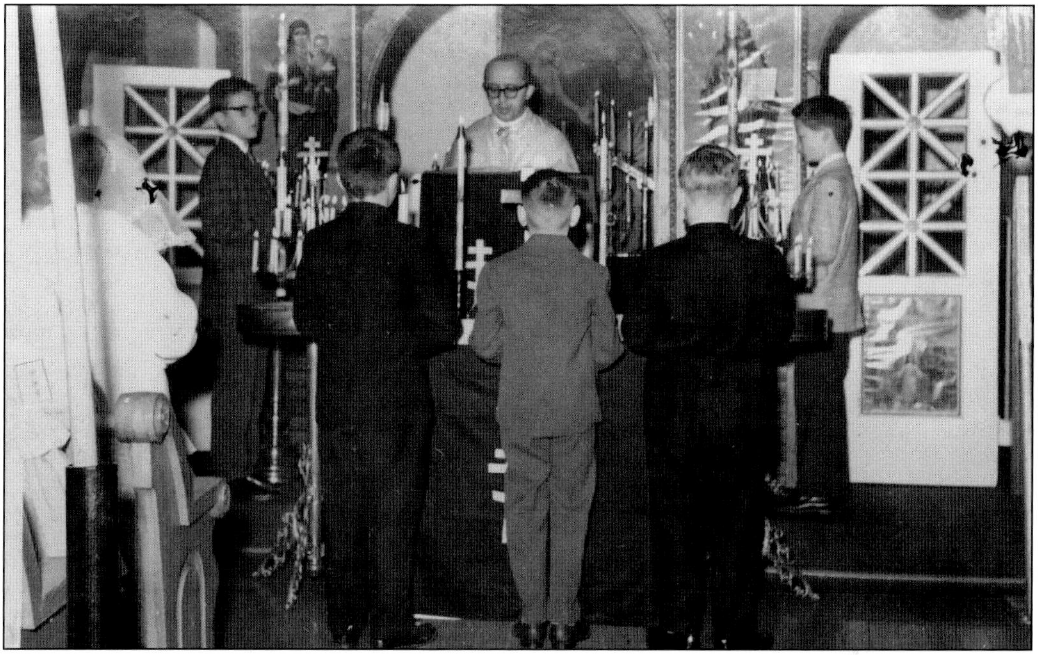

This Russian Orthodox Church on Saltsburg Road (Roosevelt Avenue) also served Serbians, Croatians, Lithuanians, and others worshipping in Export. Father Teleynos is at the podium. From left to right are John Cherepko Jr., Daniel Telysko, George Lawrence, Carl Lotinsky, and William Telysko.

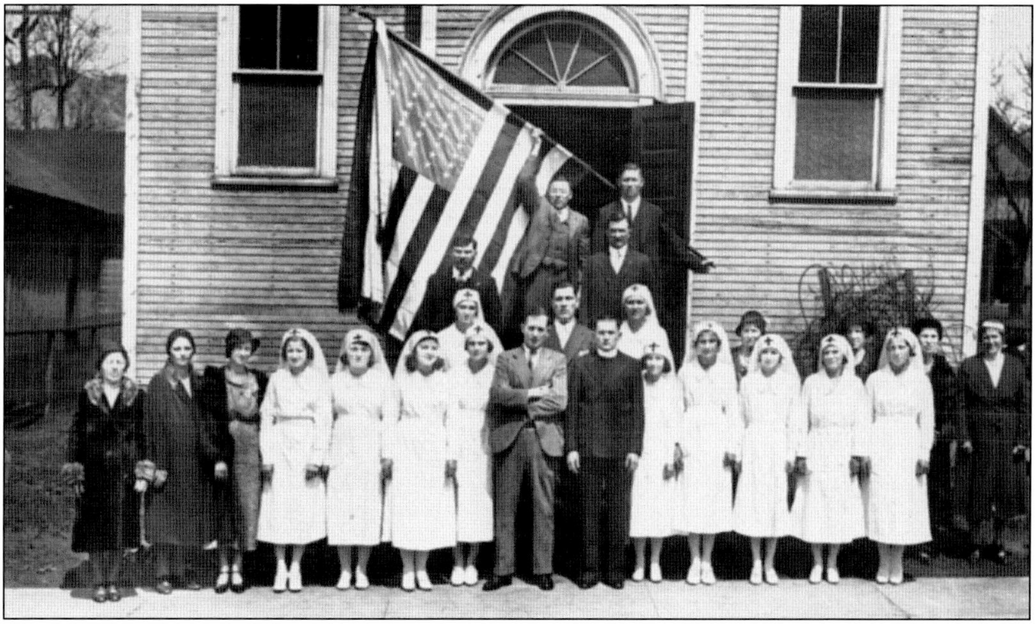

Grable's lumber company built the Export Russian Orthodox Church. This picture with nurse members in the front was taken in 1918 at the end of the World War I. After it caught fire, meetings were held temporarily in Charles Berlin's home. Members later attended St. Mary's Catholic Church, whose first congregants came from Poland. The former Russian Orthodox church is now completely boarded up for preservation.

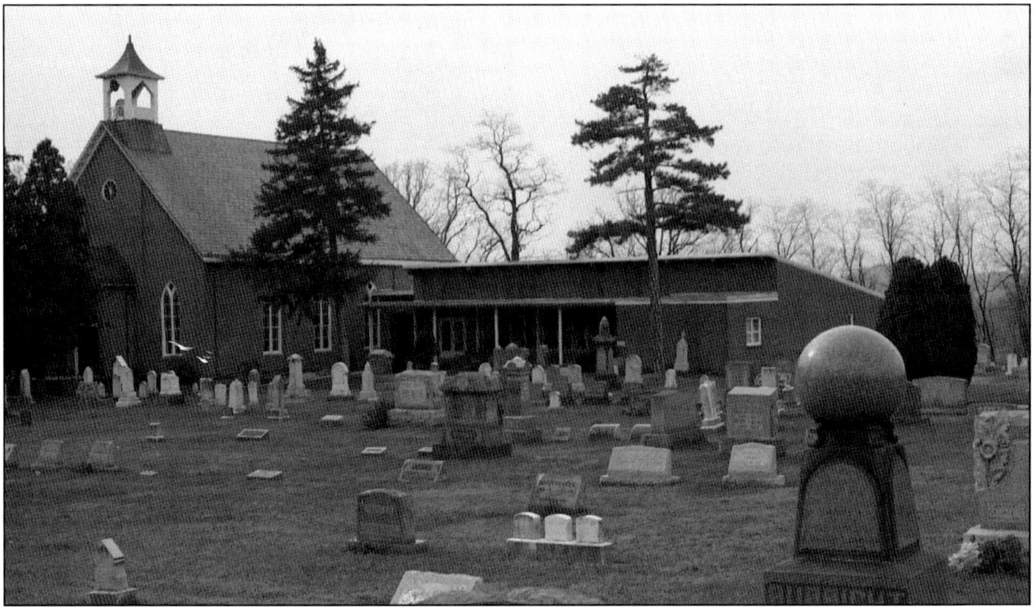

John McIlduff donated land for Hill's Emanuel Reformed congregation. A canopied tent pulpit protected itinerant ministers. First Americans defending their land once attacked an outdoor service, and victims from both sides were buried at the adjoining cemetery. Nicknamed White Valley Church, it was built in 1828 with Lutherans sharing the building, and named for the adjacent hillsides of white spring blossoms. Lutherans later built their own church on nearby land donated by Philip Drum and Peter Hill.

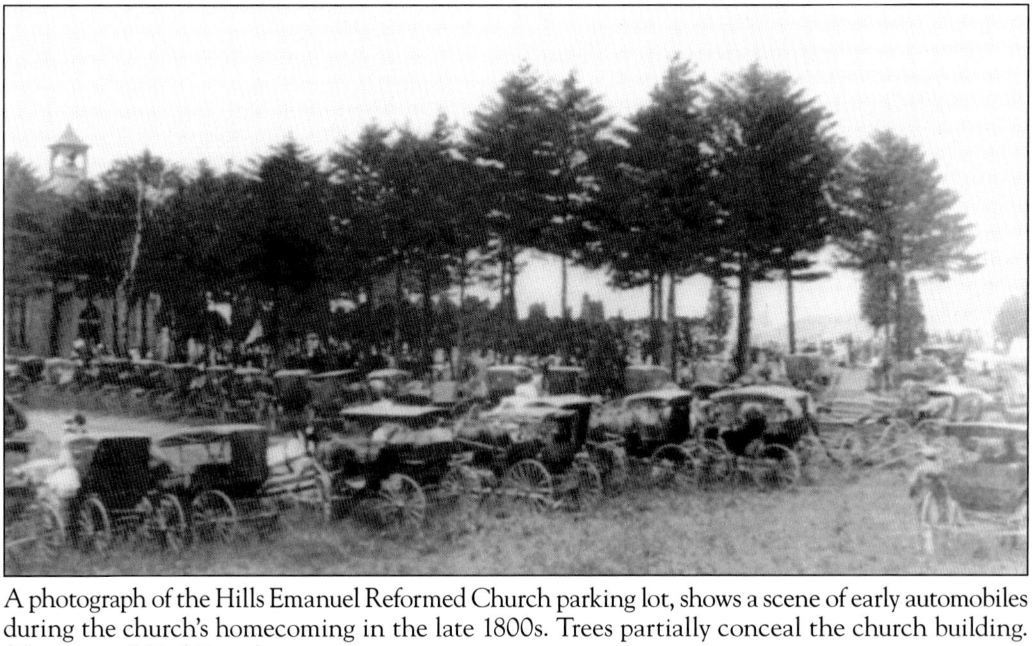

A photograph of the Hills Emanuel Reformed Church parking lot, shows a scene of early automobiles during the church's homecoming in the late 1800s. Trees partially conceal the church building. (Courtesy of Carl Patty.)

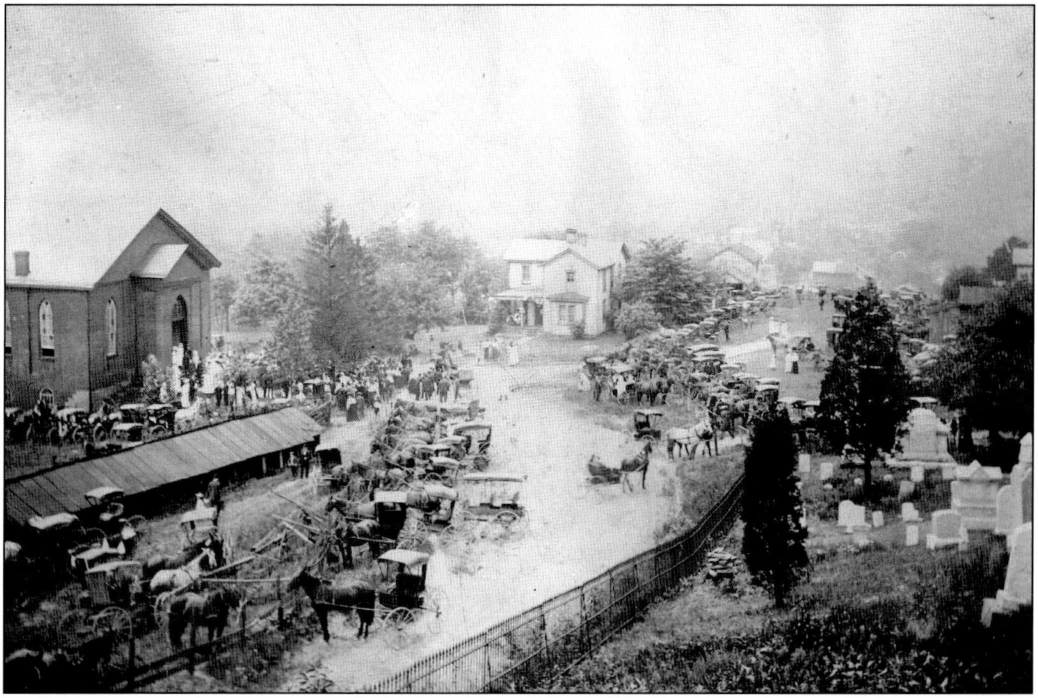

This homecoming occurred at Murrysville's First Presbyterian Church, built in 1871 at the junction of North Hills Road and Old US 22 (Northern Pike). Stables in front of the church were needed for horse transportation. The wrought-iron fence surrounding the cemetery was torn down and sold during the Depression to raise funds for maintaining the cemetery. The church was razed in 1979. (Courtesy of the Rev. John C. MacPhearson and Carolyn Krudwig.)

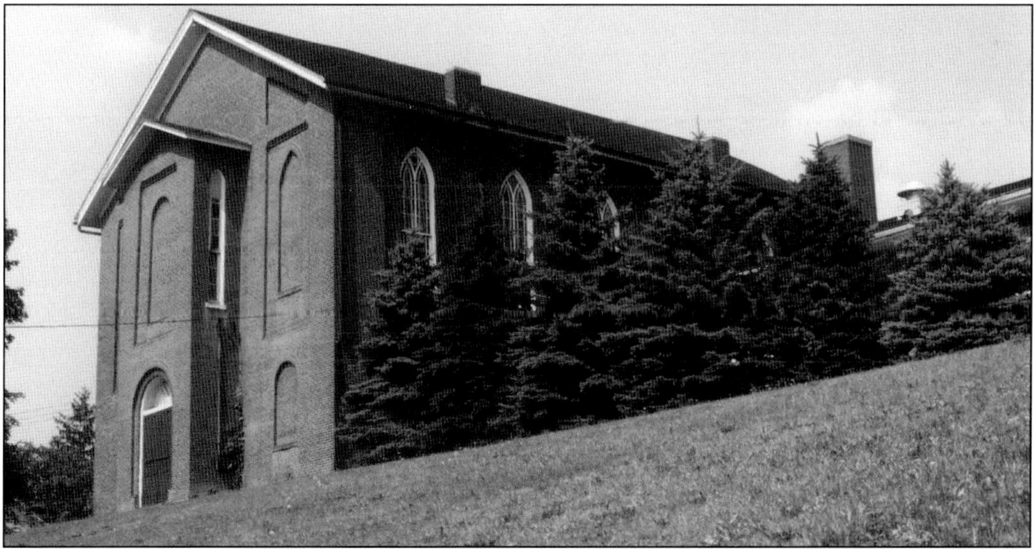

Turtle Creek Valley Academy (Laird Institute) was held in the First Presbyterian Church basement; it had been held originally in Francis Laird Stewart's home in Murrysville. This hillside cemetery is the only one in the vicinity since 1830. It is also the site of Obadiah Haymaker's grave, along with those of members of the Jeremiah Murry and Laird Stewart families. Abby Byram's memorial stone is also here. (Courtesy of Gregory Smith.)

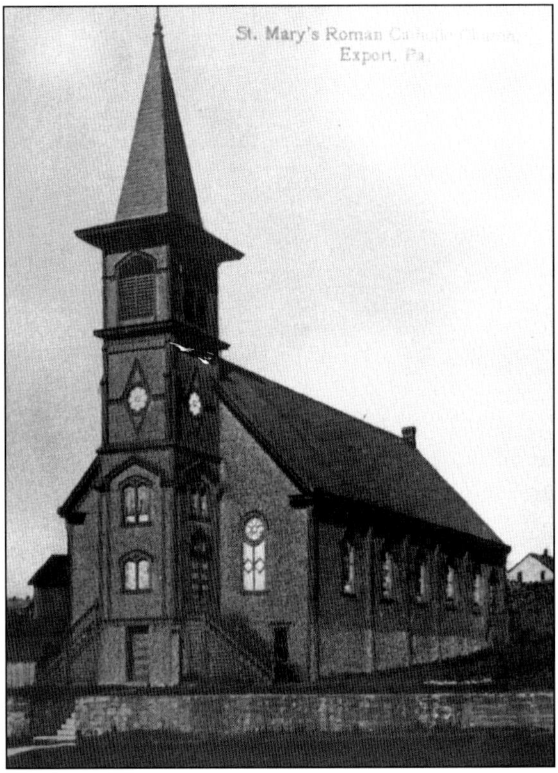

Export's St. Mary's Catholic Church was built around 1902. The first services had been held in Andrew McHugh's home. A small bell was rung if a child died, and a large bell was tolled for adults. Collections were recorded by nationality. Men sat on the right and women on the left. In 1932, pastor James Renshaw Cox led 125,000 indigent men, many unemployed steelworkers, from Pittsburgh to Washington, DC. (This should not be confused with Jacob Coxey's 100-man marches in 1894 and again in 1914, which also protested unemployment.) The church and Polish Club provided food and lodging.

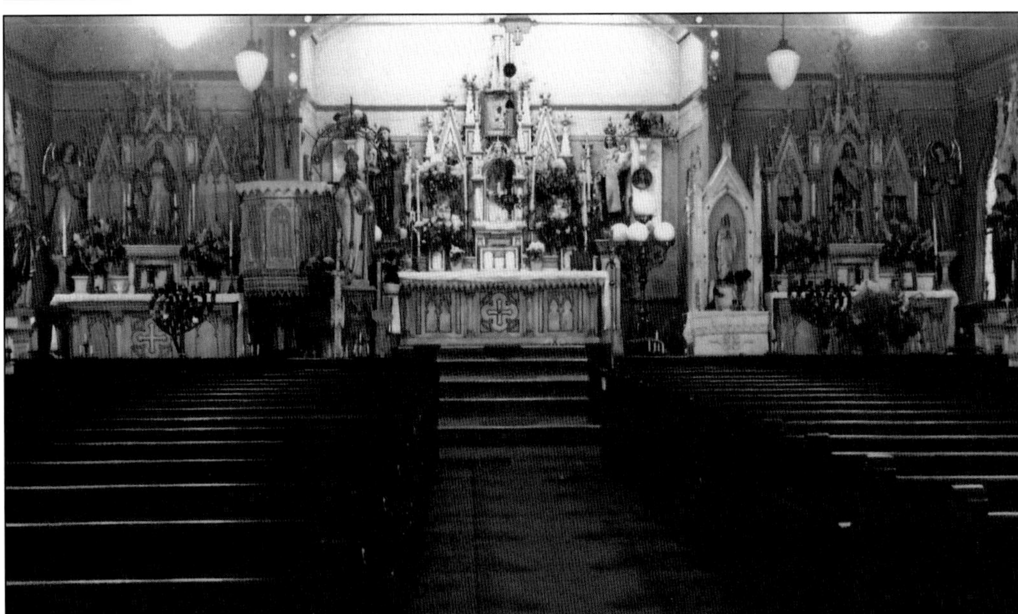

St. Mary's Catholic Church's organist, the mother of Stanley Dombrowski (a Pittsburgh Symphony Orchestra violinist), said, "During the Depression many people in Export raised vegetables and livestock." Before moving, the Reverend Peter Rendziniak painted historic murals on the walls (center front) and ethnic saints as well as wooden statues of saints and angels. He took his personal paintings with him when he went to New York City, but his murals are now painted over.

Abby Byram's cenotaph is in the Murrysville Presbyterian Church cemetery. Her grave and a marker are at Pleasant Valley Church cemetery. She and her father were captured by Indians in 1779 and taken to the British in Canada in the custody of Mohawk Chief Joseph Brant for prisoner exchange. A silver buckle from her shoe was found years later. J.C. Greer, manager of Export's company store, was Abby's descendant.

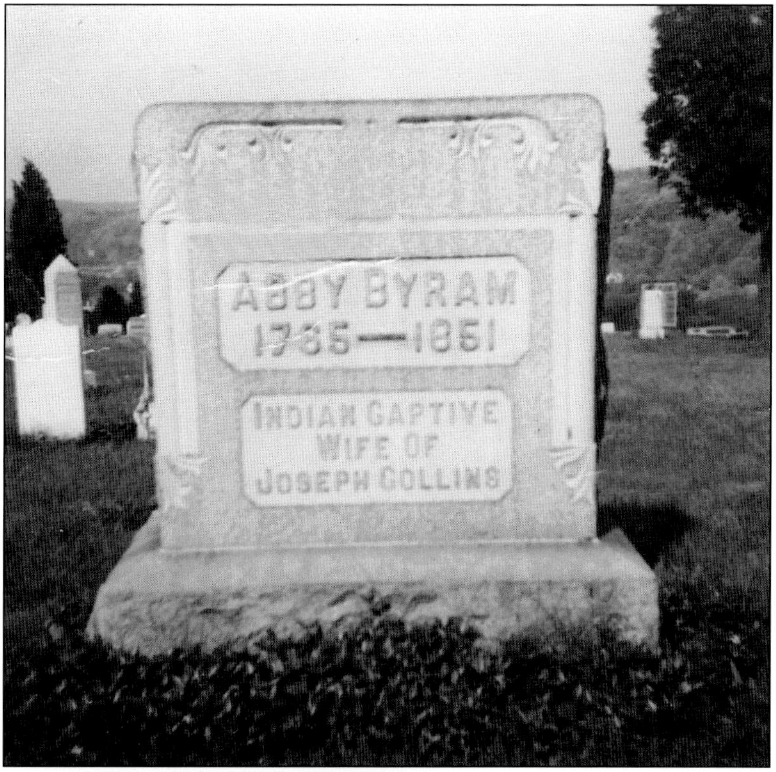

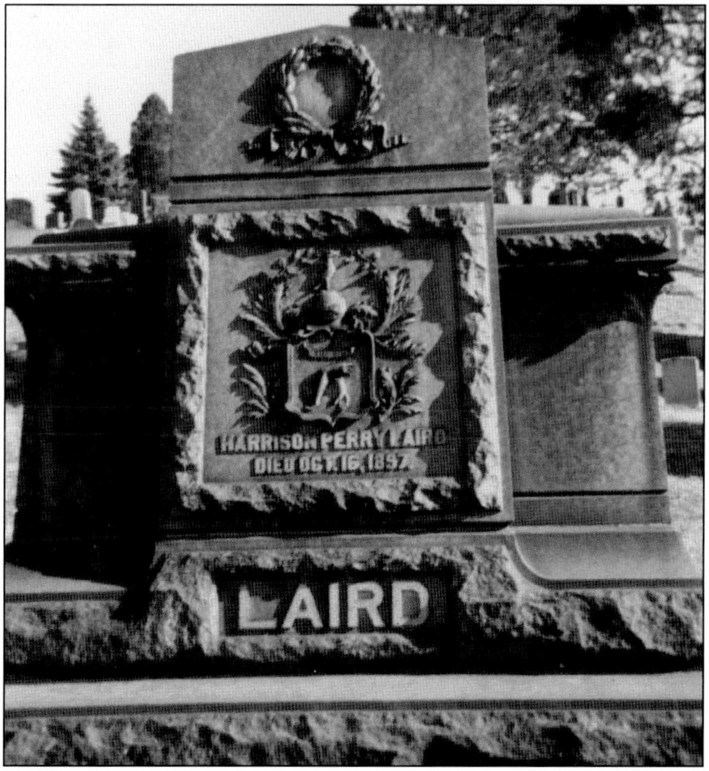

A gravestone dated 1897 in First Presbyterian Cemetery is that of Pennsylvania state senator Harrison Perry Laird. He had been lame from birth and was appalled by the surgical profession. The US National Bank Act adopted part of his 1850 Bank Law. A severed-limb coat of arms is on his stone. Byram's and Laird's memorials overlook the Murrysville tree sign. These, along with Mary Borga's wedding picture memorial in Grandview Cemetery, stand vigil over Turtle Creek Valley.

Bibliography

Albert, George Dallas. *History of the County of Westmoreland, Pennsylvania.* Philadelphia, PA: L.H. Everts, 1882.

Alexander, Edwin P. *The Pennsylvania Railroad: A Pictorial History.* New York: W.W. Norton, 1947.

Boucher, John, N. and John W. Jordan. *History of Westmoreland County.* Vol. 1, *Early History.* New York: Lewis, 1906.

Foley, Helen M. and Marion L. Berger. *This is Murrysville.* Murrysville, PA: Murrysville Women's Club, 1959.

Guyer, John P., citizen member of Pinchot Police Commission investigating citizen's rights during 1922 coal strike. *Pennsylvania's Cossacks and The State's Police.* Reading, PA: Peoples, 1924.

Hall, Charles A. *More on the History of Murrysville.* Murrysville, PA: Historical Preservation Society, 2008.

Iacocca, Lee. *Iacocca: An Autobiography.* New York: Bantam, 1984.

Jones, Mary Harris. *Autobiography of Mother Jones.* Chicago: C.H. Kerr, 1925.

Jordan, John W., ed. *History of Westmoreland County, Pennsylvania,* 3 vols. New York: Lewis, 1906.

Koch, Karl. *Memoirs of Karl Koch.* Greensburg, PA: MacDonald & Sward, 2009.

Lauck, J. W. "The Bituminous Coal Miners and Coke Workers of Western Pennsylvania." *The Survey* 26 (April 1911).

Mayo, Katherine. *Justice to All: The Story of the Pennsylvania State Police.* With an introduction by Theodore Roosevelt. New York: G.P. Putnam's Sons, 1918.

Niell, Charles P. (US Commissioner of Labor, prepared under the direction of). Report on the Miners' Strike in the Bituminous Coal Field of Westmoreland County, PA in 1910–1911. H.R. Doc. No. 62-847, vol. 97, 2nd session, (1912).

Smith, Helene. *Export, A Patch of Tapestry Out of Coal Country America.* Greensburg, PA: MacDonald & Sward, 1986.

Washlaski, Raymond A. "Export history–Westmoreland Coal Company History of no. 1 and no. 2 Mine Entrances, North and South." Article on Internet, accessed 2008.

Williams, Edward G. *Bouquet's March to the Ohio, The Forbes Road.* Pittsburgh: Historical Society of Western Pennsylvania, 1975.

INDEX

Altman, 113, 120
Berlin, 57, 73, 82, 94, 100, 103, 120, 121
Brunot, 26, 28, 34
Calisti, 117
Diffenderfer, 38, 103, 118
Dombrowski, 124
Drum, 122
Duff (McIlduff), 3, 11, 54, 61, 63, 88, 103, 109, 110, 120, 122
Fink, 11, 45, 63, 67, 86, 100
Foight, 72, 73, 106, 123
Forbes, 2, 9
Geiger, 2, 12, 62, 63, 67, 78, 79, 86, 87, 120
Glunt, 45, 78, 79, 103
Good, 63, 65, 86, 87, 98, 108
Grable, 115 121
Greer, 50, 63, 97, 114, 125
Hall, 1,44, 60, 63, 71, 103, 104, 105, 126
Hanacik, 118
Haymaker, 23–29, 31, 32, 34, 36, 41, 69, 72, 74 75, 101, 123
Hilty, 63, 82
Kemerer, 12, 45, 60, 86, 103
Koch, 1, 47, 63, 65, 98, 108, 126
Krushinski, 60, 63, 85, 88, 89, 90
Laird-Stewart, 64, 119, 123, 125
Lauffer, 61, 100
Manovich, 63, 85, 86
MacHugh, 41, 57, 84, 112, 124
Martz (Marts), 35, 63, 88
Meanor-Cole, 99
Mediate, 87, 91, 92
Mellon-Cline-Pipher, 3, 88, 109
Millberg, 57, 60, 83, 115
Moose, 62, 84
Murry, 2, 72, 77, 99, 100, 101, 114, 119, 122, 123
Norris, 17, 18
Patty (Patton), 63, 74, 75, 77, 78, 114
Remaley (Raymaley), 38, 41, 63, 88, 119, 120
Rendziniak, 90, 124
Rings, 11, 38, 91, 88, 91
Ripple, 31, 81, 82, 89
Ryckman, 106
Rugh-Miller, 101, 63
Rulyak, 73
Sampson, 13
Sartoris, 42, 85, 117
Schell, 44, 76
Skelly, 48, 49
Skena (Schena) 58
Sloan, 11, 23, 36, 67, 75, 83
Staymates, 61, 62, 64, 67, 102, 114
Torrance, 2, 3, 11, 103
Visnic, 39, 55, 63, 83, 86
Walton, 110
Watson, 118
Weigle, (Wigle), 60, 65, 66, 70, 108, 116
Wuslich, 40, 59, 78, 85, 88, 97–99

Discover Thousands of Local History Books Featuring Millions of Vintage Images

Arcadia Publishing, the leading local history publisher in the United States, is committed to making history accessible and meaningful through publishing books that celebrate and preserve the heritage of America's people and places.

Find more books like this at
www.arcadiapublishing.com

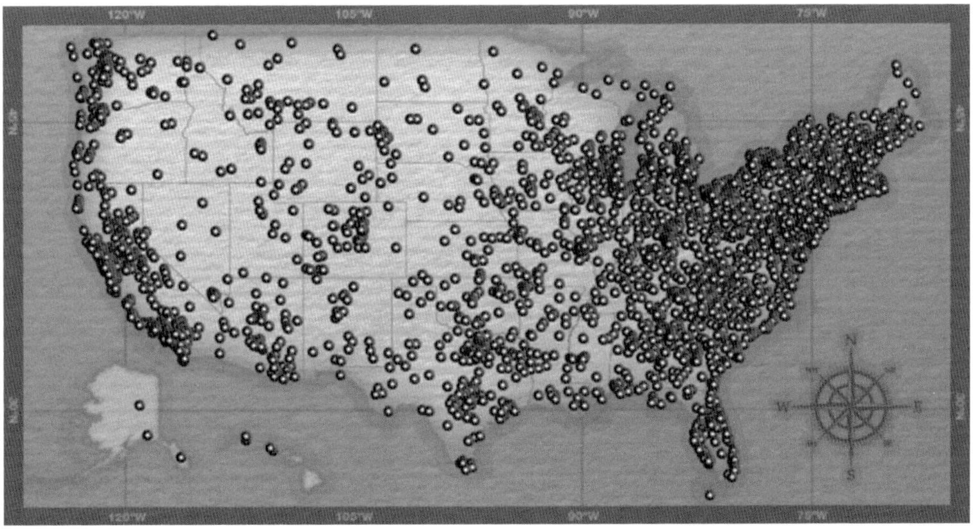

Search for your hometown history, your old stomping grounds, and even your favorite sports team.

Consistent with our mission to preserve history on a local level, this book was printed in South Carolina on American-made paper and manufactured entirely in the United States. Products carrying the accredited Forest Stewardship Council (FSC) label are printed on 100 percent FSC-certified paper.

MADE IN THE USA